D1090100

Spirit Beings in European Folklore 4
Compendium4: 270 descriptions – France, Brittany, Wallonia, Portugal, Italy, South Tyrol, Malta, Greece, Spain - Basque Country, Asturias, Catalonia, Cantabria, Galicia, Valencia
Author: © Benjamin Adamah
2022

Lay-out: Sylvia Carrilho
Editor: Orenda Bol

ISBN 978-94-92355-58-4

Publisher:

VAMzzz Publishing
P.O. Box 3340
1001 AC Amsterdam
The Netherlands
www.vamzzz.com
vamzzz@protonmail.com

– 270 DESCRIPTIONS –

France, Brittany, Wallonia, Portugal, Italy, South Tyrol, Malta, Greece, Spain – Basque Country, Asturias, Catalonia, Cantabria, Galicia, Valencia

---

SPIRIT BEINGS

IN EUROPEAN FOLKLORE 4

COMPILED & EDITED BY

BENJAMIN ADAMAH

CONTENTS

INTRODUCTION

Compendium 4 of this 4 volume-series *Spirit Beings of European Folklore* focuses on an area that starts with Wallonia and continues via France and the Pyrenees through the Iberian Peninsula to Italy and Greece – and thus covers the folklore of spirit beings of Romanesque, Basque, and Mediterranean peoples, with some Celtic influences via Brittany in particular. Initially written as a single encyclopedia of about a thousand pages, we decided to divide this manuscript into four separate compendia and use a cultural-geographical format, describing alphabetically the spirit beings of a more or less coherent segment of Europe. Each compendium is a stand-alone work, but when purchased together with the other volumes can also be enjoyed as part of the whole series – see also *From the same series* at the end of this book.

The classification into cultural-geographical formats is not solid because many creatures overlap with creatures from other areas or are (basically) the same creature under a different name, which however, almost always has elements integrated from the region and culture where it is locally known. This is especially true of *Alp* or *Mare*-like creatures, *Goblins* and dwarf-like spirits, *Spring-spirits*, which often have roots in the Greek *Nymphs*, as well as a spirit like *Lady Midday*, *Mittagsfrau* in German, of which there are also Eastern European variants such as the *Poludnitsa*.

The geographic-cultural demarcation as used in *Compendium 4* has resulted in a very diverse and colorful collection of spirit beings. Not only because of the concatenation of varied regions, but also because of the placement in time. Of a number of the Greek creatures we know that they have not been part of later folklore for some time, but nevertheless their existence in it is still strongly represented indirectly, and especially beyond the borders of Greece. Indeed, many of these creatures evolved within other European cultures into, what appear to be authentic region-specific creatures, but have their roots in ancient Greece. Even *Tartaro* for example, a one-eyed *Wild Man*-type figure of Basque folklore – one of the most intact authentic folklores of Europa – is a direct offspring of *Polyphemos*, the Cyclops mentioned in Homer's *Odyssey*. The *Kabeiroi* were at the base of many European dwarfish-humanoid creatures (*Kobold, Kabouter, Coblynau* etc., not to mention the *Goblin*) and the many types of *Nymphs* and the Greek *Strix* also found their way.

Compendium 4, the last volume of this series, is therefore, indispensable to complete the picture of the spirit beings of Europe. It is the finishing touch.

– Benjamin Adamah, Amsterdam, August 6, 2022

Aatxe

Aatxe (calf) is an *Irelu* (nature genius) in the folklore of the Basques. His name can be translated literally as "young calf". Aatxe lives in caves and usually takes the appearance of a young red calf, but because he is a shapeshifter, he can also present himself in the form of a man. At night, especially during stormy weather, he is believed to come out of his lair to attack criminals and other evil-doers. He also protects people by making them intuitively decide to stay home when danger threatens. Aatxe, like many Basque *Ireluak* (pl. of Irelu) or *genii*, is both a unique entity and a representative or manifestation of the goddess *Mari*. These Ireluak often act as the executors of her will, and punish people who somehow violate the rules of the goddess. In some regions, the name Aatxegorri (red calf) is used instead of Aatxe, a contraction of the words *aatxe* (calf) and *gorri* (red) or *Beigorri* (red cow). It was believed that Aatxe lived in caves and dens; in many caves (Isturits, Sare, Errenteria, etc.) engravings and paintings have been found depicting aurochses (extinct cattle species), bulls and oxen; this suggests that this Basque myth may have its origins in the Paleolithic period.

Addar

Addar or *Aiar*, the latter being a diminutive, is a horned and evil underground *Irelu* of Zuberoa in Basque folk belief. Its name means "branch".

Aidegaxto

Aidegaxto, Aide-gaizto, Aire-gaizto, Aide or *Lainogaixto* is an *Irelu* of Basque and Asturian folklore who, according to Labourdine beliefs, creates and directs storms. This spirit is also called *Ortzi, Ostri, Urtzi* or *Ortzilanoa*. Aidegaxto, literally means "bad sky" or "wrong sky" (Aidegaixtoa in Basque). The name is a contraction of the words *aide* (heaven) and *gaixo* (unhappy, sick). *Ortzia* means "firmament", "sky", "storm". Closely related to Ortzi, Aidegaxto (evil air, or lightning) is the Irelu *Odei*, who creates and directs thunderstorms, hurling them against men in order to harm them.

Protection against Aidegaxto

To exorcise Aidegaxto or to placate him, several procedures were used, ranging from lighting blessed candles, burning laurel branches in the home, wearing a wreath of laurel or hawthorn leaves on the head during storms, and placing an axe on the front door threshold of the house, with the edge up. Attaching a laurel cross or branches of trees such as hazel, ash or pine on the front door was also applied. One procedure used the magical influences of the herb *Rumex crispus*, or *cow's tongue*. The herb was rolled on the wrist of the left hand of the sorcerer or conjurer in question, while with the right hand he indicated to Aidegaxto the course he had to follow and where he had to unleash the wind and to unload the rain. In Brañaseca people lighted a blessed candle and placed the oven shovel on the roof, next to an axe with the edge up. In other Asturian villages *candles tenebrarias* are lit and rosemary and laurel are burned on Palm Sunday.

Aideko

Aideko is an *Irelu* in Basque folklore. It is invisible in itself, but it can take on a variety of shapes, such as fog. The spirit can act as a criminal, but also be benevolent or neutral. This is common among the *Ireluak* of Basque folklore. Aideko is derived from *airekoa* meaning "moving with the air" or "coming from the air". Other names: *Aide*, *Aidetikako*, and *Lauso* and *Lainaide* when it appears as a fog. Lainaide is composed of *Laino* (mist) and *Aideko*; "the mist of Aideko".

Aideko seems to be an autonomous entity as well as a feature of *Aidegaxto.* While the latter is feared for the material damage caused by bad weather, Aideko seems to represent the interaction of the supernatural or "airy" world in a more occult way, and the spirit is especially associated with causing diseases or epidemics. Within the scope of the Basques the world has two sides; one is "natural", all in itself, natural. The other is *aide*, "aerial" – supernatural, magical, mystical. The aerial world, home of many Ireluak, can invade the natural world in a good way or a bad one. Within this context the responsibility for all illnesses that are not revealed is the faculty of *Aide*. In addition to the Basque Country, the geographical area that preserved Aide's faith covers the whole of the Pyrenees and the Cantabrian side of the Iberian Peninsula. In Goierri it was believed that fog was bringing Aide, which is why they considered fog to be something harmful. The belief that low fog is harmful is widespread in the Basque Country. The long days of "rotten fog" can ruin crops and orchards, and can be harmful to both livestock and humans. In such cases, Aideko looks like *Lainaide.* It is the sea that sends Aide in the form of a low fog to spoil crops and grass.

The cholera-fog
According to the folk belief of Zerain and Zegama, the cholera plague was caused by Aide, who looked like a small fog bank. In the middle of the year, it is said that a low fog passed through the streets of Segura, and the next day the plague of black fever began to massacre the population. To put an end to the plague, groups of sheep were taken to Segura and passed through its streets. They believed the sheep would absorb the disease and save the people who lived there.

Akelarre

Akelarre is a controversial Basque term denoting "Witches' Sabbath" or more precise: *the place* where witches hold their meetings. The most common etymology proposes Akelarre as *"meadow of the billy goat"* – meadow is *larre* and billy goat translates as *aker*. Witches' sabbaths were envisioned as presided over by a billy goat (which in the Basque religion was not an animal but *Aker* or *Akerbeltz,* which was in turn one of the manifestations of the goddess *Mari*). Spelled as *aquelarre* the term has been used in Castilian Spanish since the witch trials of the 17th century. It is also the title of a witchcraft painting by Francisco Goya, to be seen in the *Museo del Prado,* which depicts a gathering of witches in the company of a huge black billy goat, that made the word more famous. "Aquelarre" was first attested in 1609 at an inquisitorial briefing, as a synonym to *junta diábolica,* meaning: *diabolic assembly*. Basque terms, often transcribed into Spanish texts by monolingual Spanish language copyists, were fraught with mistakes. According to J. Dueso, in *Brujería en el País Vasco* (1996), during the 1609-1612 persecution period and later, the Basques actually didn't even know what the term "akelarre", referred to by the inquisitors, meant.

The Spanish Inquisition politicized the ancient Basque religious practices as part of their conversion strategy and condemned people who worshiped a black goat by relating this to the worship of Satan. As the only true goal of the Inquisition was to bring any non-Christian people under the influence and domination of Rome, it is clear they demonized Basque goat worship into something that "justified" the horrors so many Basques would suffer in "the Name of God" when the persecutions started. In 1610, the Spanish Inquisition tribunal of Logroño initiated a large witch-hunt in Zugarramurdi and villages around Navarre, that resulted in 300 people being accused of practicing witchcraft. They took 40 of them to Logroño and burnt 12 supposed witches in Zugarramurdi at the stake (5 of them symbolically, as they had been killed by torture earlier). As a result of these major trials the term akelarre became synonymous with the word witches' sabbath, and spread into common parlance in both the Basque and Spanish language.

Places where according to folk-belief and other sources the Akelarre was organized

- *Akelarre,* a field of Mañaria, Biscay.
- *Akelarrenlezea,* a large cave of Zugarramurdi, Navarre.
- *Abadelaueta,* in Etxaguen, Zigoitia, Alava.
- *Ajunt de Bruixes,* in Canigou mountain, Catalonia, believed to be the place where the Sorginak created storms to send to the plains.
- *Akerlanda,* "Goat's meadow", in Gautegiz Arteaga, Biscay.
- *Amboto,* Álava and Biscay.
- *Atsegin* Soro, "Pleasure orchard". This was the name by which Sorginak themselves called the field of Matxarena in Errenteria (Gipuzkoa), according to inquisitorial records.
- *Balmaseda*, Biscay.
- *Bekatu-larre,* "Sinful meadow", in Ziordia, Navarre.
- *Campo de las Varillas*, Castro-Urdiales, Cantabria, Spain
- *Cernégula,* Burgos.
- *Cueva de Salamanca*, Salamanca.
- *Dantzaleku,* between Ataun and Idiazabal, Gipuzkoa.
- *Edar Iturri,* a spring in Tolosa, Gipuzkoa.
- *El Bailadero,* area in the Anaga Massif, Tenerife.
- *Eperlanda,* "Partridges' field", in Muxika, Biscay.
- *Garaigorta* in Orozko, Biscay.
- *Irantzi, Puilegi, Mairubaratza,* in Oiartzun, Gipuzkoa.
- *Jaizkibel*, mountain in Hondarribia, Gipuzkoa. The inquisition heard they celebrated Akelarre near the church of Santa Barbara. Local sayings believe that there were Akelarres in the bridges of Mendelu, Santa

Engrazi and Puntalea.
- *La Veiga'l Palu, Caboalles de Arriba,* in Laciana, León, Castilla y León
- *Larrun mountain,* here the Sorginak from Bera (Navarre), Sara and Azkaine (Lapurdi) gathered.
- *Llano de Brujas y Alcantarilla* in the Region of Murcia.
- *Macizo de Anaga* in Tenerife, Canary Islands.
- *Mandabiita* in Ataun, Gipuzkoa.
- *Matxarena* in Errenteria, Gipuzkoa, according to inquisitorial records.
- *Monasterio de Hermo* in Cangas del Narcea, Asturias.
- *Pals,* the mountains on top of the village Pals, in Andorra.
- *Petralanda* in Dima, Biscay.
- *Playa de Coiro,* Cangas de Morrazo, Pontevedra.
- *Sorginerreka,* "Sorginaks' creek", in Tolosa, Gipuzkoa.
- *Sorginetxe,* "Sorginaks' house", in Aia, Gipuzkoa.
- *Sorgintxulo,* "Sorginaks' hole", a cave in Hernani, Gipuzkoa.
- *Sorginzulo* "Sorginaks' hole", in Zegama and another one in Ataun, both in Gipuzkoa.
- *Trasmoz y Gallocanta*: in Aragón.
- *Turbon,* a mountain in Huesca.
- *Urkitza* in Urizaharra, Alava.
- *Viladrau y Cervera* in Catalonia.

Akerbeltz or Aker

Akerbeltz or *Aker* (from *aker*; billy goat, and *beltz*; black) is a deity and nature demon in the folk mythology of the Basque people, representing one of the aspects of the goddess *Mari*, but he is also known as a sovereign deity. A stone slab dating back to the Roman age already mentions *Aherbelts Deo* (the god Aherbelts). Akerbeltz had many *Ireluak* as his servants. In Christianity, Akerbeltz – the name is sometimes shortened to Aker – is the live image of "the demon" and the Inquisition identified him as *Satan*, or the *Devil* himself. The black he-goat was associated with all kinds of sexual activity, expression and exaltation, and was the central force and entity of the sabbath. Folklorists have linked Akerbeltz to some ancient deities as *Dionysus*, in terms of excesses, and Pan, in terms of sexual activity. However, originally Akerbeltz was an ancient European deity, worshiped also outside the Basque Country as the protector of animals. There were some other beliefs that say he was the animals' and houses' protector, having power over all the animals.

He was also the life image of fertility. Being black, many people from the Basque Country had a black billy-goat in their stable, in order to protect the rest of the animals and the house. Black billy-goats have always been very valuable in Aragon and in the Basque Pyrenees in general. Another quality attributed to Akerbeltz was the power of creating storms and bad weather. People from the Pyrenees thought that witches, Akerbeltz and "the demon" could go to any house and take the beard from a billy-goat in order to make hail. That is the reason for the saying: "*A la casa han tosa la cabra, aquesta tarde tindrem pedra*" (They have cut the billy goat's beard, this afternoon it is going to hail).

Serving the power of Rome, the Inquisition pushed Akerbeltz through the same kind of political distortion machine as *Pan*, thus transforming him from a nature god into the Devil. Pierre de Lancre – an inquisitor who went looking for women from Labourd and Lower Navarre who were supposed to be witches – wrote a book called *Tableu de l'Inostance* in which he documented the testimony of a supposed witch: "*Akerbeltz has a man's face, big and terrifying*". Another witch said that he had two faces; one in front and one in the back. Other inquisitors have described Akerbeltz erroneously as an enormous dog, or a big ox. During the time of the witch-hunts Akerbeltz was said to perform a parody of the Catholic mass for his followers, and during the mass, they were supposed to offer him eggs, bread and money. The ritual continued with a banquet with his witches and *elves*, where they served human meat and his horns illuminated the darkness by functioning as two gigantic candles. To continue with the celebration Akerbeltz and his followers danced together, accompanied by the sound of a tabor. And in the end the witches casted their spells.

Akerbeltz featured in several mythological tales and beliefs. He was believed to guard the entrance of the caves of Zugarramurdi where Ireluak, *Lamia*, and witches met. Once a priest entered one of those caves with a host and a snake appeared and ate his hands. From inside the cave some mysterious voices could be heard. Neighbors from Baigorri say that Akerbeltz's ghost lived in some of the caves in the area. In Urepel, from the Biurretabuxtan baserri, Juan Monakok said that there was a cave full of gold, guarded by a snake and Akerbeltz. Many times a priest had tried to exorcise the cave so that he could enter, but the snake and Akerbeltz did never leave.

Alarabi

In Basque folklore *Alarabi, Alarabie* or *Alabarri* is an *Irelu* living in the mountains in the Markina region (Biscay), where it was customary to burn an image of Alarabia every year during the Markina festivities. This creature resembles a *Cyclops* as it has only one eye in the middle of its forehead. It stands and walks with just one leg whose foot leaves a circular imprint. It is possible that *Tartalo, Tartaro, Tarto* or *Anxo* and Alarabi are variants of the same character, but the Irelu has some distinctive features. People believed that Alarabi was a shepherd before he became an evil genius, accused of feeding himself on wild beasts and humans, especially children. Because of the latter he is used as a child-Bogey in the region. Some researchers associate the word Alarabi with the Arabs. It is well known that the Basques, like the surrounding Christian peoples, fought for centuries against the Muslims of the south. A Basque legend tells the story of a shepherd being locked up in Alarabi's cave, witnessing his cannibalistic habit, and escaping in a way very similar to Odysseus' escape from *Polyphemos'* cave; by burning out Alarabi's one eye.

Aloja

An *Aloja*, also known as a *Goja*, *Goya* or *Goia* and as a *Water Maiden* (in Catalan *Dona d'Aigua*), is a female being in Catalan mythology, that has much in common with other female European *water-spirits,* like the Greek *Naiads* or Russian *Russalkas.* The word *goja* (Cat. pl. *goges*) could come from Old Catalan or perhaps Occitan, with the meaning of "young maiden" or "girl"; similar to the Latin *puella.* Of the same etymology as *gojat*, *gojata*, *mozo* and *moza.* The *Alojas* are *genies* that favor births and fertility, and are seen as givers of life and constant re-generators of nature. They are generally benevolent, although caution is required when encountering them. They are a local adaptation of the *Nymphs* as representations of the (feminine) forces of nature. They always live near icy blue waters: the ponds of the Pyrenees, torrents and waterfalls, pools, springs, damp caves, and underground streams and lakes. They take the form of beautiful maidens with blue or emerald green eyes, with long golden or coppery unbraided hair which reaches to their feet, shining under the rays of the sun or in the moonlight. Some versions attribute wings to them, like those of butterflies or dragonflies. They are usually nude or dressed in transparent tulle, showing the beautiful shapes of their bodies, although sometimes they wear bright white or golden tunics.

They are similar to women, although their nature is less corporeal, more subtle or etheric; they can appear and disappear from sight as if by magic. They have the appearance of eternal youth, and it seems there is no time or defect that can make them grow old. They are however believed to be mortal, but able to live for over a thousand years. Due to their longevity, the human concept of the passing of time is foreign to them; they have a hard time learning and remembering the names of the days of the week, for instance. Even so, they count the nights and are always very attentive to the phases of the moon, being most active when the moon is full.
In their subterranean palaces, time passes at a different pace; someone who spends a single night inside may find on leaving that tens, or even hundreds of years have passed in the outside world.

Habits
Some have spied them at midday, others at dawn, at first light, emerging from the water like shimmering shadows. On nights when the moon is full, they come out of the caves in which they hide, and organize circular dances to the sound of soft and captivating music. In some occasions, at the entrance of some of the caves, a brightness is seen as if coming from the bowels of the earth, like a filtered blue or pink halo, and strange harmonies are heard; the Alojas celebrate splendid parties at certain nights of the year. Certain stories speak of passersby who heard the tinkling of the purest crystal goblets, and smelled exquisite delicacies. They are accustomed to go out at night to wash their clothes by hand in the bed of a rushing stream, and then dry them under the moonlight, in forest clearings, on the grass of the meadows or on the rocks. Tradition says that those who manage to catch one of these pieces of clothing – unnoticed – will be lucky all the time and get all their wishes fulfilled. But if someone is caught in the attempt, he or she will be turned to stone or locked away in their subterranean mansions until the end of their days. Alojas can fall in love with humans, but are extremely jealous and distrustful. Only once a year, during the night of St. John, can they be observed by a human being without the latter being in danger of being bewitched.

Contact with humans
Interaction with humans is usually favorable, but always disturbing. For example, they are accustomed to watch over human newborns, whom they select in order to make them heroes for their people, but not infrequently this education is not exactly discreet, and they kidnap the babies and take

them away to "educate them better". They have powers that allow them to cure diseases, but also to cause them, as well as to drown and mislead people. Out of love for a human being they can attract him irresistibly, to the point of making him lose his own personality, seducing him to the point of causing madness and turning him, involuntarily, into a puppet under their complete control. It is relatively normal for them to mate with humans, however it does not appear that such unions can produce offspring. There are tales abound in which a man is married (knowingly or unknowingly) to an Aloja, who lives with her happily for years, under the commitment to respect a certain taboo (entering a specific room, following her on a full moon night...). The day the husband voluntarily or carelessly breaks the taboo, she disappears from his life.

Alseids

In Greek mythology, *Alseids* (Ἀλσηΐδες) were the *Nymphs* of glens, undergrowth and groves. Of the Classical writers, the first and perhaps only poet to refer to Alseids is Homer. Rather than *Alseid* he used the spelling *Alsea.*

> "*The Nymphs who live in the lovely groves* (ἄλσεα – alsea), *and the springs of rivers* (πηγαὶ ποταμῶν – pegai potamon) *and the grassy meadows* (πίσεα ποιήεντα – pisea poiëenta)."

> "*They* [Nymphs] *come from springs* (krênai), *they come from groves* (alsea), *they come from the sacred rivers* (ποταμοί – potamoi) *flowing seawards.*"

> "*The Nymphs* [of Mount Ida] *who haunt the pleasant woods* (alsea), *or of those who inhabit this lovely mountain* (ὄρος – oros) *and the springs of rivers* (pegai potamon) *and grassy meads* (pisea)."

Amalur

Amalur or *Ama-Lurra* (literally in Basque: Mother Earth or Mother Land – *lur* meaning "land" in Basque) is a chthonic goddess of Basque mythology, the personification or *Deva* of the Earth itself. She is closely related to *Mari* and sometimes fuses with her. Mari, who is the personification of all nature and therefore, in turn, is the official superior divinity who dominates all mythological characters, has a special relationship with the Earth and was often regarded as the personification of Amalur. The Earth was regarded as the habitat of all living beings, possessor of its own vital force that underlies the vegetable kingdom. This force strengthens the human organism sometimes through contact, sometimes through magic formulas and gestures. It ensures the preservation of livestock through offerings or sacrifices of domestic animals. It is the Earth that makes the existence of animals and plants possible, and therefore Amalur gives us humans our food and the necessary place to live. The Earth is also seen as an enormous container, an unlimited receptacle, where the souls of the deceased lived and most deities and other mythical beings had their dwelling, some of whom could manifest themselves as bulls (*zezen*), horses, boars, goats (*aker*), sheep etc. The faith in Ama-Lurra is very old among the nature orientated Basque people, prior to the invasion of the Indo-Europeans. The Indo-European cultures came to Europe from the East and brought with them the belief in the celestial divinities, residing under a more transcendental oriented spirituality.

For the Basque people the Genius of the Earth was the central deity of worship, in the past. They deposited their offerings (especially coins) in the caves, since these were seen as the doors to the interior of the Earth, so that Amalur, who was also the guardian of hidden treasures, could grant them her favors. It is in this type of worship, it seems, that some hermitages, built in caves or caverns converted into chapels, originate. The same applies to the origin of the prayers recited at the entrance to some of the country's caves. Amalur was seen as the creator of the sister Moon (*Ilazki, Ilargi* or *UIlargi Amandre*), the sister Sun (*Ekhi, Eguzki*) and the *Eguzkilore* (sun flower, *Carlina acaulis*), a flower similar to the in Basque Country very abundant thistle and which is placed in the doorways of houses to drive away the evil *Ireluak, sorginak* (witches), *Lamiak* and other evil beings. It was believed that if any evil entity intended to enter the house and found an Eguzkilore, it had to stop to count the numerous hairs or bracts of the flower, and the new day would surprise it without having finished its task.

Akerbeltz depicted in Testings (1797) by Francisco de Goya (1746-1828)

Amilamia

Amilamia is a friendly *Irelu* in Basque mythology, a supporter of Salvatierra (a town and municipality located in the province of Álava). She is said to have lived in the Lezao Cave in the Entzia Mountains. It had yellow hair (like gold) and was honest and generous in character. She was sometimes seen combing her hair with a golden comb while using the well at the side of the cave as a mirror. Her hair was reaching to the ground. She allegedly sang in an unknown language while combing and often spent the whole day doing so. She was believed to possess many wonderful secrets and tools, such as being able to extract flour from an empty sieve and was a helper to poor people. The Amilamia has a lot in common with the *Lamina*. In some cases, Amilamia is described as one special character, while in other cases, the Amilamiak are described as a group of beings.

Ana Sösana

A common *Folletto* in the provinces of Bergamo and Brescia (most common in Val San Martino & Isola / Valle Seriana) is the *Ana Sösana*, *Ana Mata* or *Mata Sösana*. Of her we know that she used to hide in the hoods of the chimneys, into which she enjoyed throwing twigs, pebbles, dry leaves and "souvenirs" while the pot with soup or polenta was on the fire. Some folklorists have suggested that this Folletto may have had its origin in an ancient tutelary divinity of Indo-European origin called "Ana" also widespread in northern Spain and France. It seems that her cult was still active during the Middle Ages and was operated by groups of women during the night, which brought them before the courts of the Inquisition with the accusation of being witches and participating in the forbidden Sabbath.

Anguana

Anguana (from Latin *aqua* = water; also *Aguana*, *Guana*, *Gana*, *Eguana*, *Agana*, *Enguana*) is the name of a demoness from the Ladin or Romance folklore and in South Tyrolean legends. Anguanas are said to bring bad luck for a lifetime if you offend them. They are mostly found near springs and streams, so a connection with *Nixen* or *Water-Nymphs* is not excluded. They can appear both as beautiful, young, attractive women, and as old, ugly women with goat feet. They show also similarities with the *Viles* and Catalonian *Alojas*. In essence, they are said to be benign, and a good luck blessing on their part is said to actually bring this about. Allegedly Anguanes live by streams, springs or in caves and wash linen. They are also said to appear only at dawn and dusk. Sometimes they are said to enter into marriages with humans, similar to the *Fairies*, but then the man is not allowed to touch their blond hair. In addition, they are said to bestow "endless gifts" (that is, things that never end). In the town of Nonsberg they were believed to be witches or other beings, and they had been banished by the Council of Trent so that they could no longer "haunt". In the Ladin language they are abbreviated as *Gana* (singular) or *Ganes* (plural). Besides the *Ganes*, there are also the *Salvans* or *Salvangs* as forest people (from the Latin *silva* 'forest').

Anjanas

In the folklore of Cantabria, *Anjanas* are a type of *Duendes* similar to the *Nymphs* of Ancient Greece. In Castille and Leon they are called *Janas*, and they are known as the *Xanas* in Asturia. They are described as extremely beautiful beings with long flowing hair that they are combing daily for long hours. Anjanas are believed to wear blue mantles, or in other versions wearing pearls and dresses made up of stars or stardust. They are very pale, and usually appear wearing a crown of flowers and a magical staff adorned with flowers, which they use to cure and protect the sick, lead the way for those that get lost in the forest. They also protect humans and other creatures from the nasty *Ogre*-like beings called *Ojancanus*. Like the ancient Greek *Dryads* or *wood-Nymphs*, the Anjanas are also believed to be protectors of the trees, and they are sometimes seen by travelers through the Cantabrian woods. They are said to strengthen the roots so the trees grow stronger, delicately tend to the branches, leaves and flowers, and safeguard their seeds to help the forests grow. Anjanas are usually small in size – not much larger than an average flower – but they can change their size and become as large as humans, or even taller; a feature also attributed to many kinds of *dwarfs* or *Goblins*. In some regions, Anjanas are always described as having the size of humans.

Anjanas are said to live in fountains, springs, rivers, ponds, lakes and caves and come out only at night when everyone is asleep. In secret caves they hide their wealth of gold and silver, which they protect and may use to help those that truly need them. They are never malignant but always benign. There are stories of *Pasiegos* (peasants and farmers, inhabitants of the area around the river Pas) who claim that at night, they have seen these Duendes visiting their villages and leaving gifts at the doorsteps of those who called for their aid and who showed good intentions. They bless the waters, trees, farms and herds. It is said that a man that spots an Anjana while she is brushing her hair is allowed to marry her and take possession of all her bountiful treasures. However, if he is unfaithful, she will disappear forever, taking all her treasures with her, leaving the man destitute for the rest of his life. The Anjanas are not to be summoned lightly. They are mighty creatures, and if their help is asked for ill-doing, or their advice is contradicted, they will issue a punishment for the aggravation. In Galicia and Portugal, a similar mythological being to the Anjanas or Xanas is called a *Moura*.

Ankou

The *Ankou* (Breton: *Ankoù*) is a spectral personification of the community of the dead, and a prominent character in Breton mythology, often recurring in Breton oral tradition and tales. The Ankou is sometimes portrayed as a very tall and skinny man, with long white hair, and a grimacing mouth that stretches from ear to ear. Instead of eyes he has two black holes, at the bottom of which burn two small white candles. His face, without a nose, is shaded by a large felt hat. Sometimes the spirit appears in the form of a skeleton draped in a shroud, and whose head turns around constantly at the top of the spine, like a weather-vane around its iron rod, so that he can embrace at a glance the whole region he has the mission to cover. On occasion, he simply appears as a shadow. He wields a scythe and is said to sit atop a cart for collecting the dead, or to drive a large, black coach pulled by four black horses and accompanied by two ghostly figures on foot. His name comes from a derivative in *-awos* and the Indo-European *n̥ku* – "the dead"; *Anghau* in Wales, Middle Welsh *Angheu*, Cornish: *Ankow*, Old Irish *ec*. He is associated with death in Lower Britain, where he does not represent death itself, but his servant: his role is to collect the souls of the dead. It is also said that whoever sees the Ankou, will die within a year. Fulfilling thus a role of "passer of souls". In other words, the Ankou is a psychopomp-entity. In case the Ankou is related to the last dead person of December, it is sometimes reported that the first dead person of the year becomes his servant (*komis an Ankou*: "the clerk of the Ankou" in Breton) to assist him in his task. Anatole Le Braz writes in his collection *La Légende de la Mort*:

"The Ankou is the worker of death (oberour ar marv). The last dead person of the year, in each parish, becomes the Ankou of this parish for the following year. When there have been more deaths than usual during the year, it is said of the Ankou in office: 'War ma fé, eman zo un Ankou drouk' ("On my faith, this one is a wicked Ankou")."

Origin

The Ankou seems to be a heritage of Celtic mythology: a god whose function is the perpetuation of vital cycles, such as birth and death, the seasons or the day-night cycle. Although he is now attributed the scythe or the pike, his canonical weapon is the "blessed mallet". Some features indicate his proximity to the Gallic god *Sucellos* and the Irish god *Eochaid Ollathair*, or *Dagda*, who kill or give life with their weapon, mallet or club. The Ankoù is a pan-Brittonic figure of this function. The word is masculine in Breton and according to Dom Le Pelletier, in his etymological dictionary published in 1752, it is simply the plural of *anken* which designates anguish, pain. In Alan Heusaff's *Geriaoueg Sant-Ivi dictionary,* Ankoù is close to *ankouaat*, or *ankounac'haat*, which means "to forget".

Annequin

The *Annequin* (also: *Hannequet*, *Hannequin* , *Harliquin*; pl.; *Annequires*) is a mysterious and evil creature from Ardennes folklore. They are said to reside mainly in the forests of Puilly. Annequires are described as a kind of *Nuton* and *Will-o'-the-wisp* whose main occupation is to lure people to swamps where they drown. The name Annequin is closely linked to the *Mesnie Hellequin* (a legendary leader of the *Wild Hunt*) and via him to the Italian figure of the harlequin. The Annequins held a round every Saturday night and on some occasions they went past the houses while blowing whistles. According to legend, anyone who accidentally encountered them ran the risk of disappearing forever.

Antaura

Antaura is a female demon from Greek and later Roman folklore that causes migraines. She rises from the sea to haunt people. The name Antaura refers to an evil headwind, such as the scirocco or the foehn (both of which are classic triggers for migraine attacks). Through a protective amulet (phylacterion) worn on the body, people tried to ward off the demon. The root to Antaura is to be found in the female demon *Abyzou* (discussed in *Spirit Beings in European Folklore - Compendium 2*), a Sumerian female demon who kills children, and who appears in the myths and tales of the Sumerian Near East. Abyzou is often blamed for miscarriages and infant mortality because, being barren herself, she envies mothers. In Jewish tradition Abyzou was identified with *Lilith*, and in Coptic Egypt with *Gylou*.

Apabardexu

In the Lakes of Somiedo, locals say there lives a kind of mountain-*Duende*. In Asturleones *Apabardexu* may translate to "Duende of the mountain or of the lake".

Apalpador

In eastern (Spanish) Galician folklore the *Apalpador*, also known by the name of *Pandigueiro* in the region of Tierra de Trives, is the mythical figure of a benevolent *coalman-spirit* who comes to the villages on the nights of December 24 and December 31. He comes to touch the bellies of children, to see if they have eaten enough during the year, leaving a lot of chestnuts or other gifts behind, and wishing them to have a new year full of happiness and food. In eastern Galicia New Year's Eve is therefore called the *Noite de Apalpadoiro* (Night of Touching).

Ardi

Ardi means "sheep" in Basque, and is also found in the form *Ardia* which means "the sheep". In Basque folklore Ardi is not an ordinary sheep but a sheep-spirit or ghostly sheep. One legend tells of a shepherd who slept in the shade of some beech trees while his sheep were scattered on Mount Okina. When it got dark, most sheep withdrew to a shelter under the rocks. Some of them did not. The shepherd went looking for the missing ones and headed for a place where he heard a ringing sound. However, when he arrived there, although he continued hearing the bells, he did not see his sheep. Suddenly it seemed to him that the sounds of sheep-bells were coming from under his feet. He stepped forward a little and slipped into a deep hole. There he saw some mysterious ghostly sheep, whose bells rang exactly like those of his own sheep. Frightened, he remembered the Virgin of Arantzazu and prayed to her for protection. The next morning he found himself under Arantzazu's bell tower. When, after a few days, he returned from Arantzazu, he found one of the missing sheep, a lamb, in the same place he had last visited. He tried to capture the animal, but when he touched it with his hand, he was pushed back by a strange force and thrown into the hole again by the little animal. He couldn't let go of it, invoked the Virgin of Arantzazu again and, at that very moment, the animal disappeared into the depths of the abyss of Mount Okinahe, leaving him behind without his lamb, but feeling liberated as well.

Argiduna

Argiduna is a *Goblin* who manifests himself at night in the form of light. Argiduna means "one who has light" in Basque, it is a contraction of the words *argi* (light) and *duna* (one who has). See also under: *Gaueko.*

Arquetu

The *Arquetu* is a mythological being that appears in Cantabrian mythology as an old man with a drawing of a green cross and seven keys on his forehead. He lends money to those foolish enough to spend their fortune, but if they waste their money again, he punishes them by cursing them with eternal poverty.

Arrainandere

The *Arrainandere*, or Fish woman, is the Basque *Mermaid* which appears for the first time in the folklore of Euskal Herria in the 15th century. Heiress of the medieval Mermaid, she retains her physical attributes – half woman, half fish – and in the same way attracts unsuspecting sailors with her beautiful songs, to capsize their ships.

Atarrabi or Atarabi

In Basque mythology *Atarabi* is a benevolent daemon, one of two sons of *Mari* and *Sugaar*. He is also known as *Atarrabio*, *Ondarrabio*, *Atxular* and *Axular*. His brother was *Mikelats.* Attarrabi was the good son while Mikelats was the bad one.

Auloniads

The *Auloniads* (Αὐλωνιάς – from the classical Greek αὐλών "valley, ravine") were *Nymphs* who were found in mountain pastures and vales, often in the company of *Pan*, the god of nature. *Eurydice*, for whom *Orpheus* traveled into dark Hades, was an Auloniad, and it was in the valley of the Thessalian river Pineios where she met her death, indirectly, at the hands of *Aristaeus*, son of the god *Apollo* and the Nymph *Cyrene*. It was Aristaeus's wish to ravish Eurydice, and either disgust or fear compelled her to run away from him without looking where she was going. Eurydice trod on a poisonous serpent and died.

Ayalga

Ayalgas are a variant of the *Xanas*, but differ primarily in that they are human beings. They are beautiful maidens who are abducted to the world of the *Elementals* and get certain abilities foreign to our understanding. Generally their mission is to guard the treasures of the grottoes, along with the fearsome *Cuélebre* (a giant winged serpent-dragon of the Asturian and Cantabrian folklore, that lives in a cave, guards treasures and keeps Xanas and Ayalgas as prisoners).

These young women initially felt a great sadness for not being with their loved ones and expressed this by singing beautiful and enigmatic songs at the entrance of the caves. Their voices attract shepherds and travelers who pass nearby, who can liberate them from their imprisonment, but only if the visitor manages to kill the Cuélebre. Folklore has a lot of stories of shepherds' encounters with these beings, in which the Ayalga fell in love and explained to the visitor how to obtain the valuable treasures of the interior. When the Ayalga marries a mortal man, she immediately loses all powers the spirits of Nature have given her, such as her beautiful voice and the understanding of the language of animals and plants. Her memories of living in the kingdom of the Fairies is also deleted. However, this did not always happen, and sometimes these escaped Ayalgas became immortal beings.

B

Badalisc

The *Badalisc* or *Badalisk* is not to be confused with the *Basiliskos* or *Basilisc*, originally a North African serpent described by Pliny the Elder, that later evolved into a mythical serpent-tailed bird, depicted in medieval bestiaries. The Badalisc is a mythical creature of the Val Camonica, Italy, in the southern central Alps. Today the creature is represented with a big head covered with a goat skin, two small horns, a huge mouth and glowing eyes. According to legend the Badalisc lives in the woods around the village of Andrista (commune of Cevo) and is supposed to annoy the community. Each year a puppet depicting the Badelisc is symbolically captured during the period of Epiphany (5 & 6 January) and led on a rope into the village by musicians and masked characters, including *il giovane* (the young man), *il vecchio* (the old man), *la vecchia* (the old woman) and the young *signorina*, who is "bait" for the animal's lust. There are also some old witches who beat drums, and bearded shepherds, and a hunchback *(un torvo gobetto)* who has a "rustic duel" with the animal. Traditionally only men take part, although some are dressed as women. In ancient times women were prohibited from participating in the exhibition, or even to see or hear the Badalisc's speech; if they did so they would be denied Holy Communion the following day.

Banyoles

The *Monster of Banyoles* is a dragon-like creature that, according to legend, dwells in the lake of Banyoles in Girona, Catalonia. It is no longer dangerous. As early as the eighth century, a French monk named St. Emeterio is said to have lured the beast out of the lake with prayers and turned it into a peaceful herbivore. It is said that the monster of Banyoles still lives in the depths of the lake today.

Barbegazi

Barbegazi are Alpine *Gnome*-type *mountain spirits* from French and Swiss folklore, with very large feet and a white fur. They reside in a network of caves and tunnels that is only accessible near the peaks of mountains through concealed entrances. The name Barbegazi is believed to be a corruption of *barbes glacées* meaning "frozen beards". Barbegazi hibernate during the Summer and become active in the Winter season. They love the cold and can dig through snow with an amazing speed. Although they even enjoy 'riding avalanches', they also warn people about these hazards, by making whistling noises, such as marmots, or noises, which may be mistaken for gusts of wind. They seem to have a friendly attitude towards humans and are said to have helped people who were buried under snow and to have guided lost cattle back to their herd.

Basajaun or Baxajaun

Basque folklore knows a kind of *Wild man* or *Woodwose* named *Basajaun* or *Baxajaun.* The *Basajaunak* (plural) lived in the most remote mountains and forests of Gorbea (Álava) and also in the Selva de Irati (Navarra) and in the area of Ataun, in Guipúzcoa. Together with *Tartalo* or *Tartaro* and the *Jentilak*, the *Basajaunak* are part of the group of mountain giants in Basque mythology. They walked in a human way, with their huge and very strong bodies covered with hair and a very long mane that reached their feet. Basajaun is the Lord of the Forest, or the "Wild Lord". This creature also appears in Aragonese folklore, in the valleys of Tena, Anso and Broto, places where Basque toponymy is preserved. In Aragon it is called *Basajarau, Bonjarau* or *Bosnerau.* His foot is said to look more like the claw of a bear than a human foot, though in other tales he is described with one humanoid foot and one horse foot.

The Basajaun could be a friendly creature, acting as the protector of flocks of sheep, and when there was a danger of a storm, he roared to the shepherds to protect the sheep; he also made sure that the wolf did not get close to the flock. In contrast, however, he has also been portrayed as a terrifying and evil creature of great strength, an entity that was best avoided. There are also stories which describe the Basajaunak as the very first settlers and farmers of the Basque country; possessors of secrets from which men learned by means of tricks; how to cultivate wheat, the manufacture and use of the saw, welding, etc. Before that, legend has it that these skills were taught to the Basajaunak by a figure called *Martin Txikik* (Martin the Little One).

Bête de Gévaudan (The Beest of Gévaudan) copper engraving (1764)

Basandere

Basandere, also *Basaandere*, *Basa Andere*. In Basque folklore *Basandere* refers to the female partner of Basajaun. She is a hairy and wild woman, living in the Basque Pyrenees, taking up residence in a labyrinth of caves and caverns. In the Basque sense, a gallery that connects the outside world to the underground world. These are so vast, that they remind us of huge castles. Basandere is especially associated with the Irati Forest. Her name literally means "Lady of the forest" or "Wild lady". Through her physical characteristics and behavior, she is similar to the *Wild women* or *Sylvan*, and is a protector of nature and agro-pastoral activities, but, just like her male companion Basajaun, also to the legendary hominids known in most traditional cultures, and more particularly in mountain areas (yeti, almasty, sasquatch and others...). Jean-Jacques Rousseau spoke of wild men from the Pyrenees in 1754 in his *Discours sur l'origine et les fondements de l'inégalité parmi les hommes*. Linnaeus classified these humans walking on all fours, not knowing how to speak, and hairy, as Homo ferus. In 1776, the engineer Leroy, responsible for the Royal Navy and the exploitation of the forests of Aspe and Iraty, wrote in his memoirs about a man in his thirties, who was hairy like a bear, probably suffering from hypertrichosis or Ambras syndrome (abnormal hair growth). Like the Asian Almas, the Basajaunak apparently walk with one foot in myth and folklore and one foot in cryptozoology. Children born from the union of a Basajaun and a human are called *Hachkos*.

The more mythical *Basandere* usually stays near the entrances of caves, or near fountains. They spend hours combing their hair, while keeping an eye on their vast amount of treasures. The theft of a golden comb by a shepherd is a frequent storytelling theme. It is almost impossible to see any of these creatures up close, because as soon as you get close to them, they magically disappear. According to some legends, but relatively rare, the Basajaunak can move extremely fast. Yet paradoxically they have to lean on a stick. They sometimes have a single eye, located in the middle of their forehead: a characteristic of the *cyclops* (*Tarto*, *Tartaro*) with whom they have gradually been assimilated. Moreover, both are often given the name *Anxo*.

Toponyms associated with Basajaun are:

- Basajaun haitza (Aia)
- Basajaunberro erreka (Auritz-Orreaga/Roncesvalles)

- Basajaun etxea koba: former mine, now abandoned (Lantz)
- Basajaundegi baserria eta erreka (Azpeitia)

Bécut

Bécut is a mythical giant, cyclops and cannibal of Gascony and the Pyrenees. Most of the stories that refer to it are set in Bigorre and Béarn and often take on the theme of the Cyclops Polyphemus. An identical character with the same type of stories is known in the Basque Country by the name of *Tartalo*, *Tartaro*, *Tartare*, *Torto* or *Anxo*, in Ariège by the name of *Ulhart*. The figure of Ullard is also known in the Alpine regions.

Befana

Befana is the name of a witch or female demon of Italian folklore who, on the night of Januari 5-6, flies from house to house on a broom in search of the baby Jesus, bringing gifts, or punishments. The name derives from *Epiphany*, the church feast of the Magi Caspar, Melchior and Balthazar. According to legend, the witch heard the Good News from the shepherds. The star of Bethlehem was supposed to lead her to the manger. However, because she left too late, she missed the star. In the course of time, the positive aspects of her figure prevailed, so that today she is primarily considered to be a good witch. She represents a parallel figure to the Alpine *Perchta* and the Central European *Frau Holle*.

Bella 'mbriana

In Neapolitan folk-belief *la Bella 'mbriana*, is the spirit of the house. She manifests herself in the form of a gecko or is seen between the curtains moved by the wind on a sunny day. It owes its name to the sundial, a symbol of the sun laid out in front of the house. Pleasant in appearance, la Bella 'mbriana reigns, controls and advises the family. Throughout the centuries, and still today, she is the antagonist of the more mischievous *Munaciello*. She is invoked in all the difficult situations that compromise the family serenity. Generally she is a good spirit, but one should never offend her, because, when insulted or maltreated she can even cause the death of several family members. In the past, one would put an extra place for her at the table. La Bella 'mbriana likes order and cleanliness and for this reason a neglected house makes her irritable. When family members decided to move, they tried to talk about it outside the house, so as not to let her know anything, not to attract her wrath. La Bella 'mbriana, along with the Munaciello and *Janara*, was the main topic of stories told on winter evenings, when the women gathered in front of the brazier *('a vrasera)* to discuss things.

Berbéch, Malasén & Sblesén

In the folklore of Tera Orobic, Northern Italy, the *Berbéch, Malasén & Sblesén* are three *Folletti*, who often accompany each other, but can also act on their own. They are sylvan Folletti, in the sense that they live in the trees and are most common in the lore of Gavarno di Nembro and Val Seriana. Berbèch owes its name to the beard in the shape of a "beak". He lives in attics of old houses and appears only when Sblesen and Malasen join him. The name Malasén originates from the term *malessere* (misery, discomfort). A frequent visitor to taverns and bad places, he often takes care of drunks who do not find their way back home. His appearance is widespread in the province of Bergamo. Sblesén is an anxious and irascible Folletto, who hates lies and when he 'smells them' caresses the blade of his saber in a very suggestive way.

Bête du Gévaudan

La Bête du Gévaudan or in Occitan *la Bèstia de Gavaudan* (the Beast of the Gévaudan) is the nickname of a mysterious canine predator (a wolf of dog; probably several of them) that was/are responsible for a series of attacks on humans (between 88 and 124 according to the sources) between June 30, 1764 and June 19, 1767. Most of the attacks took place in the northern part of the Gévaudan (southern France) with usually fatal results. Some other cases were reported in southern Auvergne, northern Vivarais, Rouergue and southern Velay. The Gévaudan was a sparsely populated historical province in the Massif Central; its boundaries largely corresponded to those of the present-day department of Lozère. Some historians assume that several animals were involved in the attacks. At the time the Beast roamed the Gévaudan, people speculated about a serial killer or *Werewolf* who was invulnerable to bullets. There have been about a hundred similar attacks in the history of France. In the second half of the 18th century the kingdom was populated by about 20,000 wolves. But this tragedy came at a propitious time for the press, which was in need of interesting news after the Seven Years' War: the *Courrier d'Avignon*, then the *Gazette de France*, and the international gazettes plunged into the matter and published hundreds of articles within a few months.

The attacks led to a targeted hunt for the monster. Among the many animals then killed, two canines were suspected of being *the Beast*. The first was a large wolf, shot in September 1765 by François Antoine, Louis XV's harquebus bearer, on the grounds of the Royal Abbey of Les Chazes. Once the animal was stuffed and taken to Versailles, the newspapers and the Court lost interest in the affair. But the attacks on peasants continued. In June 1767, Jean Chastel (1708-1789), a literate farmer from Darne, shot the second animal, identified as a wolf or a large shaggy dog that resembled a wolf, at La Besseyre-Saint-Mary. According to tradition, this animal was the Beast of Gévaudan, as no more fatal attacks were reported in the province after this date. Not a bullet proof Werewolf, but a mortal creature. What remains is the mystery of the enormous scale at which these brutal attacks on humans occurred.

Beuffenie

Beuffenie is an evil *Fairy* in the legends and folklore of Burgundy, France. She was mainly a punishing spinner, *Bogey*-figure and boiler of children. In Clamerey (Côte-d'Or in the Bourgogne-Franche-Comté region) she is seen as a night spinner. In Noidan (also Côte-d'Or in the region Bourgogne-Franche-Comté) she is seen as a Bogey, because she has the reputation of boiling children in her fireplace. *Rocher de la beuffenie* (Vic-sous-Thil, Côte-d'Or in the region Bourgogne-Franche-Comté) is a granite set in a forest, that was named after her, connected to a local legend; Beuffenie had eaten all the children of a certain woman, who then prayed to the Virgin Mary. She put a curse on Beuffenie and the Fairy, her companion, who then were transformed into stone.

Bildur aize

Bildur aize or *Beldur aize* is an *Irelu* of Basque mythology of the *Alp*-type who makes people dream and sometimes oppresses the chest of people who are sleeping. *Beldur aize* means "frightening wind" in Basque. *Beldur* means "fear". To get rid of it, the people of Goiherri (Gipuzkoa/Guipuzcoa) go to certain churches in Olaberria, Arriarán and Mutiloa to have the priests of these places say a prayer for them. In the same way, they consider it useful before going to bed to recite a special prayer three times:

Amandere Santanes	Grandmother Sainte Iñes
Bart egin det ametz	Last night I had a dream
Ones edo gaitzez	Good or bad
Egin ba-det gaitzez.	If I did it wrong
Biurr egidazu on	Make it good

Birao

Birao means "curse" or "to swear" in the Basque language. It was a common belief that a Birao could cause people's deaths. The Birao was not an entity itself, but introduced evil spirits called *Gaixtoak* into the bodies of the targeted persons. In some villages it is believed that on a particular time of day the uttered curse could be totally effective. Nowadays a curse or the Evil Eye is regarded as superstitious nonsense, thus evil spirits carrying out the curse are even more dismissed as fantasy. The reality however, is that the effect of a curse can actually be photographed. Joe H. Slate Ph.D in his book *Psychic Vampires – Protection from Energy Predators and Parasites*, Llwellyn Publications 2002, on page 82, published a Kirlian picture taken of a so called *vampire-shadow*. The photo was taken during an experiment whereby students deliberately send very negative energy to a test-person, that shows a black mycelium-like structure which almost entirely blocks the energy field around a fingertip and blurring the border between energy and (an acutely created) entity.

Borda

The *Borda* is a kind of witch-like creature, whose existence possibly roots in a swamp-spirit in the folklore of the Emilia-Romagna and other areas of the Po Valley in Italy. It can appear both as a female or a male witch, blindfolded and horrible, at night as well as on foggy days killing anyone who has the misfortune to meet her. She is a personification of the fear related to swamps and marshlands, and to ponds and canals, invoked by adults to scare children off and keep them away from such potentially dangerous places. The Borda, known by this name especially in Modenese, is also known as *Bourda* in Bolognese, *Bùrda* in Ferrarese and *Bûrda* or *Burdâna* in Emelian. The masculine form takes the name of *Bordón* in Parma, *Bordö* or *Bordoeu* in Milan (meaning *Ogre*) and *Bordò* in Bormiese. In Milanese, as well as in the dialects Cremasco and Bormiese, the word *borda* means "fog". In Bergamese the name has the meaning of "fog" as well as that of "paper mask". Some scholars of local folklore trace the etymology of the term Borda to the root *bor-* which can be traced back to *Borvo*, of Celtic mythology, who presided over thermal and spring waters, and would be found in a vast area united by an ancient Celtic presence, in toponyms and terms related to the water element. Examples being: the river Bormida, spa resorts such as Bormio, Bourbon-Lancy, Bourbon-l'Archambault, words in French such as *brouillard* and *brume* (fog) or bourbe (slime).

Broxa

In Portugese Jewish folklore, *Broxa* or *Bruxa* is a vampiric bird-like entity that is said to suck the milk of goats and sometimes human blood during the night. In medieval Portugal, the Broxa was considered to be a shape shifting entity as a witch or demon that could appear in both a female and male form.

Brouculaka

In 1721 the bishop of Avranches explained the etymology of the term *Brouculaka* or *Brucolaka* as a compound of the Greek *bourcos* (mud) and *laucos* (ditch, sewer) because this creature of the *Revenant-Vampire*-type emerged from a mud filled grave. When its grave was opened it could be recognized by its missing nose bone and a split lower lip. According to a 1703 London dictionary (by Moreri, Baile, Hoffman, Danet – printed for J. Hartley), the Brouculakas were the bodies of the excommunicated that were animated by the Devil. To destroy a Brouculaka one had to dig up the body, cut its heart into pieces and rebury it again.

Buffardello

According to the *Vocabolario Lucchese* of Idelfonso Nieri, the *Buffardello* is an *Imp*, or a curious devilish or even vampiric *Alp*, almost like the *Linchetto,* and present in the folklore traditions of Val di Serchio, Garfagnana, Versilia (Province of Lucca) and Lunigiana (Provinces of Massa Carrara and La Spezia). Variants of the name are *Bufardello,*

Buffardella, Bufardella, Baffardello, Bafardello, Baffardella, Baffardelle, Bafarded, Beffardello, Baffardejo, etc. In Gorfigliano, a hamlet of Minucciano, it is called *Pappardello*, in Sillano *Piffardello*. In the area closest to the city of Lucca the Buffardello is certainly known in Val Pedogna (Municipality of Pescaglia) in the valley of Camaiore, in the northern part of the municipality of Massarosa and in some villages of the Pizzorne Plateau (for example Corsagna di Borgo a Mozzano). Tales about the Buffardello have been recorded in 1984-1987 by Oscar Guidi in the towns of Camporgiano, Careggine, Castelnuovo di Garfagnana, Castiglione di Garfagnana, Fabbriche di Vallico, Fosciandora, Gallicano, Giuncugnano, Minucciano, Molazzana, Piazza al Serchio, Pieve Fosciana, San Romano in Garfagnana, Sillano, Vagli Sotto, Vergemoli, and Villa Collemandina. In the villages his typically sarcastic laughter can be heard near the houses; in Gallicano it is said that once he had occupied a house, he spent the whole time opening and closing the windows almost laughing himself to death.

Appearances

It is generally believed that the Buffardello is invisible, but there are testimonies of those who have seen it in person: according to them, the strange creature lives in the stables or in the trees (especially in walnut trees); sometimes it is seen entering from a window, at other times it walks while jumping and kicking. The Buffardello has different appearances. He is generally described as an anthropomorphic being of small size (around half a meter, so that it can be compared to a Gnome or a dwarf) and dressed in red clothes (sometimes the whole dress, other times only a cap) wearing pointed shoes. In other descriptions he is as a child, or just without a beard, in others as an old man with a beard or red beard. He can have animal features as well, though not well defined, generally he mimics a "beast of the woods" or other animal, like a fox, cat, dog, badger, stone-marten, a big night bird or at least a "bad bird", or even in one case a "gray wad". Sometimes the Buffardello appears as a completely fantastic creature: in Minucciano it is described as a horned night bird that lives in the church tower of the village (so much so, that at night you can hear its breath), while in Pianacci, in the municipality of Villa Collemandina, the Buffardello is described as a bird with the head of a mouse. When in his anthropomorphic shape, his hands were pierced by Saint John so that he would no longer suffocate people during the night. Sometimes he is seen sitting on a pile of hay or in a tree.

His evil deeds

The Buffardello can be a real pest to domestic animals housed in stables: it sucks the milk from the udders of cows, transforms the milk into oil, tangles the tails of cows and horses and makes them immune to fire, makes the cages of birds falter, makes the cows nervous, scares the sheep and can suck the blood of domestic animals until they die. It has sometimes been seen riding a mare at night through the streets of the country. With boys and children he seems to have an ambivalent relationship; sometimes he frightens them, throws them on the ground or kidnaps them, or loosens the swaddling clothes of newborns, sometimes he shows affection towards the smallest so much, that he goes to sleep in the bed next to them. He has the same ambivalence with women and girls: in some cases he pulls out their hair or tangles it up in such an inextricable way that they are forced to cut it, he unravels the braids or loosens the apron they are wearing, hinders the weaving of wool; in others he falls in love with them and takes care of them by bringing them food and drink, combing their hair, making them beautiful. In this case, however, the relationship must remain secret, otherwise the Buffardello takes revenge by making the girl die. It is not uncommon that a pair of girls, one of which is ugly and the other beautiful, is said to be the work of the buffardello (as well as a pair of children, one healthy and strong, the other weak and sickly). It seems that priests are his worst enemies, so he visits them, breaks their glasses and tries to scare them with animal noises (grunts, brays, meows). It is thought to cause a strong and whirling wind (called *scontronello* in Magliano in Garfagnana), so that in some places the name Buffardello has passed to identify this type of wind or the wind that makes the windows vibrate.

Protection measures

To prevent him from entering the house, at sunset the windows are closed and the clothes are hung up to dry to prevent them from "witching"; then a broom is placed upside down against the inside of the door, or a priest's stole is hung there. On the outer side of the door people hang a branch of juniper, so that the Buffardello, when he arrives, is forced to count the berries, forgetting the person he wants to harass and then goes away. This remedy is also used to protect domestic animals, by hanging a branch of juniper in the stable. If the Buffardello is already in the house, there are several remedies to make him run away; the light could be turned off, one could sit next to a candle made of three different qualities of wax, or one could put a plate containing juniper berries on the staircase leading to the bedroom. When the Buffardello stumbled on it and one ordered him to pick them all up, the Buffardello would usually run away. In the most desperate cases one could take a slice of bread and a slice of cheese and eat them at the toilet while performing ones bodily needs, pronouncing at the same time the formula: *"Io mangio pane e cacio, e te buffardello, ti rincaco!"* (I eat bread and cheese, and you Buffardello, are going to get sick!) If the Buffardello is at home but a woman did not want him to climb on the bed, she could put a broom on the side of the bed, or she could put a piece of men's clothing (pants or hat) and keep it at the end of the bed or use a white nightgown with the sleeves arranged into a cross. In case you already felt the presence of the Buffardello on your chest or stomach while sleeping, there is a phrase you could use: *"Run away! Don't you know what St. John did to you?"* (with reference to the hands of the Buffardello that were believed to have been pierced once by St. John) and so do not suffocate me", whereupon the Buffardello, knowing himself discovered, runs away. Iron also scares the creature.

Bugul-noz

The *Bugul-noz*, *Bugul-nôz* (Shepherd of the night) or *Bugel-noz* (Child of the night) is a nocturnal creature in Breton folklore, close to the *Goblin* and the *Werewolf*, and known to appear in the form of a metamorphic shepherd wearing a large hat. The creature is mentioned since the seventeenth century. Joseph Loth studied the etymology in his Breton-French Dictionary of the Vannes dialect, in 1894. The name has changed its meaning in Breton Vannetais, since *bugel*, which designates the child, is the same word as *bugul*, the shepherd, of which the meaning is different in the other dialects. The form *Bugel-noz* is found in 1633, and that of *Bugul-noz* in Vannetais from 1732.

Descriptions

According to some descriptions, the Bugul-noz is a Werewolf. According to other descriptions the creature is an "evil Goblin" who frightens humans with his appearances, sometimes donning a wolf skin to run around at night. The Bugul-noz is also described as a wolf. Bretons who return late from plowing are likely to encounter it and dread this moment. The Bugul-noz is especially known in the Vannetais region (southern Brittany), where one way to protect oneself from it was to *"quickly entrench oneself behind a Christian door, the horizontal and vertical bars of which form a cross"*, or to stay in a ploughed field, previously sown with blessed grains. A spirit of the night, the Bugul-noz sees the height of his power at midnight and frequents the woods and paths, hidden under a hat "wider than a cartwheel" and with a large white cloak dragging on the ground. Just like the *Cauchemar*, he grows as one approaches him. He possesses the gift of metamorphosis in order to surprise his victims, and can change, for example, into a horse. He is sometimes accompanied by *Korrigans* singing their marching song. Anatole Le Braz says that in Riantec, when you hear him whistling behind you, you must be careful not to whistle too. But the Bugul-noz is not always evil. He is said to also have protected people against demons, by putting them under his coat. In other stories, he is a *Werewolf* who carries off children by hiding them in his hat. Paul Sébillot gives a version according to which a farmer notices that his brother is "Bugul-noz" and goes out every night in the shape of a wolf. On the advice of a priest, he goes to meet him one night and pricks him with a two-pronged fork. The Bugul-noz is sometimes linked to the sea, where he is said to officiate, "armed to the teeth ", and that he fears the hawthorn, whose power puts an end to enchantments. He would be a cursed man who performs a penance. The American Walter Evans-Wentz was interested in the Bugul-noz, whom he described as a "Fairy man," but was unable to find a description of the herd that accompanied him, nor what his encounter portended, although he noted that the Bretons preferred to avoid him. He suggests, as does Pierre Dubois, that the Bugul-noz took his flock of shadows to graze at nightfall to signify to the shepherd that it is time to return, and would not be evil, but would urge men to leave the territories he haunts with the spirits of the night.

Most of the information concerning the Bugul-noz comes from various Briton collections. Joseph Frison collected several for the *Revue des traditions populaires*: *Le petit boudeur* in April 1908, *Le berger de nuit* in July 1910, *Le Bugul-nôz* in November of the same year, and *La délivrance du Bugul-nôz* in February 1911. He learned from a servant of about twenty years old that one of these creatures once haunted the church of Cléguer. However, the popular belief is already disappearing: a peasant from Lorient says that he has heard of the Bugul-noz but does not remember it, adding that it may be a songbird, but that this name is no longer used. Joseph Frison is told that the creature would have lived with his wife near Hennebont, but would have since disappeared. Yves Le Diberder collected new anecdotes in the Kemenet-Héboé, the Porhoët, and in the Rhuys peninsula in 1912. The Bugul-noz is said to be an archaic pagan, allergic to the sign of the Redemption.

Busgoso

The *Busgoso*, also known as *Busgosu* or *Musgosu*, is a being of Asturian folklore and considered to be a tall bearded *Duende*, lord and defender of the forests, who protects and controls the flora and fauna. The creature dwells deep in the woods and in caves. Physically the Busgoso is identical to the *Fauns* and *Satyrs* of Greek mythology; he is a humanoid figure, covered with thick hair and has goat's legs and little horns. However it seems he sometimes dresses himself up. Some tell of having seen him wearing a hat made of leaves and a green moss suit. In some areas, he is described in a quite different way; like a batrachian (hence the expressive name *Mufosu*, for his appearance as a giant frog, as in Piloña).

The Busgoso-myth has also spread to parts of Cantabria where the Busgosu is a kind being, who helps people, especially shepherds, whom he guides when they get lost. He even helps them to fix the huts they use when they are in the countryside. In western Asturias Busgoso is a bitter enemy of the woodcutters and hunters. He tries to frighten or mislead those who enter his domain, or even chases them until they fall off cliffs. He also abducts women from the villages to take them to his cave to enjoy them. He does not mind being hunted down because he cannot be caught. In the east of Asturias, the Busgoso presents more positive aspects, undoubtedly due to the influence of the Cantabrian version. There, the Busgoso is a kind and beneficent being and guides the shepherds when they get lost, or helps to fix the huts of the brañas (meadows or pastures located high in the mountains) that have collapsed during the storms in winter and he also cleans the springs so that the cattle can safely drink and bathe in the water. He is dressed in a dry moss jacket, a hat of leaves and wolf-skin booties. He plays sad and sweet songs on a wooden flute that he takes out of his bag, and these melodies help to guide the lost shepherds and urges them to shelter their flocks before the arrival of storms.

Butoni

El Butoni is a traditional phantom from Huerta (Horta) de Valencia. He is also known locally as *Botoni* (Safor), *Bataroni* (Ribera Alta and Ribera Baja), *El Toni* (Comtat), *Butatoni* (Campo de Murviedro) and *Batoni* (Tierra Alta). El Butoni is described as a spirit, devil, little demon, ghost and served mainly as *Bogey* to keep children from all kinds of mischief. Sometimes he is depicted with two faces and hands and feet with claws. It was said that he could enter any room through the keyhole.

Etymologically, Butoni is probably an amalgamation of "bu" and the name "Toni". *Bu, bo* or *boe* (or *pu*) is a European letter compound/sound common in the names of Bogeys – see for example the Dutch *Boeman* and German *Busemann* or Austrian *Putz*. El Butoni has been around for centuries and who this historical "Toni" may have been remains unclear. As early as the Middle Ages, El Butoni was used as a threat to children who misbehaved, did not empty their plates, cried all the time, or would not go to bed. A historical example of the use of the word Butoni as a deterrent is the so-called *ronda del Butoni*, the popular name of the police force or vigilante group created in Valencia by Captain General Elío after the French War to fight bandits, and which was known for the cruel methods they used. In 2014, the screenwriter Ricardo Vilbor and the cartoonist Paco Zarco created a comic called *Butoni*, based on this character. In 2019, the short film *Espantacriaturas* by Valencian director Javier Guillot premiered, starring El Butoni and sharing the screen with other creatures from Valencian folklore.

C

Caballi

Caballi or *Cabales* is mentioned in Nevill Drury's *Dictionary of the Esoteric* and in two other sources. It is a vampiric being of the astral plane that preys on other astral beings, and occasionally humans passing in their projected double through the astral plane, and sexually driven mediums or "projectors" as John Kreiter has recently named them. The Caballi, similar to the *Incubus/Succubus*, seeks out those who share its passion for satisfying its needs, latching on to those humans and utilizing their bodies during sexual activity. These beings are said to be created when someone dies before it is his or her natural time. The soul travels to a lower section of the astral plane, retaining its intellect and a desire to interact with the world again. For this purpose a Caballi will sometimes possess a psychic medium, so that – for a little while at least – it will have some sense of sensation. Something comparable are ancestral spirits, or *Lwas*, possessing practitioners of Vodou, Winti, Umbanda or other Afro-American religions. Theory has it, that the Caballi will in that case only remain as such until the day that it would have died naturally.

Cabeiri

In Greek mythology, the *Cabeiri* or *Cabiri* (sing. *Cabeiro* or *Cabeira*; also transliterated *Kabeiri* or *Kabiri*; Ancient Greek: Κάβειροι, *Kábeiroi*) were a group of enigmatic chthonic deities of pre-Greek (Pelasgic) origin, who were worshipped in mystery cults, especially on the islands of Lemnos, Imbros and Samothrake. They offered protection from storms, but as descendants of *Hephaistos* they were also considered good craftsmen. They were often associated with fertility cults. Presumably the cult of the Cabeiri existed even before the arrival of the Hellenes in Greece and the word "kabeiroi" is originally pre-Greek, possibly Phrygian or Semitic. Josephus Justus Scaliger associated the name with the Semitic *kabir* (great), as early as the 16th century. But many other explanations of the name have also been proposed. For example, a connection with the Sumerian-Hurritic *kabar* or *kibir* (copper, bronze) has been assumed, and the name has been equated with that of the ancient Indian god *Kúbera*.

The nature of the Cabeiri

The number of Cabeiri, their nature and the composition of their company had been rather unclear ever since the earliest antiquity. Several sources mention one Cabeiro or Cabeira, a daughter of *Proteus*, as the mother of the Cabeirs at Hephaistos. They were, however, represented as *dwarf*-like helpers of Hephaistos. The Cabeiri were perhaps originally lower deities who were helpers to a mother goddess, variously referred to as *Demeter*, *Rhea*, *Cybele*, *Hecate*, or *Persephone*. In that respect they would then be similar to the *Corybants* and the *Curets* (with whom they were also equated). But later they were also regarded as gods in their own right and put on a par with the "Great Gods". The names of the Cabeirs on Samothrake are mentioned: *Axieros*, *Axiokersa* and *Axiokersos*. The writer Mnaseas, who is the source of this information, equates the first with Demeter, the second with Persephone and the third with Hades. Perhaps this was originally a triad of gods, but often a fourth is added, *Cadmilus* (or *Casmilus*), an ithyphallic (that is, with erect penis) god, who was equated with *Hermes*. During the mysteries at Samothrake, revelations were probably made to the initiates about the sexual relationship between *Persephone* and *Hermes*. In Boeotia, an older "Kabeiros" was worshipped along with a child (Greek "pais"), as evidenced by wisdom-gifts found in the Kabeirion (temple of the Cabeiri) which was about 10 km east of Thebes. In Berytos (present-day Beirut), according to Philo of Byblos, seven Cabeiri were worshipped, to whom the Phoenician god *Esmun* was added as the 8th. By the Romans their *Penates*, their household gods, were sometimes considered equal to the Cabeiri, or to the *Dioscures* (with whom the Cabeiri were also confused). The Roman writer Varro made it out that the Penates had been brought from the Arcadian city of Pheneos to Samothrace by Dardanus and from there taken to Italy by Aeneas.

In myth, the Cabeiri bear many similarities to other fabulous races, such as the *Telchines* of Rhodes, the *Cyclopes*, the *Dactyls*, the *Korybantes*, and the *Kuretes*. These different groups were often confused or identified with one another since many of them, like the Cyclopes and Telchines, were also associated with metallurgy. Diodorus Siculus said of the Cabeiri that they were *Idaioi Dactyloi* (Idaian Dactyls). The Idaian Dactyls were a race of divine beings associated with the Mother Goddess and with Mount Ida, a mountain in Phrygia sacred to the goddess. Hesychius of Alexandria wrote that the Cabeiri were *karkinoi* (crabs). The Cabeiri

as Karkinoi were apparently thought of as amphibious beings (again recalling the Telchines). They had pincers instead of hands, which they used as tongs (Greek: karkina) in metalworking. It has been suggested by Comyns Beaumont (in: *Britain The Key To World History*, 1948) that the Orphic mysteries may have had their origins with the Cabeiri.

Cama-Crusa

The *Cama-Crusa*, *Came Cruse*, *Came Crude* ("Raw Leg" in Gascon) or *Òs-de-la-Mala-Cama* (Bone of the Bad Leg) was a nocturnal "child eating" *Croque-mitaine* (Bogey) of French folklore, that could be found in Gascony, notable around Aire-sur-L'Adour in the Landes. Its role has largely been usurped by more traditional Croque-mitaines such as the poltergeist-like *Ramponneau* and the *Sopatard* or *Soupetard,* that emerged from soup eating Spanish immigrants in 1852. The Cama-Crusa however had a unique and perhaps the most horrifying appearance of all Croque-mitaine-variants, as it presented itself as a gruesome disembodied leg, sometimes with its skin ripped off. Despite its appearance as just one leg, the Camacrusa was described as very rapid in movement, capable of hiding behind hay-bales, jumping over ditches and hedges, and easily running down its prey – mainly children who remained outside after dark. How it ate children without a mouth remains unspecified.

Local names and interpretations

- **Gascony, Béarn**: *Came-Crue* or *Came-Crude*, "raw leg" or "cruel", a *Bogeyman*; a kind of *Croquemitaine* for children. According to Abbé Vincent Foix, the *Came-Crude* hides behind piles of straw or hay.
- **Gers** and **Landes**: according to Abbé Dambielle, the *Camo-Cruso* is said to be a *pèth* ("skin" or disguise, the appearance a sorcerer would assume). The creature evokes the idea of a *Vampire*, and prowls around houses with terrifying ferocity to grab small children.
- **Ariège**: *Camba Crusa et Uelh Dobert* (The Rough Leg and the Open Eye) is certainly one of the most widespread Croquemitaines of Ariège. It is a leg with an open eye and a horn, which runs faster than anyone else, a raw leg, which has only the bone or a red leg ugly and all bloody.
- **Agenais**: the two stories, *La jambe d'or* and *La Goulue*, by folklorist Jean-François Bladé (1827-1900) on this theme are collected in Lot-et-Garonne:

Cama Crusa (2022) by Benjamin Adamah

La Goulue (the Ghoul)
In this story, *La Goulue* is the nickname of a young girl who eats large portions of raw meat, and who loses her temper when she stays deprived of it. When her parents leave for town one day, she asks them to bring some meat for her. When they return, they realize that they have forgotten the meat. When they pass a cemetery, they dig up a newly buried dead man, cut off his leg, and bring it to their daughter, who immediately devours it raw. The next day, however, the dead man comes to claim his leg and drags the La Goule to his grave, where he in turn devours the girl. Bladé indicates in a note that this story is called *La Camo Cruso* by some of his informants.

La jambe d'or (The Golden Leg)
This story takes place in Agen. A rich man has a very beautiful wife. One day the woman falls and breaks her leg. To replace the broken leg, the gentleman has a golden leg made for her, which enables her to walk with the same grace and lightness as before. But after seven years the woman dies, and is buried with her golden leg. A greedy servant, however, goes out in the night to steal her leg. In the cemetery a voice is heard groaning, *"D'or, d'or, rendez-moi ma jambe d'or"* (Gold, gold, give me back my golden leg). This is heard by the gravedigger, who warns the husband, who goes to the grave of his wife and promises her to have Mass celebrated, but the complaint keeps coming back, *"Gold, gold, give me back my golden leg"*. The next day, the man sends his servant, with the same result. On the third day, he sends the servant again. The man, somewhat worried, asks, *"What do you want, madam?"* and the lady jumps out of her grave and says, *"You I will have!"*, she pulls him into the grave and devours him.

Camenae

In ancient Roman mythology the *Camenae* (also *Casmenae*, *Camoenae*) play a complex role, which is interesting in the sense that their history shows how supernatural entities can "refresh" their label. The Camenae were originally goddesses of childbirth, wells and fountains, and also prophetic deities and later on they became Water-Nymphs before making their final transition to *Muses*. There were four Camenae:

- *Carmenta*, or *Carmenti*
- *Egeria*, or *Ægeria*, or *Aegeria*

- *Antevorta*, or *Porrima*
- *Postverta*, or *Postvorta*, or *Prorsa*

The last two were sometimes specifically referred to as the *Carmentae* and in ancient times might have been two aspects of Carmenta rather than separate figures; in later times, however, they are distinct beings believed to protect women in labor. Carmenta was chief among the *Nymphs*. Her festival day, the *Carmentalia*, featured water ritually drawn by *Vestal Virgins* from the spring outside the Porta Capena. The Camenae were later identified with the Greek *Muses*; in his translation of Homer's Odyssey, Livius Andronicus rendered the Greek word *Mousa* as *Camena* and Horace refers to poetic inspiration as the *"soft breath of the Greek Camena" (spiritum Graiae tenuem Camenae)* in *Odes II.16.*

Cauchemar

Cauchemar is derived from *cauquemaire*, used in the 15th century. It is formed from *caucher* and *mare*. According to Dubosquet, the word *Cauchemar* itself comes from the words *calca* (Low Latin, for *calcatio* "the action of treading") and *mar*, softened from the Celtic *march* (horse). Another etymology however states that *caucher* derives from *cauchier* (to press), which is a probable cross between 17th century Old French *chauchier* (to whip, to press), Latin *calcare* (to stomp, to trample), and the Picardic form *cauquer*. *Mare* comes from the Picard word *mare*, borrowed from Middle Dutch *mare* (ghost), with the same meaning in German and English. The *Mara* or Mare is a type of malevolent female spectre in Germanic, Scandinavian and – under different names – Eastern European folklore. Cauchemar has had different spellings, depending on locality and time: *Cochemare* 1694; *Cochemar* 1718; *Cauchemare*; *Cauquemare* (Picardie); *Cauquevieille* (Lyon); *Chauchi-vieilli* (Isère); *Chauche-vieille* (Rhône); *Chaouche-vielio* (Languedoc), *Cauquemare, Quauquemaire* (witch), *Cochemar*; *Coche-Mares*; *Cochomaren*; *Cochomares*; *Couchemache*; *Couchemal*; *Gaukemares* and *Macouche.*

The Cauchemar is the French version of the classical *Succubus* (more than the Mare, which mainly exerts pressure) and seems to prefer men as its victim, though I know at least one actual report of an attack on a woman. At night the Cauchemar slips into the bed of what it perceives to be an evil person. Then it sexually stimulates the person to orgasm, enslaving the person to its will and draining him or her of life-energy. In the morning, the victim will awake with drool descending from either side of his mouth and with evidence of having experienced a nocturnal emission. Other signs include feeling overly tired and suffering leg cramps. To prevent the Cauchemar from attacking, a person can place some salt under his pillow or dried beans or stones under his bed every night. A broom propped in the corner will offer protection, as will sleeping on one's stomach. Saying prayers before going to bed and keeping religious items in the room will prevent it from entering. If all else fails, one can put screens on the windows. If the Cauchemar cannot be prevented from entering the room and attacking, it is vital that no one ever so much as touches the victim during one of the assaults. To do so can cause the Cauchemar to kill the victim as it flees.

Centaur

The *Centaur,* a creature with the body of a horse, except for the part of the horse's neck and head that has been replaced by the upper body of a human being, is much more a creature of Greek mythology than folklore. It is included in this compendium because the Centaur probably functions as the source of some creatures in Mediterranean and Basque folklore, that share this hybrid appearance of being part human, part horse, mule, donkey or even part cow. See for example the Catalan *Muladona,* the Andalusian *Juancaballos,* the Basque *Oiartzun* of Intxisua, that appears half human half cow, and even the *Kallikantzaros,* a kind of vampiric creature of Greece, Turkey and the southern Balkan, that is sometimes described with horse legs.

Cheval Mallet

Le Cheval Mallet describes a fabulous and evil horse mentioned in folklore around the French Vendée, Poitou, and more frequently in the Pays de Retz, near Lac de Grand Lieu. This animal is said to appear in the evening or in the middle of the night in the form of a magnificent white or black horse, properly saddled and bridled, tempting travelers that are exhausted from a long journey to climb on its back. Several very similar legends circulate about the unwary who ride this horse. They never return, unless they have the ransom for the journey, or a protective charm such as a medal of St. Benedict. The Mallet horse is seen as an instrument of the Devil, or even a form of Satan himself. Perhaps originating from *Sleipnir* and the wild hunt, its legend is very similar to that of other fabulous horses such as *Lou drapé* or the white mare. The name *Mallet*, and by corruption *Merlet*, could be derived from *mail* which means "trunk" or "suitcase" in the ancient Celtic languages. Taking the word from Breton roots, a Celtic language, we find *Marc'h Klet*, meaning the "comfortable horse". A saddled and bridled horse is in fact more comfortable than a bareback horse. And this temptation of the comfortable trip on a horse seals the loss of the one who gives in to it. When spoken, the "k" preceded by the "c'h" becomes silent, which gives *mar'let*. "Mallet" could also come from *mallier*, meaning "a horse that carries trunks" in Middle French.

Description

The Cheval Mallet is a beautiful horse, usually white, rarely black (it is said to be white as fog in the Vendée and black in Saintonge). It is sometimes described as a ghost-horse, always evil or cursed, which appears carefully saddled and bridled, sometimes in the evening, and most often in the middle of the night, in front of a person tired from a long journey. It then represents a temptation for the traveler. If the traveler rides this horse, this ride ends in the morning with his death. The rider is thrown to the ground, and usually dies on the spot. He may be trampled to death by the horse, thrown into a precipice or into any type of water source. Traces of a "strangely shaped" hoof can be found next to the body. The eyes of the Mallet horse are said to emit a glow that illuminates its path when it gallops. There would be only one way to stop this animal: throwing six coins marked with a cross in front of it. A medal of St. Benedict (known as a "witch's cross") is said to be the only effective protection that allows one to take control of it for a night.

A feast was also known to be called a horse Merlette, Merlet or Mallet in the town of Saint-Lumine-de-Coutais, where it had a military function, as a cathartic celebration of renewal, or carnival, and featured several actors around one oak, one of them disguised as a horse. It was opposed by the ecclesiastical authorities and banned in 1791.

Chevêche

According to Perel Wilgowicz in *Le vampirisme, 2e édition*. Broché – March 20, 2000, the *Chevêche* (also: *Chevche, Chevecsch, Chevesche*) is a vampiric witch from France that preys on little children, drinking their blood. According to the *Dictionnaire du moyen français of the Trésor de la langue française*, the word *chevêche* has the same root as *chat-huant* and *chouette*, i.e. it is derived from the Latin *cavannus* (tawny owl).

Coco

The *Coco* or *Coca* (also known as the *Cucuy, Cuco, Cuca, Cucu* or *Cucuí*) is a mythical ghost-monster, a kind of *Bogeyman*, found in many Spanish-speaking and Portuguese-speaking countries. The Cucuy is a male creature while Cuca is a female version of this mythical monster, notorious for visiting the homes of disobedient children and makes them "disappear." The Coco is variously described as a shapeless figure, sometimes a hairy monster, that hides in closets or under beds and eats children who misbehave when they are told to go to bed. There is no general description of the Cucuy, in terms of facial or body descriptions, but it is stated that this shape-shifting creature is hideous to look at. The myth of the Coco, or Cucuy, probably originated in northern Portugal and Galicia. According to the Real Academia Española, the word Coco is derived from the Galician and Portuguese *côco*, which means "coconut." The word *coco* is popularly used in Spanish to refer to the human head or a skull. The oldest reference to the Coca is in the 1274 book *Livro Terceiro de Doações e Direitos Reais*. In this book, the Coca is described as a stranded large fish that dies on the shore:

> *"And if by chance a whale or sperm whale or mermaid or coca or dolphin or Musaranha or other large fish resembling some of these, dies in Sesimbra or Silves or elsewhere".*

In Catalonia, the *Cuca fera de Tortosa* was first documented in 1457 as a zoomorphic figure resembling a turtle with a horned backbone, dragon claws and a dragon's head. According to legend, Cuca fera had to feed on three cats and three children every night. This legend of the Coca can be compared to that of the *Peluda* or *Tarasque*. Traditionally in Portugal, the Coco is represented by an iron pan with holes, to represent a face, with a light inside; or by a lantern carved from a pumpkin with two eyes and a mouth, left in dark places with a light inside to scare people. In the Beiras, heads carved on pumpkins, called *coca*, were carried around by the village boys, stuck atop wooden poles. The famous Halloween pumpkin, therefore, did not cross over from the U.S. to the Iberian Peninsula but is an authentic tradition. The spooky carved pumpkin heads are thought to root in the Celtic cult of severed heads. This custom was first mentioned by Diodorus Siculus (XIII.56.5;57.3), with Iberian warriors hanging the heads of enemies from their spears after the battle of Selinunte, in 469 BCE. According to João de Barros, the name of the "coconut" is derived from coco and was given to the fruit by Vasco da Gama's sailors, ca. 1498, because it reminded them of this mythical creature. The Bogey of the Iberian Peninsula thus has a curious relationship with the coco nut and the (severed) head from the Celtiberian regions, from where the Coco spread throughout the Iberian Peninsula. In the first half of the 20th century, the Coca was still an integral part of festivities such as All Souls' Day and the ritual begging of Pão-por-Deus. The tradition of Pão-por-Deus, mentioned as early as the 15th century, is a ritual begging for bread and pastries done door-to-door by children, although in the past poor beggars also participated. The purpose is to share the bread or delicacies collected from door to door with the dead of the community, who were eagerly awaited and who arrived at night in the form of butterflies or small animals.

Couzzietti

The *Couzzietti* is a kind of *Lutin* in the folklore of the Ardennes who sets traps for washerwomen to steal their laundry. His presence is accompanied by cries like *"O Couzzietti, O Moule de Coutteni!"* This creature is described by Paul Sébillot, Albert Meyrac and Pierre Dubois in *La Grande Encyclopédie des lutins.*

Craqueuhhe

The Lorraine or Lotharingen has its own beast: the *Craqueuhhe.* In several localities of Moselle, the Craqueuhhe or *Craqueuhle* was known by other names: *Chan-Crochet* in Châtel-Saint-Germain, *Cappermann* or *Kapermann* in the vicinity of Condé-Northen, or *Père Tôsô* in the Saulnois. The Lorraine author André Jeanmaire describes it in his book *Superstitions populaires dans la Lorraine d'autrefois* (1985) as *"a fantastic being, a sort of Croquemitaine with enormous jaws, wolf's teeth and a bushy beard"*. He continues: *"During the day, he would hide in the deepest part of the woods, in old quarries, and even at the bottom of wells; all dangerous places for small children"*. At dusk, the Craqueuhhe would leave his lair and approach the villages. He would stand in observation behind a bush, a wall, and watch for children who were delayed. When he saw one, he would pounce on it, quick as lightning, and bite it. If he was standing at the bottom of a well and a disobedient child leaned over the edge, he would pull it towards him, grab it and drown it.

Crinaeae

In Greek and Roman mythology, the *Crinaeae* (Ancient Greek: Κρηναῖαι) were a type of *Naiads* or *Water-Nymphs* associated with fountains or wells. Etymologically Crinaeae comes from the Greek *krini*, which in turn comes from the Proto-Indo-European *kr̥s-neh*, from *kres-* (spring, fount). There were a lot of these *Fountain* or *Well-Nymphs*, but only of a few of them we have a more specific description.

- **Aganippe**

  Aganippe (Ancient Greek: Ἀγανίππη, meaning: "mare who kills mercifully") was the name of both a spring and the Crinaeae associated with it. The spring is in Boeotia, near Thespiae, at the base of Mount Helicon, and was associated with the Muses who were sometimes called Aganippides. Drinking from her well was considered to be a source of poetic inspiration. The Crinaeae is called a daughter of the river-god Permessus (called Termessus by Pausanias). Ovid associates Aganippe with Hippocrene.

- **Appias**

  In ancient Rome, *Appias* was a statue of a Nymph near the Appiades Fountain in the Forum of Caesar. Ovid wrote that the fountain was in the middle of the Temple of Venus Genetrix and surrounded by statues of Nymphs who were called the *Appiades* (plural of Appias). Traditionally the Appiades are said to be of *Concordia*, *Minerva*, *Pax*, *Venus*, and *Vesta*. In Roman mythology, Appias was a Naiad who lived in the Appian Well outside the temple to *Venus Genitrix* (Venus Foundress of the Family) in the Roman Forum. In one of his letters, Cicero refers to a statue of *Minerva* as "Appias". In this case, he derived this surname from the name of Appius Claudius Pulcher, whom he intended to flatter.

- **Myrtoessa**

  In Greek mythology, *Myrtoessa* (Ancient Greek: Μυρτωέσσης) was an Arcadian Nymph, specifically a Crinaeae, who together with other Nymphs, *Neda*, *Anthracia*, *Hagno* and *Anchirhoe*, were nurses of the god Zeus. She was depicted carrying water-pots with what is meant to be water flowing down from her.

- **The Sithnides**

  The *Sithnides* were Crinaeae of the springs and fountains of the town of Megara and Mount Gerania in Attika (southern Greece). Pausanias wrote:

  "There is in the city [of Megara] a fountain, which was built for the citizens by Theagenes... This Theagenes upon becoming a tyrant built the fountain, which is noteworthy for its size, beauty and the number of its pillars. Water flows into it called the water of the Nymphai (Nymphs) Sithnides. The Megarians say that the Nymphai Sithnides are native, and that one of them mated with Zeus; that Megaros (Megarus), a son of Zeus and of this Nymphe, escaped the flood in the time of Deukalion (Deucalion), and made his escape to the heights of Gerania. The mountain had not yet received this name, but was since then named Gerania (Crane Hill) because cranes were flying and Megaros swam towards the cry of the birds."

  (*Description of Greece 1.40.1* (trans. Jones) – *Greek travelogue* C2nd A.D.)

Croque-Mitaine

The *Croque-Mitaine* is basically a *child-Bogey* and known all over France. Children are often – for their own safety – threatened with this frightening and evil creature, to forbid them going somewhere they shouldn't. Croque-Mitaines hide in rivers or lakes and in the winter they eat little children's noses and fingers. This figure is present in popular folktales all over France and has many different names.

Most etymological dictionaries avoid the question of its origin or simply mention "obscure origin". Among the etymologies that are proposed, none is really convincing. The word *croque-mitaine* appeared in literature at the beginning of the 19th century. Collin de Plancy devotes an article to it in his *Dictionnaire Infernal* (1818), with a reference to the entry "Babau". It is found many times in Victor Hugo's work, and in Pierre-Jean de Béranger's song *Les myrmidons*, dated December 1819. The term is made up of two words: *croque*, from the verb *croquer* (to bite, to eat) or *crocher* (to catch with a fang), and *mitaine*, which is more difficult to interpret. *Mitaine* could derive from the Old French *mite*, which means "cat". It would therefore be a "cat-eater" whose purpose would be to scare children. *Mitaine* also refers to a glove with cut fingers, or, to use the previous interpretation, a cat's paw with retracted claws. The word could suggest the idea of a finger eater, the monster being invoked by parents to encourage their toddlers to stop sucking their thumbs. Another interpretation would see *mitten* as a distortion of the German *Mädchen* or Dutch *meisje* (meaning "girl" in these languages). Spread out over the many French provinces there are about eighty local varieties of the Croque-Mitaine. Some more interesting ones are for example:

- *Le Suédois* (the Swede), a distant memory of the Thirty Years' War, threatened disobedient children: *"Kindele bet, sunscht kummt d'r Schwed"* (Say your prayers, little one, or the Swede will come).
- The *Nòchtgròbbe*, or night crow, that is supposed to attack children if they stay out too late; a variety of the German *Nachtkrabb* (Alsace).
- *La Mère Tire-Bras*, is supposed to "pull by the arms" the children who come too close to the wells (Sologne, Brittany).
- *Picolaton* (also known as *Pique-au-mollet*, *Quiperlibresson*, and *Cacalambri*), an imaginary bird using its beak to prick the buttocks and heels of lazy children (Franche-Comté).
- *Le Snouck*, a giant pike that eats children who come too close to the water (Brouckerque region of waterways and canals),Vliet (Nord-Pas-de-Calais).
- *Le Lébérou*, a large hairy creature that hides in the woods at night and watches for stray walkers to eat them (Nouvelle-Aquitaine, Périgord).
- *La Ganipote*, a protean creature related to the Werewolf, haunting the countryside of Charentes, Poitou and Guyenne, Nouvelle-Aquitaine.
- *Banya Verde,* a kind of green devil with one horn (Garrotxa, Ampurdan, Catalan Pyrenees).
- *Camuchech*, a kind of big black ball that chases night walkers until they die of exhaustion (Comminges).
- *Garamiauta*, a character or animal, sometimes a cat (Couserans).
- *Cambacrusa*, a creature with a *"naked leg with an eye at the knee"* (Gascony).

- *Rampono, Ramponneau*, poltergeist-like creature that manifests itself by knocking on a floor, a ceiling, or a door (Occitania and Spanish Pyrenees).
- *L'Ome pelut* (the hairy man), a hairy Bogeyman who kidnaps children and sells them as slaves (Occitania and Spanish Pyrenees).
- *Chapacan, Chiapacan,* a dog thief (Marseille).
- *La Garaoude*, an old woman who lives in a caravan; she takes children from the street and puts them in her big bag (Hautes-Alpes).
- *Garamaoude*, a monster of the wells and pits (Bouches-du-Rhône).
- *Marronne*, an old woman holding a lantern (Hautes-Alpes).
- *Le Bègue*, a kind of horned wolf, with big white teeth and a green tail ; it steals children to eat them in the woods (Frontonas).
- *Carabi-bounet,* a character wearing a cap and catching children with a long pole (Isère).
- *La Faye daou mau-parti* (The Fee of the bad hole) and *La Fée Caramogne*: they hide in the cracks of the rocks (Isère).
- The *Tiro-nègo* (in Occitan, *Tire-noie*) and the *Tire-gosse*, drown children in wells (Saint-Paul-Trois-Châteaux).
- *Mâchecroute*, a monster who lived in Lyon under the Guillotière bridge and caused floods (Lyon).

Cuegle

El Cuegle is a strange monster in Cantabrian folklore. It walks on two legs and has a more or less humanoid shape, has black skin, a long beard, gray hair, three arms without hands or fingers, five rows of teeth, a stubby horn, and usually three eyes in its head (sometimes one). Despite its small size, it has great strength. The Cuegle can attack livestock, and is notorious for stealing babies from the cradle. Babies can be protected by placing oak wood or holly leaves in the cradle, which promote an apotropaic effect. El Cuegle can see the past, present and future. It sees the future with the eye on the forehead, the present with the right eye and the past with the left eye.

D

Daktyloi

In Greek mythology, the *Daktyloi* or *Dactyls* (Ancient Greek: Δάκτυλοι Dáktuloi "fingers") were an archaic mythical race of male beings associated with the *Great Mother*, known as *Cybele* or *Rhea*. Their numbers vary, but often they were ten of these spirit-men. The Dactyls were both ancient smiths and healing magicians. In some myths, they are in Hephaestus' employ, and they taught metalworking, mathematics, and the alphabet to humans. When the pregnant *Ankhiale* knew her time of delivery had come, she went to Psychro Cave, on Cretan Mount Ida. As she squatted in labor, she dug her fingers into the earth (Gaia), which brought forth these *Daktyloi Idaioi* (Δάκτυλοι Ἰδαῖοι "Idaean fingers"), thus often ten in number, or sometimes multiplied into a race of ten tens. However, three is just as often given as their number, or they are sometimes also numbered as thirty-three. When Greeks offered a most solemn oath, often they would press their hands against the earth as they uttered it. The Dactyls of Mount Ida in Crete invented the art of working metals into usable shapes with fire.

Dames blanches

Dames blanches in general were female spirits or supernatural beings, comparable to the *White Women* of both Dutch *(Witte wieven)* and Germanic *(Weiße Frauen)* mythology. Dames blanches were reported in the region of Lorraine (Lotharingen) and Normandy. They appear as *Damas Blancas*, in Occitan, in the Pyrenees mountains, where they were supposed to appear near caves and caverns. Sometimes Dame Blanches act as the French version of the Irish *Banshee,* as a family-attached female ghost, that only appears to herald the death of a family member. In the Pyrenean legend, one finds Dame Blanches related to people of royal or princely blood (or their spectres), where they play a protective role. This is the case in Andorra, where a Dame Blanche appeared near the waterfall of Auvinyà. She lived in a nearby tower and appeared several times to defend the Andorran territory against the aims of a bishop of Urgel, and a bit later also against the attacks of a monstrous wolf, who was none other than this metamorphosed bishop.

Thomas Keightley, in his *Fairy Mythology* (1870), describes the Dames blanches as a type of *Fée* known in Normandy *"who are of a less benevolent character"*. They lurk in narrow places such as ravines, fords, and on bridges, and try to attract the attention of passerby. They may require someone to join them in dance, or assist her, in order to pass. If assisted, she *"makes him many courtesies, and then vanishes"*. One such Dame was known as *La Dame d'Apringy*, who appeared in a ravine at the Rue Quentin at Bayeux in Normandy, where one must dance with her a few rounds to pass. Those who refused were thrown into the thistles and briar, while those who danced were not harmed. Another Dame was known on a narrow bridge in the district of Falaise, named the Pont d'Angot. She only allowed people to pass if they went on their knees for her. Anyone who refused was tormented by the lutins, cats, owls, and other creatures who helped her.

One variety of Dames blanches are *Les Lavandières de Nuit* (The Night Washerwomen). It is a myth that is present, not only in France, but in many parts of Europe, under various names: *Kannerez-noz, Night Washerwoman, Bean nighe, Lavandeira Da Noite, Lamina, Bugadiero, Gollières à noz*, etc. According to Jacques Collin de Plancy, Night Washerwomen wash their clothes in fountains while singing in the moonlight. They ask for the help of passers-by to wring their clothes and sometimes break the arms of those who help them.

Nowadays, the Dames blanches seem to have stopped announcing aristocratic deaths, but they remain very present as ghosts and haunt certain locations, where they are frequently supposed to guard a legendary treasure. In several places Dames blanches walk around, especially seeking the vicinity of old castles:

- le château de Puilaurens (France, Aude)
- le château de Puymartin (France, Dordogne)
- le château de Trécesson (France, Morbihan)
- le château de la Boursidière (France, Hauts-de-Seine)
- le château d'Arlempdes (France, Haute-Loire)
- le château du Hohenbourg (France, Bas-Rhin)
- le château de Pouancé (France, Maine-et-Loire)
- le château de Landreville (France, Ardennes)
- le château de Frœningen (France, Haut-Rhin)
- le château de Greifenstein (France, Bas-Rhin)

- le château de Fougères-sur-Bièvre (France, Loir-et-Cher)
- le château de Rouelbeau (Suisse, Canton de Genève)
- le château de Savy-Berlette (France, Pas-de-Calais)

Debru

Debru means "devil" in Basque. Other appellations are *Etsai* and *Tusuri* (Soule). Apart from the Christian cliche, it is a *Irelu* of a tyrannical character who confines souls. It sometimes has a human appearance or that of the snake (Sugaar), the goat (Aker), the red bull (Zezengorri), etc. As a particular Irelu, one of his functions is to encourage people to behave badly towards their neighbors, so that they can do them some harm, both to the person and to their property. Debru is usually represented as a male figure, however, the demon was once represented as a woman in one of the statues of the church of Elkano (Navarre).

Diaños

In Spanish folklore, *Diaños* are mischievous *Duendes*. They are active during the night, scaring those who walk around at odd hours. They can adopt the figure of a horse, a cow, a ram or any other animal, even a human baby. It displays its activity during the night, frightening the walker who wanders in the dark, disorienting the farmer who is looking for lost livestock, annoying the miller who grinds by moonlight, or making fun of the young men who return late from a party. Among its most common pranks is that of the white donkey offering itself as a mount to the traveler, and that once mounted grows and grows without ceasing. Disguised as a horse, after a hellish gallop it returns the rider to the same place from where they left, throws the rider headfirst into the river, or burns his pants. Diaños may also turn into a black dog that chases a walker or turn into a toad that runs faster than horses. They love to turn themselves into babies that play naked in the snow. They may also be the cause of *poltergeist*-like phenomena, like endless noises, mysterious lights and other disturbing phenomena that frighten the nocturnal walker.

Diañu burlón

In Asturian folklore the figure of the *Diañu burlón* is extremely complex. On the one hand it seems to have absorbed attributes of various *Goblins* and minor *Genies* specialized in different tasks (such as, for example, preventing the clearing of land and digging in the mountains, causing snow avalanches and earthquakes, braiding the manes of horses, spoiling the nets of fishermen, or squeezing the chest of sleepers until they almost choke). *Diañu burlón* is sometimes mistaken for Satan, the Lord of the Hells, whose demonic figure constitutes the incarnation of evil propagated by the Catholic Church. However the Asturian Diañu burlón is mainly a prankster Genius and to a certain extent funny, who enjoys teasing people with his nocturnal pranks.

Dip

The *Dip* is a Catalan mythological being. Some kind of evil and hairy dog, an emissary of the devil, who, like so many others, is lame in one leg. It feeds itself by sucking people's blood. On the coat of arms of the Catalan town of Pratdip (Tarragona), you can see an image of this animal. It is precisely in this village that it is a living legend. In the altarpiece of Santa Marina de Pratdip, dating from 1602, images of these *Vampire-dogs* can already be seen. They also appear in another 1730 altarpiece, cut from a gold background.

According to legend, the dips sucked the blood out of cattle. They only went out at night and among their victims were nocturnal drunks, who went to the taverns of the town. There is no reliable evidence, no documented witnesses. It is believed that this legend was only intended to frighten the alcoholics of the town and prevent them from wandering around at night. According to tradition, the name of the village has its origin precisely in these animals (Pratdip = Prado de dips), which seem to have disappeared during the 19th century. At the entrance to Pratdip there is a monument devoted to this being. Because of his thirst for blood, the dip served to inspire Joan Perucho in his novel *Les històries naturals* (Natural Stories, 1960), which tells the story of Onofre de Dip, a Vampire with the ability to transform into many different animals. The central part of the work takes place in Pratdip at the beginning of the 19th century, in the midst of the First Carlist War, and the dip is actually an ambassador of James I the Conqueror, who 700 years earlier had gone to the Carpathians on a diplomatic mission where he had been attacked by a noble Vampire. In other parts of Spain, such as Tenerife (Canary Islands) there was also a belief in a being or evil spirit in the form of a woolly dog known as Guayota (the demon).

DRYAS

Doñas de fuera

In the historical folklore of Sicily, *Doñas de fuera* (Spanish for "Ladies from the Outside" or "Ladies from Abroad" – Sicily was under Spanish rule at the time) were supernatural female beings comparable to the *Fairies* of English folklore. In the 16th to mid-17th centuries, the Doñas de fuera also played a role in the witch trials in Sicily. In historical Sicilian folklore, the Doñas de fuera would make contact with humans, mostly women, whom they took to Benevento, the "Blockula of Sicily", famous for its gatherings of witches around an ancient walnut tree. They were described as beautiful creatures, dressed in white, red or black. Despite the fact that the people addressed them as "doñas", they could be female or male. Their feet were the paws of cats, horses or just of a peculiar "round" shape. They came in groups of five or seven and a male Fairy played the lute or the guitar while they were dancing. Every Tuesday, Thursday and Saturday, the Fairies would meet the humans, belonging to their congregation in the woods. In March, several congregations gathered, and their "Prince" instructed them to be benevolent creatures. A special congregation called *Le Sette Fate* (The Seven Fairies) could transform themselves into cats, or something called an *Aydon. Ayodons*, that were able to kill. The Fairies could easily be offended by humans.

Between 1579 and 1651 there were a number of recorded witch trials in Sicily. The trial summaries, sent to the Spanish Inquisition's Suprema in Madrid by the Sicilian tribunal, reflected a total of 65 people, eight of them male, many of whom were believed to be associates of Fairies, who were put on trial for sorcery. The Inquisition denounced them as witches, but often did not take these cases seriously, as the accused never mentioned the Devil in their confessions. The Inquisition did occasionally associate meetings with the *Elves* as events similar to a Witches' Sabbath, but as the local population generally held a positive view of the phenomenon, the Inquisition did not press the matter. The accused said that they had become associated with the Fairies because they had *sangue dolce* (sweet blood), and that in most cases they went to the meetings in a non-corporeal fashion, leaving their actual bodies behind. This is similar to the concept of astral projection and was something they had in common with the *Benandanti*, a related group that also faced scrutiny by the Inquisition.

Dryad (1564) by Cornelis Cort (1533-1578), after Frans Floris I

Donyet

In Catalan folklore a *Donyet* is a spirit that inhabits in certain houses or places and frightens the people who live there by making noises and causing all sorts of disturbances. It is considered a type of *Goblin*, but not as small as the majority of them, and it is especially fond of playing with horses' manes and riding horses very fast. It loves speed. Traditionally the *Donyets* are dressed in a skirt, a *jupetí* (waistcoat) and a mukador tied to the head with a esquellerinc at the end. In the Valencian towns of Relleu (la Marina Baixa) and La Torre de les Maçanes (l'Alacantí) there is talk of *Cerdets*, a type of Donyet that appears at night and also likes to ride horses and to scare away the genets (a predator of the feline-family).

Dryad

A *Dryad* (Greek: Δρυάδες, *Dryades*; single: Δρυάς, *Dryas*) is a young and beautiful *Tree-Nymph* or tree-spirit in Greek mythology. *Drys* signifies "oak" in Greek, and Dryads are specifically the Nymphs of oak trees, but later in history the term has come to be used for Tree-Nymphs in general, or human-tree hybrids in fantasy stories. They were normally considered to be very shy creatures, except around the goddess Artemis, who was known to be a friend to most Nymphs. The Dryads were supposed to dwell in trees, groves and forests, and, according to tradition, were wont to inflict injuries upon people who dared to injure the trees they inhabited and protected. Notwithstanding this, however, they frequently left their leafy habitats, to wander around and mingle with the wood-Nymphs in their rural sports and dances. They are represented veiled and crowned with flowers. Long before the Dryads and Oreads had received their perfection of human form and face from the sculpturesque Greek mind, trees were said to have woman-like inhabitants, capable of doing good and ill, and with the power of banning and blessing. Therefore was it that they were worshiped, and that people made an appeal to them by way of certain rites. Similar ideas and practices prevailed all over ancient Europe and Asia – an example are the *Tree Mothers*, worshiped by the Celts and their druids.

Duende

The *Duende* – apart from the flamenco cultural context (the inexplicable and mysterious character that this art and its interpreters and great artists in general acquire, a mysterious power that everyone feels and no philosopher is able to explain) described by Federico Garcia Lorca in his *Teoría y juego del duende* – is a humanoid figure in Iberian folklore. It is comparable to the *Gnome* or *Leprechaun* and sometimes also to the *Incubus/Succubus*. In Spanish, Duende originated as a contraction of the phrase *dueño de casa or duen de casa*, effectively "master of the house", or perhaps derived from some similar mythical being of the Visigoth or Swabian culture, given its similarity with the *Tomte* of the Swedish language, conceptualized as a mischievous spirit inhabiting a dwelling.

Spanish folklore is rich in tales and legends about various types of Duendes: *Anjanas*, *Busgosos*, *Diaños*, *Enanos*, *Elfos*, *Hadas*, *Nomos*, *Nuberus*, *Tentirujus*, *Trasgos/Trasgus*, *Trastolillus*, *Trentis*, *Tronantes*, *Ventolines* and others. In some regions of Spain, Duendes may have other names like *Trasnos* in Galicia, *Follets* in Catalonia, *Iratxoak* in the Basque Country and Navarra, *Trasgus* in Asturias, *Menutos* or *Mendos* in Valle de Hecho and in other parts of Alto Aragón, *Mengues* (South of Spain). Duendes also appear in Portuguese folklore, as beings of small stature wearing big hats, whistling a mystical song, often walking in the forest. These Duendes use their talents to lure young children to the forest, who then lose their way home. It is possible to distinguish different Castilian Duendes: *Martinicos*, *Diaños*, *Trasgos*, *Gnomos*, *Encantadas* (Enchanted ladies), *Hadas* and *Elfos*. Engraved in some of Goya's *Caprichos*, are big-headed dwarfs with large hands that are usually disguised by the Franciscan habit they wear. They make noises in the cupboards, displace and lose objects and love to pull (cruel) pranks. The Gnomes inhabit the cavities of the earth. The first mention of an Elf in Spanish literature is made in the *Cantar de Mio Cid*, where it speaks of *Caños de Elfa*, meaning Elfa's cave. The first to extensively deal with *Goblins* was the demonologist Fray Antonio de Fuentelapeña in *El ente dilucidado: discurso único novísimo que muestra que hay en naturaleza animales irracionales invisibles y quales sean* (1676).

Dusios

In the Gaulish language, *Dusios* (pl.: *Dusioi*; Latin pl.: *Dusii*) was a *Satyr*-like *demon* among the continental Celts, although according to a writing of Richarius – born ca. 560 – the *Dusi*, called *Maones* in northern Gaul, are accused of stealing crops and damaging orchards. These beings appear in other medieval sources as *Mavones*, *Maones*, *Manes* and *Magonians*, the latter being airborne crop-raiders from a mythical land located in the clouds. Dusios is however primordially identified with the Greek god *Pan* and the Roman *Faunus, Inuus, Silvanus*, and *Incubus*. All notorious for having the ability to impregnate animals and women, usually by surprise and force. Dusii continued to play a role in the magico-religious belief systems of Gaul and Francia as a type of *Incubus* in early-medieval paganism and Christianity. Etymologically Dusios/Dusii is related to a semantic field of Indo-European words, some meaning "phantom, vapor", as for example Lithuanian *dvãse* (spirit, phantom), and *dùsas* (vapor); the Slavic *dusi* (spirits), *dusa* (soul), *dusmus* (devil) and others meaning "fury" (Old Irish *dás-*, "to be in a fury"). The Breton word *Duz*, a type of *Fairy, Goblin*, or *changeling* is – according to many scholars – derived from *Dusios. Duz* sometimes has been proffered as the origin of deuce as a name for "devil" in the expression *"What the Deuce!"*. The Dusii, becoming a synonym for *Fauns* in later writings, possibly root in an ancient fertility-cult wherein the fig plays an important role. Papias, in a writing from 1040, says that the Dusii are those whom the Romans call *Fauni ficarii*. The adjective *ficarius* comes from *ficus*, "fig", and is applied to Faunus frequently enough to suggest a divine epithet. "Figgy" may refer to the god's fructifying power, or may be a lewd reference to the Fauns' well-known habits of random penetration, as "fig" was Greek slang for "anus" and Latin slang for both "sore anus" and later "vagina". A fertility ritual involving twigs and sap from the male fig tree was carried out by Roman matrons for *Juno Caprotina*, later identified with the goatskin-wearing *Juno Sospita*. Pliny notes that the wild fig (called *caprificus)*, was often called "goat-fig" because it was used as food for goats. Spawns "flies" or fig wasps were called *ficarii*. The adjective *ficarius* characterizes the "figgy Fauns", and their counterparts the *Dusii*, by their swarming, serial acts of fertilization.

Later evolutions

As is often the case with supernatural creatures in European folklore rooted in Antiquity, the Dusii also evolved during the ages and fused with other spirit beings. References to the Dusii appear in the writings of the Church Fathers, where they are treated as demons. Saint Augustine (354-430) writes:

> *"One often hears talk, the reliability of which must not be doubted, since it is confirmed by a number of people who know from their own*

or others' experience, that Silvani and Pans, commonly called incubi, have often appeared to women as wicked men, trying to sleep with them and succeeding. These same demons, whom the Gauls name Dusii, are relentlessly committed to this defilement, attempting and achieving so many things of such a kind that to deny it would seem brazen. Based on this, I dare not risk a definitive statement as to whether there might be some spirits, aerial in substance (for this substance, when it is set in motion by a fan, is perceived as sensation within the body and as touch), who take bodily form and even experience this sexual desire, so that, by any means they can, they mingle with women sensually. But that the holy angels of God in no way fell in like manner during that era — that I would believe."

Archbishop Isidore of Seville (ca 560-636) echoes Augustine closely, but expands the identifications with other divine figures:

"The 'hairy ones' (pilosi) are called in Greek Pans, in Latin Incubi, or Inui from their entry (ineundo) with animals everywhere. Hence also Incubi are so called because wrongful sex is incumbent on them. For often the wicked ones come into the presence of women also, and succeed in sleeping with them. The Gauls call these demons Dusii, because they seduce relentlessly."

In 882 AD, Hincmar, Archbishop of Reims, sees the Dusii as a threat to marriages. In his *De divortio Lotharii regis et Theutbergae reginae* (On the divorce of King Lothar and Queen Theutberga) he writes:

"Certain women have even been found to have submitted to sleeping with Dusii in the form of men who were burning with love."

So in the 9th century the Dusii have become identical with the *Incubi*. In later centuries the definition gets more diffuse. Gervase of Tilbury (ca. 1150–1228) deals with Dusii in his chapter on *Lamiae* and "nocturnal larvae" *(Otia Imperialia, tertia decisio LXXXVI)*. Although he draws directly on Augustine, calling the Dusii Incubi and comparing them to Silvanuses and Pans, he regards them as sexually threatening to both men and women, thus adding the *Succubus* to the Incubus. In the 13th century the Dusios merges with the concept of the *Wild Man* or a forest-spirit one had to stay on friendly terms with. Thomas of Cantimpré (1201-1272) a Flemish Dominican, writer, preacher, and theologian, claimed (in his allegory on bees) Dusii were still an active part of cult practice and belief in Prussia:

> *"We see the many works of the demon Dusii, and it is for these that the folk used to consecrate the cultivated groves of antiquity. The folk in Prussia still reckon that the forests are consecrated to them; they don't dare cut them down, and never set foot in them, except for when they wish to make sacrifice in them to their own gods."*

In the 17th century the philologist and historian of the Middle Ages and Byzantium, Charles du Fresne, sieur du Cange (1610-1688) writes:

> *"Sunt aliqui rustici homines, qui credunt aliquas mulieres, quod vulgum dicitur strias, esse debeant, et ad infantes vel pecora nocere possint, vel dusiolus, vel Aquatiquus, vel geniscus esse debeat."*
>
> (There are some country people who have a belief in certain women, because it is commonly said that they must be witches and able to harm infants and cattle, and the Dusiolus or Aquatiquus or Geniscus must too.)

The form *dusiolus*, a diminutive, appears in a sermon with the beings *Aquatiquus* (from aqua, "water") and *geniscus*, possibly a form of the Roman *Genius* or the Gallic *Genius Cucullatus*, whose hooded form suggested or represented a phallus. According to "country people", these and *Striae* threatened their infants and cattle. This 17th century association is not incompatible with the Dusii-definition of 19th century Irish folklorist Thomas Crofton Croker. He describes the Dusii as a kind of *Woodland* or *Household-spirits*, and deals with them in his chapter on *Elves*.

E

Eate

Eate is a herald of natural disaster. Legends of this Basque *Irelu* are told in the region of Goiherri and Azpeitia in Guipuzcoa, and in Arakil in Navarra. He is a Irelu of the storm, the fire, the floods and the hurricane wind. His voice sounded dull and imposing when hail, a flood, or a devastating fire was approaching. There were people who believed they had the power to tell Eate where to unload his fury by means of an incantation: with a *rainbow herb* in their left hand, they would point out to Eate with their right hand where he should go. Other names associated with the Genius are: *Egata* in Zegama (Guipuscoa), *Ereeta* in Azpeitia (Guipuscoa), *Erots* in Arakil (Navarre) or *Erreate*. The Genius *Eate* may have its roots in *Edelate* or *Edelat,* a god of the Pyrenees in Roman times. His name appears on some of the inscriptions. An altar was found with an inscription addressed to the god *Edelat* in Luscan.

Egoi

Egoi, sometimes also spelled *Hegoi*, is the *Irelu* of the south wind in Basque folklore. The south wind often blows in the mountains, forests and villages. The Egoi wind causes damage to crops and trees due to its violence. In Baztan people believed that when the south wind blows, the gates of Hell are open for a sinner to enter.

Eguen or Egu

Eguen or *Egu* was a *deity* or *Irelu* in Basque mythology representing the (day)light and the blue sky. The root *egu* seems to have meant *light* but also *blue sky*. In Biscayan, some names of the days are dedicated to the god Egu: *eguen* (Thursday), *eguazten* (Wednesday). There are also many Basque terms related to the name *Egu*: *eguantza* (dawn), *eguerdi* (morning and evening art), *eguargi* (light day), *eguarte* (daylight, especially dusk), *egubakoizt* (Friday), *eguberri* (winter solstice), *egunabar* (dawn), *egunaldi* (weather), *egunari* (calendar), etc.

Ehiztari beltza

Ehiztari beltza, "The Black Hunter", is a character (and myth) that often appears in Basque folklore. During the Basque version of the myth *The Wild Hunt*, he will walk through the mountains and valleys in search of prey. The myth is quite widespread throughout the Basque Country. He is also known by other names: *Martin* or *Mateo Txistu*, *Joanito* or *Juaniko Txistularia* in Zerain, *Salomon* or *Errege-Xalomon* in Zuberoa, *Oiartzun* and *Dohoztin*, *Salomon-apaiza*, *Prixki-Joan Usurbilen*, *Martin-abade* in Gesalibar. *The Abbot's Dogs* is another name for the myth, in which case the dogs are accompanied by a Black Hunter, giving them prominence. In Catalan legends the figure is known as *Caçador Negre* (Black Hunter), *Mal Caçador* (Evil Hunter) or *El vent del caçador* (The Hunter's Wind; *Ehiztariaren haizea* in Basque). *Los Encantats* are two steep peaks in the Pallars Sobira region. Legend has it that two brothers were often avid hunters and went after a beast instead of going to Sunday Mass. A priest cursed them for this and turned them into stone. This story coincides with the tales of the cursed hunters of the Pyrenees. In Aragon there is the *Cazataire maldito* (Cursed Hunter), *O Siñó d'Espés* (Lord of Espés) or *Barón d'Espés* (Baron of Espés) in Bal d'Isabena, and *Roberto El Diablo*, elsewhere.

Wild Hunt

The myth of the Black Hunter, or Mateo Txistu, is known throughout Europe as *The Wild Hunt*. It takes different forms in the north, west and center of the continent. The general picture of all the Wild Hunt-myths is always the same: a group of ghostly hunters and their hunting dogs and horses, pass across the sky in a wild hunt. Sometimes they touch the ground, but mostly they stay in the air, often accompanied by a violent storm. The hunters of the wild hunt were the dead, errant souls and certain gods and goddesses. Their leader could often be a historical dead king, or mystical figure like *Hellequin*, or a god like the Germanic god *Wotan* or the Celtic *Arawn*. This myth is widespread in Basque Country, but also throughout Europe. Seeing the Wild Hunt passing by was considered a bad omen, it could be an omen of war or a plague, or the death of a hunter or someone close to you. Humans who were on the path of the wild hunters or following them, could be taken to the world of the dead.

El Broosha

In Spanish-Jewish folk-lore *El Broosha* is a demonic vampiric black cat. In fact, the *Vampire*-cat was seen as a manifestation of the Semitic demon-queen *Lilith*, Adam's first wife, who refused to give him her obedience and left him, later becoming a Vampire. She still lives, and assumes the form of a huge black cat named El Broosha when she seizes a new-born human baby, her favorite prey, and sucks its blood.

The *Vampire-cat* is a rather rare phenomenon. Apart from the mythical Vampire-cat, there exists a strange story in the *Lord Halifax Ghost Book*, first edition Glasgow, 1936, compiled by Charles Lindley, about the encounters of Lord Halifax. On page 201 we find the story *The Vampire Cat*, a true story, delivered to Lord Halifax by his nephew Mr. Everard Meynell. Meynell, who suffered from sleepless nights, managed to escape from busy London and went down to Eastbourne, to stay with some friends. Somehow a large black cat seems to like him more than any other person in the mansion and it starts to follow him everywhere – while making almost desperate attempts to climb up to his neck. Meynell even has to use force to keep the cat out of his bedroom and locks the door. However, this door was opened accidentally by the footman at 6 am, mistaking the time for 7 am, and closed it again when he realized the mistake. But then the cat had already slipped into the room unnoticed:

> "*...Benefiting doubtless by the sea air and the quiet surroundings, he at once fell into a deep and dreamless sleep, a thing which he had not been able to do for many weeks. He was awakened very gradually by a curious drawn feeling down one side of him. In his own words he felt as though he was 'breathing only on one side of his body'. At the same time he had a feeling of faintness and languor which tempted him to turn over and go off to sleep again, but a sharp pricking sensation over his heart caused him to place his hand to his side, where he felt something warm and furry. He started up and found the cat pressed closely against him, with its head buried under his arm, and the whole of one side of his night shirt drenched with blood. He sprang out of bed and said something to the cat, which at once stopped purring, came to the end of the bed, and began to spit and curse at him with a hatred that more than equaled its previous affection. Needless to say, it was the work of a moment to throw the creature out of the room...*"

Eleionómai

Eleionómai (ancient Greek Ἐλειονόμαι; Latin: *Eleionomae*) are, according to literary sources, "marsh-dwellers" (from ἕλειος éleios, "marshy" and νομός nomós, "residence, territory"). In the *Argonautika* of Apollonios of Rhodes, swamp-dwelling *Nymphs* are mentioned to be observed in two places. They are also mentioned in a study about the *Iliad*. This was the basis for modern mythographers, to place Eleionómai as Nymphs of the swamps and marshes on an equal footing with the *Naiads*, *Nereids*, and *Okeanids*, which is regarded as controversial by some scholars, as the term Naiad is specific to Nymphs, while Eleionómai denotes *swamp-dwellers* in general, thus also human inhabitants of a swampy area.

Elfos

In Spain the *Elfos* (Elfs) are probably not pre-Roman mythological beings of the Iberian peninsula, but were most likely imported by Germanic tribes like the Vandals, Suevi and Visigoths, that settled into Spain during the Roman period and after the fall of Rome. The oldest mention of Elfos are in the famous *Cantar de Mio Cid*, a medieval tale of a Castilian knight named Rodrigo Diaz de Vivar, known best as El Cid. Elfos have very similar characteristics as *Anjanas* and were most likely readily mistaken for them by locals.

Empusa

Empusa or *Empousa* (Ancient Greek: Ἔμπουσα; pl.: Ἔμπουσαι, *Empousai*; Latin *Empusae*) is a shape-shifting female being in Greek mythology, whose precise nature is a bit obscure. Sometimes she is regarded as similar to the *Lamia* or *Mormolyke*. The Empusa is said to be one-legged, namely, having one brass leg, or a donkey's leg, thus being known by the alias *Onokole*. A folk etymology construes the name to mean "one-footed" (from Greek ἑμπούς, empous: *en*-, one + *pous*, foot). The creature was a being sent by *Hecate*, or it was Hecate herself, according to a fragment of Aristophanes's lost play *Tagenistae* (Men of the Frying-pan). According to Rick Riordan *Empousai* are the daughters of Hecate, with hair set on fire. In Late Antiquity, the *Empousai* have been described as a category of vampiric or man-eating phantoms or specters, equated with the *Lamiai* and *Mormolykeia*, thought to seduce and feed on young men for the freshness of their blood. The primary sources for the *Empousa* in

Antiquity are Aristophanes and Philostratus. In Aristophanes's comedy *The Frogs and Ecclesiazusae*, the Empousa is a "demonic phantom" with shape-shifting abilities, able to change appearance from various beasts to a woman. She appears before Dionysus and his slave Xanthias on their way to the underworld, although this may be the slave's practical joke to frighten his master. Xanthias thus sees (or pretends to see) the Empousa transform into a bull, a mule, a beautiful woman, and a dog. The slave also reassures his master that the being indeed had one brass leg, and another leg of cow dung. According to 1st century *Life of Apollonius of Tyana*, the Empusa is a phantom (phasma) that took on the appearance of an attractive woman and seduced Menippus, a young philosophy student, in order to eventually devour him. This episode of the *Life of Apollonius*, known as *The Bride of Corinth*, has inspired several authors, such as John Keats. Keats dedicated one of his narrative poems, *Lamia*, to her. In a different passage of the same work, when Apollonius was journeying from Persia to India, he encountered an Empousa, hurled insults at it, coaxing his fellow travelers to join him, whereby it ran and hid, uttering high-pitched screams.

According to Robert Graves *(The Greek Myths, 1955)* Empusa was a demigoddess, the beautiful daughter of the goddess *Hecate* and the spirit *Mormo*, half *Vampire* and half *Succubus*. She feasted on blood by seducing young men as they slept (see sleep paralysis), before drinking their blood and eating their flesh. Once, when she spotted a man sleeping by the roadside, she attacked him, not knowing he was Zeus, king of the gods. Zeus awoke and visited his wrath on her and Empusa was killed. A 1985 field study by Charles Stewart *(The Exotica: Greek Values and their Supernatural Antitheses)* finds that *Empousa* is a term that is rarely used in oral tradition, compared to other terms such as *Gello*, which has a similar meaning.

Enanos

Enanos (dwarfs) are diminutive beings from Spanish folklore who toil night and day in the forests, guard the immense riches that the subterranean world hides and, mockingly, tempt the greed of peasants by offering them gold combs, bags full of silver, that later becomes piles of withered fern leaves and white pebbles. Some Enanos, like the *Duende de los Extravios*, helps good people find their lost possessions.

Etsai

Etsai means "*Devil* or *enemy*". In Basque folk-mythology Etsai is a diabolic teacher, who lives in a cave. He has many names, like *Deabru* (Devil), *Gaizkiñ* (evil), *Galtzagorri* (red pants), *Kapagorri* (red cape), *Gorritxiki* (little red cape), *Kattan*, *Addar* (branch, horn), *Beste mutil* (other young man), and furthermore *Txerren*, *Tusuri*, *Plaga*, *Kinkilimarro* and *Iruadarreko*. He represents the Devil in Basque mythology and has also been depicted in the form of a dragon. He was believed to live in the Leiza cave in Sare (Labourd) where he ran a school and taught science, art and literature. *Atarrabi* and *Mikelats*, as well as others, were educated there. When the education was finished, Etsai could remain a servant of a former student when this was decided by fate. It was believed that this Genius appears at night, sometimes as a bull (*zezen* in Basque), a horse *(zaldi)*, a pig *(xerri)* or a goat *(ahuntz)*. The word is also used in a modern sense to denote a person who has a different opinion then the masses and who is therefore treated as an enemy of the people, or a social outcast.

Etxajaun

Etxajaun or *Etxejaun* is the Basque term for "Lord of the house" or "Householder". *Etxeko jaun* comes from the words *etxe* (house), *ko* (de) and *jaun* (master). It is a *household-spirit*, but the plurals Etxajaunak or *Etxekojaunak* (Lords of the house) also refer to ancestors. They visit the fireplace after people have gone to bed. They are the guardians of the house as well as the benefactors, but they also know how to show their annoyance, when the fire in the home has been put out, when the house is dirty, or the dishes of the meal have been left lying around. They can also get annoyed when they have not been offered anything.

Oceanide (1909) by Gustave Adolf Mossa (1883-1971)

GVSTAV ADOLF MOSSA
NICIENSIS PINSIT 190

F

Falugas

Las Falugas are very small female Catalan demons that enter a persons ear to cause sleepiness or forgetfullness. Their male counterpart is the *Nitus*.

Fantasti

The *Fantasti* is a Provençal barn-spirit and *Lutin*, which bears a strong resemblance to the *Gripet*, the creature settles in stables and barns and then looks after the livestock. It is mentioned by Claude Lecouteux in *Nos bons voisins les lutins: Nains, Elfes, lutins, gnomes, Kobolds et compagnie*, Paris, 2010.

Fantines

Fantines are benevolent *nature-spirits* of the Vaudois Valley in Switzerland. They are associated with taking care of flowers and bring good crops. They also watch over the herds that graze on the Alpine pastures and make tiny bells for the cattle, to keep them from getting lost in the woods.

Farfadets

Farfadets are creatures of French folklore. Farfadets are described as being small (about 40 inches in size), wrinkled and brown-skinned; they generally wear tattered brown clothing, or go naked. Farfadets are said to be helpful rather than malicious, although playful and sometimes mischievous. They like to tend horses, which they will groom, or weave ringlets into their manes. They live in woodland, but will also attach themselves to a neighboring farm or homestead, and complete odd tasks in the fields, in return for a bowl of milk or cream left on the doorstep at night. However, they can be frightened away by too much kindness, such as leaving new clothes out for them. The word *Farfadet* translates as *Sprite*, *Imp*, *Brownie*, or *Leprechaun*, although they also resemble the Pixies of Britain's western countryside. The term is in general use throughout France, but the creature is local particularly to the Vendée and Poitou regions. Farfadets also feature in Occitan mythology, particularly in the Provence, where they are known as *Fadets*. Despite this benign reputation, the (most likely paranoid schizophrenic) 18th century French author and demonologist Alexis Vincent Charles Berbiguier de Terre-Neuve du Thym (1765-1851) believed he was tormented by them after having unsuccessfully visited some fortune tellers, and wrote extensively about the Farfadets and their depredations. In 1821 he felt constrained to publish an autobiography, *Les Farfadets ou Tous les démons ne sont pas de l'autre monde* (The Imps or All the demons are not from the other world), originally published in three volumes between 1818 and 1820. The book was intended as a warning *"To all the Emperors, Kings, Princes and Sovereigns of the Four Parts of the World"*. The autobiography relates Berbiguier's struggles with the Farfadets. He was able to capture some of them, and confine them in bottles. Sulphur and thyme were two odors he found were effective to repel them. The book tells of an adventure he had with firefighters during a sojourn in Paris, where he attracted the alarmed notice of neighbors by burning sulphur to keep the Farfadets at bay. Notwithstanding his efforts, the Farfadets continued to tempt and torment him. The title *Terre-Neuve du Thym* was self-bestowed; it means "New World of Thyme," and shows his hope that revealing his methods will renew the world and purge it of impish influences. He also bestowed upon himself the title *Le Fléau des Farfadets*, (the Scourge of the Farfadets).

Faunus

Faunus was the ancient Italian god of nature and the forest, the protector of farmers and shepherds, their cattle and their fields. He appears in many guises and under many names. Silvanus corresponds to him and in Greek mythology the shepherd god *Pan* corresponds to him. The female counterpart to Faunus is *Fauna*, who was considered Faunus' wife, sister or daughter. In some cases she was also identified with the goddess *Bona Dea*. Later, Faunus was depicted as a mythical creature from Greek mythology similar to the *Satyr* (*Faun* can therefore also be used synonymously for *Satyr*); a shawm or flute-playing horned forest-spirit, a hybrid creature, half-man, half-goat, usually depicted with a human torso, buck feet and tail. As the god Pan was accompanied by the *Paniskoi*, or "little Pans", so the existence of many *Fauni* was assumed, beside the chief Faunus. Fauni are place-spirits (genii) of untamed woodland. They are also said to watch over grain fields and encourage their growth. Educated Hellenizing Romans connected their Fauni with the Greek Satyrs, who were wild and orgiastic drunken followers of Dionysus, with a distinct origin.

Marcus Junianus Justinus Frontinus, a Latin writer who lived in the Roman Empire in the second (or according to others third or fourth) century AD, identified Faunus with *Lupercus* (he who wards off the wolf), who was seen as a priest of Faunus. Livy named *Inuus* as the god that was originally worshiped at the celebration of *Lupercalia*, February 15, when his priests *(Luperci)* wore goat-skins and hit passers-by with goatskin whips. Two festivals, called *Faunalia*, were celebrated in Faunus' honour; one on February 13, in the temple of Faunus on the island in the Tiber, the other on December 5, when the peasants brought him rustic offerings and amused themselves with dancing.

Fées

In French folklore *Fées* are half goddesses, half witches and some kind of *Fairies*. They have an obvious relationship with *Queen Guinevere* of the Arthurian legend and the Fairy *Melusine*. They inhabit moors and forests and sometimes attack rare passers-by at night. From the Jesuit scholar Martín Antonio Delrío:

> *"There are a kind of specter's that are not very dangerous and appear as white women in the woods and meadows; sometimes they are seen in the stables, holding lit candles from which they let drops fall on the hair of the horses, which they comb and then weave in a very neat way".*

They are still known in Tonneville (France, Manche), Lake Paladru (France, Isère) and many places in the Pyrenees *(Daunas Blancas, Damas Blancas)*, including caves which constituted prehistoric habitats, such as the one at Massabielle in Lourdes before the visions of Bernadette Soubirous, and caves in Comminges; the Aubegas, in Barousse; the Blanquetas.

Fées des Houles

Often described in Breton folklore, *Les Fées des Houles* (The Swell Fairies) are *Fées* specific to the coast of the English Channel which extends from Cancale to Tréveneuc in Upper Brittany, to the Channel

Islands, and known by some fragments of stories in the Cotentin. They would live in the caves and coastal caverns called swells. Reputedly magnificent, immortal and very powerful, they are sensitive to salt. Rather benevolent, the Fées des Houles described in local stories live near human communities, take care of their laundry, bake their bread or guard their herd, marry with Fairy gods and are served by warrior Goblins called the Fions. They come to the aid of humans in many ways, providing food and enchanted objects, but become angry if any of them disrespects them or acquire the ability to see their disguises without their consent. Paul Sébillot's collections, in French and in Gallo, have made it possible to gather about fifty tales and fragments of legends evoking these creatures. The Fées des Houles, considered to be "semi-divinities", were probably venerated locally by the High Breton people. The belief receded greatly in the 19th century, under the religious influence of Christianity and its teachers. They are most often described as tall, beautiful blonde ladies. Most of the Fées des Houles are dressed in gray clothing. Some of them are similar to old *Groac'h-Fairies*, who are adepts of metamorphosis and whose role is more obscure. When they become old, they are more stunted and hide themselves. Christendom tried to demonize these pagan creatures by stating that as long as they are not baptized (and therefore immortal), these Fairies carry worms in their mouths.

Feltue

The *Felteu*, *Fouilletout* or *Feuilleteu* is a prankster *Lutin* from the folklore of Bassigny in Champagne, France. The original legend is told by Dr. Gustave Sarcaud / Dr Auguste Causard in the *Contes et Légendes du Bassigny Champenois* (1844). The Felteux are large Lutins of almost 7 feet tall. According to legend, a young cook once saw more than sixty of them together. They had arranged themselves in three concentric circles around a large fire. Some of the Felteux were brushing the manes of horses, others were playing the violin and some were plucking the feathers of chickens, which the cook realized had been stolen from her. Nevertheless, she helped the Felteux cook their meal, for which they rewarded her with a large sum of money. With this money she was able to open her own inn, which she named "Au bon Felteu".

Fions

The *Fions* are creatures of the small people, especially mentioned in the maritime folklore of Haute-Bretagne, of the Lutin-type. They are perhaps of English origin. Most of the stories about them come from the collections of Paul Sébillot, at the end of the 19th century. Characterized by their habitat in the rocks and caves of the northern shore of Brittany, the Fions lead a military life in community with the *Fées des Houles* (Fairies of the Swells), whose servants they are. Organized in battalions, they would war on a golden ship. According to the tales, they own cattle that they graze and sometimes they give enchanted objects or food to humans. The origin of the name "Fions" is not known, and its usage remains unclear. For Walter Evans-Wentz, this term seems to originally designate Fairies, but it can be applied to creatures of the little people of both sexes. Opinions differ on this subject, but according to Paul Sébillot *"there were no female Fions, at least not in the swells"*. In contrast to the other *Lutins* of Brittany, the Fions are clearly characterized. They can only be compared to the *Jetins*. They do not belong to the same family of creatures as the *Fairies of the Swells*, whom they serve. They are the only Goblins reputed to live with fées, in a state of domesticity.

Folletto

Folletto (pl.: *Folletti*) is a generic Italian term which covers all kinds of *Alps*, *Goblins*, *Kobolds*, *Sprites* and other *nature-spirits* comparable to the Spanish term *Duende*, the British *Fairy* etc. Locally we distinguish the *Aùra* (Puglia), *Barabén* (var. *Barabanén*), *Mazapécc* and *Sèltapécc* (Appennino Bolognese), *Berbèch* (province of Bergamo), *Buffardello* or *Beffardello* (province of Lucca), *Cardinalen* or *Barabanén* (Imola and Dintorni), *Cjalcjùt* (Friuli), *Culèis* (Piemonte), *Fajettu* (Calabria), *Fuddhittu* e *Mazzamareddu* (Sicilia), *Fulëtt* (Piacentino), *Gnefro* (Terni and Valnerina), *Lauru* (Puglia), *Lenghelo* (Castelli Romani), *Linchetto* (province of Lucca), *Mazapégul* (Romagna), *Mazaròl, Mazariòl*, *Massaruol* or *Massariòl* (province of Belluno and Treviso), *Mazzamurello* (Marche), *Mazzemarelle* (Abruzzo), *Munaciello* (Napoli), *Monachicchio* (Basilicata), *Pàpolo* (province of Massa and Carrara), *Ru Mazzamauriegliel* or *Mazzamauriell* (Molise), *Sarvanot* (Piemonte – Valle Varaita), *Sbilf* (Carnia – Friuli), *Squàsc* (eastern Lombardia), *Sa Surtore* (Sardegna), *Salbanello* and *Salvanel* (Veneto and Trentino), *Scazzamurrieddhru* (Salento) or *Scazzamurrill* (province of Foggia),

Spremìngolo or *Sprevéngolo* (central Marche), *Sprenaggio* (Uscio – Valle del Recco), *Tramontino* (Valdarno in Toscana), *Tummà* (tableau of Puglia). A lot of different kinds of Folletti we find in the province of Bergamo, like the *Sgranf*, *Farfarèl*, *Folet*, *Ana Sösana* or *Mata Sösana*, *Gata Carogna*, *Gambastorta*, *Zöbia* or *Zöbiana*, *Fuì* and *Quacio*.

Fuì

Fuì or *Foeci* are a kind of *Imps* or *Folletti* of the region around Lallio, province of Bergamo, Italy. They have been seen throwing stones at travelers and local farmers, an art in which they seem to be very skilled. Very often they amuse themselves by raising the skirts of girls in public places, pretending to be a gust of wind, and then go away laughing.

G

Gaizkiñ

Gaizkiñ or *Gaizkina* is an evil *Irelu* who, according to Basque mythology, causes illness. Gaizkiñ literally means "does harm" in the Basque language. The creature hides in the feathers of bed pillows in the shape of a rooster's head. It then announces a mysterious illness to the child that sleeps in this bed. Only by burning this imprint of the "rooster's head" can one get rid of the illness from which the child may be suffering. In some places it is also called *Mamur*.

Gallu de la Muerte

The *Gallu de la Muerte* is an evil black rooster with a white crest and blue and red spots, which kills whoever hears its crowing on the following day, when the sun goes down. According to Asturian tradition, once every hundred years one of the chickens lays a colored egg in the *nial* (nest made in the haystacks). From this egg hatches a half-white, half-black bird, larger than a normal hen, whose life expectancy is 50 years. When it dies, a green worm is born from its putrefying flesh, which will gradually grow and blacken until it finally becomes the Gallu de la Muerte. If its song is heard, the only cure is to boil in rosemary water some herbs with blue leaves and black roots, that only grow in spring near wild apple trees, and make the person who has heard the song drink the infusion while listening to prayers. A disappointing hint, as according to Asturian folklore, is that these herbs have never been seen or found.

Galtzagorri

Galtzagorri is a contraction of the words *galtza* (pants) and *gorri* (red), thus Galtzagorri literally means "*the one with the red pants*". He is a tiny *Irelu* of Basque folklore, located in Guipúzcoa, in the countryside of Lower Navarre. Like the *Mamurrak* and *Prakagorri*, his tiny relatives, the Galtzagorri helps humans with its amazing capabilities. As their name suggests these creatures wear red pants and they hide in a comb. They start whispering to their owner: "*Eta orain zer? Eta orain zer?*" (And now what? And now what?) And at some point they obey the orders of the master, even the most horrible ones. The term is also used to denote familiar genii, such as the *Aidetikako* of Saran, *Aiharra* or *Haio* of Lapurdin/Labourd, the *Beste Mutilak* of Gernika/Guernica, and *Patuek* of Muxika/Múgica.

Gambastorta

A *Folletto* that abundantly populates the Orobic regions in northern Italy surely is the *Gambastorta*, particularly active in Grumello del Monte. It is a tiny creature with a stocky and hairy body, its small, mischievous and reddish eyes are hollowed in a wrinkled face, while its name is due to its typical lopsided gait. His favorite prank is to hide objects from young women, and if the women get angry, you can hear the Gambastorta laughing out loud as he runs away satisfied. If, on the other hand, the unfortunate woman pretends not to care about it, he puts the stolen object back in its place. During the night it amuses itself instead with making the glasses in the houses tinkle, or by removing the blankets of the sleeping to tickle them. You can also find him tying together the tails of cows or the strings of shoes and cutting the belts of peasants' pants, leaving them in their underwear. The Gambastorta is also widespread in the area of the lake of Varese, and in this case it is described as a particularly pestiferous Folletto who loves to hide objects from human beings. In order to find them, the tradition is to take a thread, make three knots in it and put it in a dark drawer. This method nullifies the power of the *Goblin*. The Gambastorta does not like this punishment at all and tries to persuade the human to free him, so that he will help to find the hidden objects. At this point you only need to break the thread and the missing objects will magically be found in their original places.

Gambosins

In the folklore of Valencia *Gambosins* are a type of *Goblins* with the appearance of little men or small animals. They live hidden in forests located near the cities. They like to approach people's residences to observe them and mimic their gestures and actions. They also approach camping grounds or other places where food is eaten to steal the leftovers. Some say they have a tail and that they howl and dance during the full moon.

Gatipedro

In Galician folklore *el Gatipedro* (the kittenpedro) is a white phantom-cat that is characterized by having a dark-colored horn on the forehead and also by walking with its tongue, in addition to its paws. The Gatipedro enters homes at night, and visits sleeping children. Once inside the house it uses its horn to release, little by little, drops of water in the rooms where small children sleep. The children, in their dreams, hear the constant dripping, start to dream that they pee, and then really pee, wetting their bed. To prevent the Gatipedro from entering children's rooms, it is enough to sprinkle a little salt under the doors of the room and at the bottom of the windows. Since the Gatipedro walks leaning on his tongue, he notices the taste of salt, which he dislikes very much, so he turns around and continues his nightly walk, without disturbing the sleep of the infants. The Gatipedro is most likely a thought form without roots in some older spirit, at one time invented – including the method to ward him off – to train children in this magical / NLP-like manner not to wet their beds.

Gaueko

In Basque mythology and folklore, *Gaueko* (the One of the Night) is not only a representation of the night, but also a god/demon of darkness. He was represented as an invisible presence, a black wolf (*Otsobeltza* or *Otsobaltza*) that sometimes stands on two legs, or another type of animal, like a cow, owl, or sheep. Gaueko represents all kinds of mysterious forces, demons, fantastic beings, who then gain all their powers from the Gaueko. Many legends, such as that of Xaindia, tell of the kidnapping of a woman or a young girl by spirits, devils, the *Basajaun*, or Gaueko, as himself, or in one of his various guises. Sometimes the Gaueko appeared as a mysterious light in the night, on heights, hovering above the tree tops, or above the rocks, and in that case it was called *Gauargi*. Later Gauargi became the guardian of the night, then a kind of *Irelu* of the night without a precise function.

Another Irelu or night-Goblin, also manifested by lights, is called *Argiduna*. It was said that Gaueko ate shepherds as well as their sheep, and for this reason this Irelu was greatly feared. According to Basque mythology, it was this fear that made the local population ask the goddess Mari to help them. She blessed them with the light of her first daughter, *Ilargi* (the moon), but her light was insufficient, and the humans asked Mari again for her help. This time the Goddess blessed them with her second daughter, *Eguzki* (the sun). But the night remained dangerous, and Mari blessed them with her protection of any dwelling that had an *Eguzkilore* ("sun flower", *Carlina acaulis*, a thistle-like flower, very abundant in the Basque Country) at the entrance. If any evil spirit tried to enter the house and found an Eguzkilore, it had to stop in order to count the numerous hairs and bracts of this plant and the daylight would then surprise the spirit without it having finished its intended task. Gaueko was believed to reign from midnight till dawn, while the rest of the day belonged to the humans. During the night it reigned with its own laws, which specified that no man or woman should abandon the ancestral protection of the home, or boast, or steal. Its accomplices could be *Sorginak*, *Jentilak* or even *Basajaun* himself. Several legends about Gaueko circulated:

- In a hamlet of Ataun, a spinner was challenged by her companions, and she accepted. The objective of her challenge was to reach the nearest spring and bring fresh water. When she set off and entered the thick forest, a scream was heard, and a terrifying breeze brought what would become Gaueko's hymn: "*Gaua gauekoentzat eta eguna egunekoentzat*" (Night for those of the night and day for those of the day).

- In Berástegui, a young girl named Kattalin, opened the window of the Elaunde farmhouse to spin in the moonlight, but before she knew it she was kidnapped by a group of *Jentilak* who took her to a nearby chasm and murdered her there, while shouting: "*Night for Gaueko and Kattalin for us*".

- In another legend, a charcoal burner from Eskoriatza stumbled at night with a bull blocking the path. After trying to pass three times and asking the beast to let him pass, the bull stood up and chased the man, shouting: *"Gaua gauekoentzat eta eguna egunekoentzat"*. In the end the man managed to escape from the Gaueko.

Gello

In Greek mythology and folklore, *Gello* (Ancient Greek: Γελλώ) is a female demon who threatens the reproductive cycle by causing infertility, miscarriages, and infant mortality. In the Byzantine era, the *Gelloudes* (γελλούδες) were also considered a class of demonic beings. Women who believed to be possessed by Gelloudes had to stand trial or were subjected to exorcism. The name Gello is also preserved in the later word *Ghoul*. *Gyllou*, *Gylou*, *Gillo*, or *Gelu* are some of its alternate forms. *Gellones* became the Latinized form of Gelloudes. The Gello could be regarded an "unclean spirit" *(akátharton pneuma)* subject to demonic excorcism, according to a text about exorcism, recorded by 17th century writer Leon Allatios/Leone Allacci (1586-1669). A woman could also be regarded as being a Gello by the populace, but these charges were dismissed in an ecclesiastical trial in the 8th century. The orthodox theology of the Church, expounded by Psellos or Ignatius, held that a woman's gendered nature precluded her from turning into a demon, since a demon was officially considered genderless. Sarah Iles Johnston, in *Restless Dead: Encounters Between the Living and the Dead in Ancient Greece* (2013), prefers to use the Greek word *aōros* or *aōrē* (untimely dead), for this form of transgressive or liminal soul or entity, finding the usual phrase "child-killing demon" to be misleading.

The Gello and aōrē in general are often portrayed as the personification of *envy* itself. That the aōrē were regarded as envious can be concluded from Greek grave-markers that blame "envious demons" for robbing a young child of its life. Along this line some protective Byzantine amulets have a design that is supposed to ward off the Gello, or one of its related demons (*Mormo*, *Lamia*, the *Stryggai*), as well as the "Evil Eye of Envy". The ancient folk-belief in the Gelloudes and the danger they posed to children continued during the Middle Ages, which may be concluded from various writings and protective charms. Somehow this ancient demon was feared so much that she survived, where the belief in so many other demons perished. In one Christian exorcism of the Gello, no fewer than 36 saints were invoked by name, along with Mary and the "318 Saints of the Fathers", with a final addendum of "all the saints". Some prayers resemble magic spells in attempting to command or compel the saints, rather than humbly requesting aid. Exorcisms emphasize that Christian families deserved exclusive protection. Thus the Gello continued to be named in exorcisms into the 20th century. One exorcism text dating from around the turn of the 19th-20th century gives *Baskania* as a name for the Gello as well as for the Evil Eye.

Origins

Gello possibly derives from *Gallû*, a Babylonian-Assyrian demon, believed to bring sickness and death. The theory was advanced by Carl Frank (1881-1945) and supported by M.L. West, Walter Burkert, and others. In Sumerian and ancient Mesopotamian religion, *Gallûs* (also called *Gallas*; Akkadian: *Gallû;* Sumerian: *Gal.lu*) were demons or devils of the underworld. Some texts list the *Galla* as a group of seven demons, that is, seven evil spirits that plague the Earth, and they are sometimes depicted in taurine forms. The main function of these beings was to carry human spirits and gods to the underworld. Thus, for example, in the poem of *Inanna's Descent into the Underworld*, these demons pursue and flank the goddess Inanna when she escapes from the netherworld, and it is they, too, who drag *Dumuzi* there, when she condemns him;

> *"The Galla are demons who do not take food, who do not drink,*
> *who do not eat offerings, who do not drink libations,*
> *who do not accept gifts.*
> *They do not enjoy sex.*
> *They have no sweet children to kiss.*
> *They tear the wife from the husband's arms,*
> *They snatch the child from his father's knee,*
> *They steal the bride from the marital home."*

Babylonian theology stated that the Galla could be appeased by the sacrifice of a lamb at their altars. Another angle to explain the term Gello is via Greek folk etymology, which links the word to the root *gel-*, (grin, laugh), in the sense of mocking or grimacing, like the expression often found on the face of the Gorgon, to which Barb linked the reproductive demons in origin (A.A. Barb, *Antaura. The Mermaid and the Devil's Grandmother: A Lecture*). Such demons are often associated with or said to come from the sea, and demonologies identify *Gyllou* with *Abyzou*, whose name is related to *abyssos*, the abyss or "deep".

Classical Antiquity and the Byzantine Era

In Classical Antiquity Gello had a lot in common with the orthodox Jewish version of Lilith, in her role as a threat to women, especially women in labor, and with newborns. According to ancient myth, Gello was a young woman who died a virgin, and returned as a ghost (φάντασμα, *Phantasma*) to do harm to the children of others. The myth is given as an explanation to a proverb by the 2nd century compiler Zenobius. It is noted that Sappho mentioned her, implying that Gello was a feared bane of children, at least as far back as the 6th century BC. The lexicographer Hesychius, who wrote in the 5th or 6th century AD but drew from earlier lexicons, glossed Gello (Γελλώ) as an "*Eidolon*" (here in the sense of a demonic being) who attacked both virgins and newborn babies. Gello, Lamia, and Mormo, due to their similar nature, have often been confounded since the Early Middle Ages. Each of these three originated as a single individual woman (with her own origin myth) in Ancient Greece, but later developed into a type of frightening apparitions or demons.

In the Byzantine Period (330-1453 AD), the Gello eventually came to be regarded as a type of being, rather than an individual. The plural form *Gelloudes*, not found in Ancient Greek, came into existence in the Byzantine period, and was used in the 7th-8th century by the patriarch John of Damascus (Ιωάννης ὁ Δαμασκηνός), in his treatise *Peri Stryggōn* (περί Στρυγγῶν, "Regarding Striges"). He considered the Gelloudes to be synonymous to the *Stryggai* (στρίγγαι, Στρῦγγαι) or "witches", and described them as beings that flew nocturnally, slipped unhindered into people's homes, even when windows and doors were barred, and strangled infants. Although the different reports of Gello's behavior are consistent, her nature is less determinate. In the 7-8th century, John of Damascus equated the Gello with the Stryggai that sometimes appeared in spirit form, while at other times had solid bodies and wore clothing. The 11th century Byzantine polymath Michael Psellus (Μιχαήλ Ψελλός) inherited the notion that the Stryggai and Gelloudes were "interchangeable". He described them as beings that *"suck blood and devour all the vital fluids which are in the little infant"*. Psellus documents a widened scope of the Gello's victims in the beliefs of the 11th century.

Gello were being held responsible for the deaths of pregnant women, and their fetuses as well. Gello (or Gillo) was also blamed for the condition of newborn infants who wasted away, and such infants were called *Gillobrota* (Γιλλόβρωτα), according to Psellus. Psellus sought in vain for Ancient Greek sources of these beliefs, and formulated the theory that the Gello derived from the Hebrew Lilith. Psellus further stated that the name "Gillo" could not be discovered in his usual sources for demonic names in antiquity, but were to be found in an esoteric or "occult" (ἀπόκρυφος) Hebrew book ascribed to Solomon. It has been pointed out by modern commentators that even though the original Gello was a young woman who died a virgin, the Gelloudes which became synonymous with Stryggai or "witches" in the Christian era, were generally regarded as being old envious crones. Gello or Gylou's curse has further been associated with the Evil Eye (of Envy) at least since the Byzantine period.

Different ways of protection against the Gello

- In the Byzantine period, mothers who had given birth customarily relied on amulets designed to protect her newborn from evil, including the Gello or Gyllou. The woman who would shun these charms and invest her faith entirely on the power of the Cross was a rare exeption.
- Leon Allatios criticized such remnants of sorcery, such as these charms, or the hanging of red coral or a head of garlic, and prescribed strictly Christian prophylactics, such as a cross or image of Christ placed by a child's bed to ward off Gello or demons in general, or burning lamps to illuminate sacred images. The practice of baptizing infants was thought to offer protection against demon-snatching, and specifically against the Gello, according to Allatios.
- The magico-medical compilation *Cyranides* from the Imperial period also provided instructions on how to defend against the Gelloudes. The eyeballs of a hyena in a purple pouch was said to be an effective amulet against *"all nocturnal terrors, also Gello, that strangle infants and trouble women in childbed"*. Using an ass's skin as a bedsheet to sleep on was also prescribed as effective against the Gello.
- The *Lithica* of the late Hellenistic to early Imperial Period listed magical stones as effective charms as well, although they do not explicitly mention the Gello. However, in these texts, *galactite* is said to protect against either *Megaira* (Envy), or "frightful woman" *(horrida mulier)* who attacked infants.
- Some Byzantine amulets against female reproductive demons are said to

Lamia, 17th century depiction from Edward Topsell's *The History of Four-Footed Beasts*

depict the Gello. This is sometimes asserted as a rule of thumb, without providing any reasoning. As no Byzantine amulet exists that actually labels the demon as a Gello or Gyllou, the inference is made that these are Gello by association with other figures labeled in the amulets, namely the demon Abyzou, the *Saint Sisinnios*, or the *"Evil Eye of Envy"*.

- Numerous early Byzantine amulets (6th to 7th century) label its demon as "Abyzou", identifiable with *Obyzouth*, a demon that strangles newborns according to the 1st to 3rd century Greek text called the *Testament of Solomon*. This Abyzou (Obyzouth) has been equated with the Gello (Gyllou), albeit in later literature, for example, in the writings of Michael Psellos of the 11th century.
- Some Byzantine amulets also invoke the name of Saint Sisinnios, who is known foremost as the vanquisher of Gello. Again, the textual evidence that connect Sissinios to Gyllou are from much later dates, the oldest version of the "Melitine charm" or Legend of St. Sisinnios dating back to the 15th century.
- The Virgin Mary was invoked against the child-harming demon *Gylo*:

"Therefore I pray, my Lady, for your swiftest aid, so that the children of these your servants N and N may grow up, and that they may live and give thanks in the sight of the Lord for all the days of their lives. Thus let it be, my Lady. Listen to me, a sinner and unworthy servant and although I am a sinner, do not despise my poor and miserable prayer but protect the children of your servants and let them live and send the Angel of Light so that he may protect and defend them from all evil, from wicked spirits, and from fiends which are in the air, and do not let them be singled out by other [demons] and by the accursed gylo lest harm comes to them and their children."

The Legend of Saint Sisinnios

The story of St. Sisinnios, assisting his sister Melitene against the demon *Gyllou*, occurs in a group of different texts (these are also the texts in which Gyllou is compelled to reveal its *"twelve and a half names"*). A spell which invokes a mythical narrative, asking for the events it describes to be enacted, has been variously referred to as the a *Historiola*, where in *"the Greek tradition the woman is usually called Melitene"* (Jeffrey Spier, *Medieval Byzantine Magical Amulets and Their Tradition*, 1993). In a 15th century manuscript version, the tale is set in the time of "Trajan the King". After losing six children to the Gyllou, Melitene gives birth to a seventh child, inside a fortification she built at Chalcopratia (a part of Constantinople). When her brothers, *Sisinnios*, *Sines*, and *Sinodoros* demand admittance, the "filthy" Gyllou gains entry by transforming itself into a fly clinging to the horse, and kills the child. The saints pray and an angel appears who instructs them to pursue the Gyllou to Lebanon. The Saints compel the demon to bring back to life all of Melitene's children, which the demon accomplishes after obtaining the mother's milk from Melitene. The saints continue to beat Gyllou, who begs for mercy in return for revealing that she could be kept away with a charm inscribed with the names of the saints and with all of her different names. Then she proceeds to divulge her "twelve and a half names" (although what is meant by a "half name" is unclear, and one name is missing, due to a lacune in the manuscript):

> *"My first and special name is called Gyllou; the second Amorphous; the third Abyzou; the fourth Karkhous; the fifth Brianê; the sixth Bardellous; the seventh Aigyptianê; the eighth Barna; the ninth Kharkhanistrea; the tenth Adikia; (...) the twelfth Myia; the half Petomene."*

A different version of this story was given by Leon Allatius. In his version of the Legend of St. Sisinnos, the "twelve-and-a-half names" are given as *Gylo*, *Morrha*, *Byzo*, *Marmaro*, *Petasia*, *Pelagia*, *Bordona*, *Apleto*, *Chomodracaena*, *Anabardalaea*, *Psychoanaspastria*, *Paedopniktria*, and *Strigla*. Although magic words (voces magicae) have often been corrupted in transmission, or deliberately exoticized, several of these names suggest recognizable Greek elements and can be deciphered as functional epithets: Petasia, "she who strikes"; *Apleto*, "boundless, limitless"; *Paedopniktria*, "child suffocator." Byzo is a form of Abyzou, abyssos, "the Deep," to which *Pelagia* (She of the Sea) is equivalent. The names of Gylo also include *Chomodracaena*, containing *drakaina* (female dragon). In one text dealing with the Gello, she is banished to the mountains to drink the blood of the *drako*; in another, she becomes a dragon and in this form attacks human beings. In other texts, the child itself is addressed as *Abouzin* (Abyzou). Parallels to the lore of a child-killing demon forced to confess its secret names occur as historiola, or folktales surrounding magic spells, in medieval manuscripts of many languages, including Greek, Coptic, Ethiopian, Armenian, Romanian, Slavonic, Arabic, Syriac, and Hebrew.

Genius

In Roman religion, the *Genius* (pl. *Genii*) was the personal guardian spirit of a man and an expression of his personality, his destiny, and especially his procreative power. With the death of the man the Genius expired. Originally, the Genii were ancestral spirits who watched over their descendants. They evolved into personal guardian spirits to whom people sacrificed and from whom they hoped for help and inspiration in difficult life situations. The most important celebration for the Genius was the birthday of the person it protected. Since the genius was understood as a kind of principle of action, other collectives such as troop units and colleges, but also places *(Genius loci)* such as provinces, cities, markets and theaters could have a Genius. From there to the overarching genius of Rome *(Genius urbis Romae or Genius populi Romani)* is only a small step. Finally, in the imperial cult, the *Genius Augusti* was worshipped.

To the Genius corresponded in the Aramaic language *gny'*, vocalized *ginnaya* (pl. *ginnayē*). These were comparable guardian spirits in northern Arabia, thought of as human beings and often addressed in pairs. At the time, they resembled the Arabic concept of the *Jinn*. Both terms originally denoted full-fledged deities; they were worshipped as such, or at least as serving and protecting angels. It was only under the influence of Islam that the *Ginnayē* were relegated to spirits of rather limited utility.

The Genius was usually depicted bearded (in later times also as a boy), with a free upper body, cornucopia (horn of plenty), and usually a sacrificial bowl. The genius loci often appears in the form of a snake. In Roman art, genii are also depicted as winged beings. To the male genius corresponded the female *Juno*. To the Roman genius corresponds the Greek *Daimon*. Also the *Daimonion*, the alleged inner voice of Socrates, is called Genius in Latin.

Genius loci

The Latin term *Genius loci* literally means "the spirit of the place". In Roman mythology, spirit originally meant a guardian spirit (genius), who was often depicted in the form of a snake. In Roman Antiquity, the term Genius loci referred not only to religious places such as temples and places of worship, but also to profane areas such as provinces, cities, squares, buildings or individual rooms within these structures. In modern occultism the genius loci has an overlap with the *Deva*, or spirit of a certain ecosystem or (natural) environment, like a mountain or forest. It are the Deva's who work as the morphogenetic umbrella-force to keep a certain area in its unique homeostasis, whilst nature-spirits are active to nurture and protect the specific parts and entities of the ecosystem.

In the tradition of monotheistic Christianity, the term spirit is defined differently; as a spirituality that cannot be precisely defined. In this sense, genius loci refers to the spiritual atmosphere of a place, which is said to be shaped by the spirit of the people that have stayed – or are still staying – there. For example, the genius loci of Maulbronn Monastery is a central theme in the works of Hermann Hesse; especially in *Unterm Rad* (Beneath the Wheel) and *Narziß und Goldmund* (Narcissus and Goldmund).

In architecture and spatial planning, the term also refers to the structural specifications and characteristics of a site, which can be decisive in determining the design. For every plot of land is first defined by its location and its embedding in its surroundings, from which it derives its value, its character and its potential uses. But the genius loci is not only made up of soil quality, the size of an area and other measurable factors, but also includes the atmosphere and aura of a place. In this sense, the genius loci is a construct in which knowledge, memory, perception and interpretation merge as an interpretative achievement of the human mind. In order to achieve an unique development with its own character and ambience, the genius loci is often incorporated into the designing process for a building. A *Zeitgeist* can be regarded as the Genius loci of a certain epoch or time-frame.

Gerixeti

Gerixeti, from the word *geriza* (shadow), is an entity in Basque folklore. It is a shadow that represents the broken or wandering souls of the dead in some parts of Bizkaia. The souls of the dead are often associated with lights or gusts of wind. *Erio*, the character who represents death, separates the soul and the body, and from that moment on, the soul goes to the underworld. However, sometimes a soul returns home at night to help their family, to consume the offerings offered to them, or to settle their unpaid bills before they die. This Basque view of the soul is most likely influenced by the Romans.

Gizotsoa

Gizotsoa, Gizotso or *Gizon otsoa* means "wolf-man" or "Werewolf" in Basque – the word being a contraction of *gizon* (man), and *otso* (wolf). He is a monster, half-man and half-wolf, that lives in the woods, and sometimes appears at night, rattling its many chains. In the Luzaide region, it is assumed that he has superhuman strength. It has a strange circular foot, like *Alarabi* or *Tartaro*. Its nature is cruel and verocious. In Bizkaia people believed that the Gizotsoa was the result of sexual intercourse between wolves and humans. Legend has it that some farmers in Urkia on their way home saw a woman on the Aginao farm, and that a *Gizotsoa* was walking towards her from Bidarbinieta. To warn her they shouted, *"Hurry up! The werewolf is coming to you!"* The woman tried to get home as quickly as she could , but was caught by the creature, who ripped her breasts off.

Gnefro

The *Gnefro* or *Gnèfru* is, in the folklore of Umbria, Italy – and in particular the area of the city of Terni, Valnerina, and the city of Rieti – a legendary creature that usually lived in groups near the Marmore Falls and along the Black River, between the waterfall itself and the end of Valnerina. It is described as a kind of *Elf* or *Gnome* of low stature (less than a meter tall). According to some theories it appears to the wayfarers exclusively at night, sometimes with the aspect of a graceful child and others with the features of a kind of small Gnome, with a coarse type of skin. The Gnomes are said to have fun bothering the lonely travelers with jokes, mostly aimed at frightening them without ever causing serious harm. The Gnefroi are endowed with weak magical powers. Some people consider them as protectors of homes.

Gorgons

The *Gorgons* (ancient Greek γοργόνες *Gorgónes*, from γοργώς gorgṓs, "terrible"; sing. Gorgon, Γοργών Gorgṓn or Gorgo Γοργώ), in Greek mythology, are three winged terrors with serpentine hair that turn anyone who looks at them to stone. The Gorgons are the daughters of *Phorkys* and *Keto*. Their names are: *Stheno* (also *Stheino* and *Sthele*), *Euryale* and *Medusa*. Medusa is the only mortal among them and was beheaded by *Perseus*. The head of this Gorgon was brought to the goddess *Athena*.

Numerous portraits of Athena show her with the Aigis and Gorgon's head on her chest. Homer still speaks of only one *Gorgo*. However, Hesiod then names three Gorgons around 700 B.C., namely Stheno (the Powerful One), Euryale (the Long Jumper) and the "long-suffering" Medusa (the Queen). Their home was the far western edge of the then known world (the Atlas Mountains), later mythographers also name Libya as their home.

Gorri txiki

Gorri txiki is a Basque term, meaning "little red"; it is the name given to some *Jentilak* in the region of Aia and Orio in the province of Guipuscoa. Gorri means "red" in Basque. *Txiki*, *ttippi* or *txippi* are variants for "small". They are said to move quickly through the heights of Aia. However, one legend tells of the inhabitants of Leoia, a municipality in Biscay, Basque Country, in northern Spain, who seized the last Gorri txiki and burned it in their lime *kiln* (a type of oven). Before the *Irelu* died in the flames, he cursed them: *"As long as the world is a world, in Leioa, there will be no shortage of disabled people!"*

Grand Bissetere

Mentioned in *Vampires: A Field Guide to the Creatures That Stalk the Night* by Bob Curran, the *Grand Bissetere* is said to be a kind of *energy-Vampire* that appears near forest roads and woodland pools in the rural parts of the Provence. It makes low moaning sounds, like a screech owl and may attack passersby and drain them of their vital energies.

Gripet

In the folklore of Provence and Languedoc, the *Gripet* or *Gripé* (from *gripa*, "to seize," according to Frédéric Mistral) is a *household-spirit* or *Lutin*, who manifests himself as both helpful and mischievous. According to Paul Sébillot, he crawls under the beds of women in labor and bites the calves of those who care for them. In Vivarais – like the Provençal *Fantasti* – he also occupies stables to care for and guard horses and keep out unwanted intruders.

Groac'h

A *Groac'h* or *Grac'h* (according to Anatole Le Braz, Breton for "old witch" or "old woman", pl. *Groagez*) is a Breton *Fée* linked to water. Multiform, she is often old and nocturnal, related to ogres and sorceresses, sometimes with walrus teeth. Reputed to live in caves, under the sand or under the sea, the Groac'h has power over the elements of nature and masters metamorphosis. She is best known as a malevolent figure, particularly because of Emile Souvestre's tale *La Groac'h de l'île du Lok.* The Fée seduces men who she changes into fish, and serves them as a meal to her guests, on one of the islands of the Glénan archipelago. Other tales present them as old solitary Fées who can bestow the humans who visit them with gifts and donations.

The origin of these Fées belonging to the archetype of *la Vieille* (the Old One) is to be sought in ancient female deities, demonized with Christianity. The influence of Breton writers in the 19th century brought them closer to the classical Fée figure. The Groac'h appears regularly in recent literary works, such as *La Pâleur et le Sang* (1983) by Nicolas Bréhal. The Groagez are the Fées most often met in Brittany, generally in the forests and near the fountains; the Breton Well-Fées. A certain number of *Fées des mers* (sea-Fairies) also bear the name of Groac'h, sometimes interchangeably with those of *Mary Morgane* or *Sirène* (Mermaid). Joseph Mahé speaks (1825) of an evil creature that he was afraid of as a child, reputed to live in wells in which it submerges small children who fall in. According to Marc Gontard, the Groac'h bears witness to the demonization of ancient female deities under the influence of Christianity: she was changed into a witch, just as other deities were changed into lost daughters and Sirènes. Her palace at the bottom of the waters is a typical motif of fairy tales and stories, which can be found among others in the texts of the Arthurian legend, Irish folklore and several Hispanic tales. Pierre Dubois brings the Groac'h closer to a large number of evil water-Fairies, such as *Peg Powler*, *Jenny Greenteeth*, *Mother Engueule* and the *Green Ogresses of Cosge* that pull people underwater to devour them.

Appeareance

Because of their multifaceted character, Groagez are difficult to define. One Groac'h is said to frequent the vicinity of Kerodi, but descriptions differ quite a bit; an old woman bent over and leaning on a crutch, or a richly dressed princess, accompanied by *Korrigans* (dwarfish creatures). The descriptions often insist on the aspect of an old woman. Françoise Morvan notes cases where the Groagez have exceptionally long "walrus" teeth, from the length of a finger to dragging across the ground. In other cases, they have no teeth or nothing is mentioned about this attribute. Sometimes they are hunchbacked. The storyteller Pierre Dubois describes them as shapeshifters, capable of taking on appearances from the most flattering to the most repulsive: beautiful swans or short-sighted and flabby *Larvae*. He attributes to them green or, much more rarely, red teeth. For Morvan, the variety of these descriptions comes from two phenomena. On the one hand, it could be that these Fées change their appearance as they grow older, taking on the appearance of pustular frogs or toads. On the other hand, a Russian tradition, reported by André Siniavski, says that Fées go through cycles of rejuvenation and aging according to the cycles of the moon: a similar tradition may have existed in Brittany.

Pierre Dubois compares the Groac'h to an ogress or a water witch. André-François Ruaud associates her with the Undines, Richard Ely and Amélie Tsaag Valren with witches, and Édouard Brasey describes her as a *Lake-Fée*. Whatever the case, the Groac'h is one of the most powerful Breton Water-Fées. From her aquatic habitat as well as on land, she has power over the elements. The Groac'h of the Lanascol castle could make the dead leaves move in autumn and turn them into gold, or make the trees bow and the ponds shiver in her path. Although it is mostly known by negative representations, the Groac'h is not necessarily an evil creature. She sometimes politely receives humans in her lair and offers them magic items (usually in threes), treasures and healing. Like many other Fées, she also does her laundry and spins. They are bossy, but generally full of good intentions. Most often, Groagez are described as loners in their retreat under the sea, in a rock or in the sand. Some tales tell of a family life that is only female. The Groagez do not abandon their children and do not leave changelings. They are sometimes accompanied by a *cheval d'eau vert* (green Water-Horse) and a *homme-brochet* (pike-man). They are more fickle and sensitive than the other Breton Fées, and can easily take offense. In Finistère, Groagez reveal to miners the existence of silver and lead.

Several story collections mention a Groac'h in various places in Brittany. Souvestre evokes one of these Fées, assimilated to a *Naiad*, in a well in Vannes: this legend seems to have been quite popular, and could have the same sources as the tale of the Well-Fées. A story collected by Anatole Le Braz makes one of these Fairies the personification of the plague: an old man from Plestin finds a Groac'h asking for his help to cross the river. The old man carries it, but it becomes heavier and heavier, so much so that he puts it down again where he took it, thus avoiding an epidemic of plague in the country of Lannion. François-Marie Luzel also gathers several traditions around the Groagez, from which the inhabitants would flee like the Ankou. Some are reputed to be able to change into foals, or to haunt the forest of *Coat-ann-Noz* (Forest of the Night). The Duke's pond in Vannes is said to be the home of a Groac'h; a former princess who threw herself into the water to escape an over-enterprising lover, and who is sometimes seen untangling her long blond hair with a golden comb.

The Groac'h in place names in Lower Brittany

Many place names in Lower Brittany are attributed to a Groac'h. The Great Menhir called *Men Er Groah*, in Locmariaquer, probably owes its name to an amalgam between the Breton name of the cave (groh) and that of this old Fée. Pierre Saintyves cites in the same commune a "table of the old woman", a dolmen named *Daul ar Groac'h*. In Maël-Pestivien, three stones of two meters high, placed next to each other in the village of Kermorvan, are known as *Ty-ar-Groac'h* (the house of the Fée). In 1868, an eight meter high menhir named *Min-ar-Groach* was destroyed in Plourac'h. In Cavan, the tomb of the *Groac'h Ahès*, or *Be Ar Groac'h*, is attributed to the giantess Ahès. There is a "Tomb of the Red Groac'h" in Prat, attributed to a "red Fée" who would have brought the stones in her apron. This megalith is however almost destroyed. The island of Groix owes its name (in Breton) to Groagez, described as "druidesses" and now seen as old women or old witches. A rock of *Croac'h Coz*, that is to say the "island of the old Fée" attached to Plougrescant, would be inhabited by an old Groac'h who spins from time to time. Sébillot tells us that the fishermen of Loguivy (in Ploubazlanec) were once afraid to pass near the cave named *Toul ar Groac'h* (hole of the Fée), and preferred to lie down under their boat turned over on the shore while waiting for the next tide, rather than risk angering the Fairy. In the same way, Anatole Le Braz cites Barr-ann-Hëol, near Penvénan, as a dangerous place with a Groac'h ready to seize people who have strayed from the shore, and stands guard at the corner of two crossroads. In the area of Ouessant, many place names refer to it, including the *Pointe de la Groac'h* and the Vieille lighthouse, in reference – according to Georges Guénin – to "a kind of witch". Some traces of possible cults associated to these Fairies have been recorded. Paul-Yves Sébillot tells us that the sick used to come and rub themselves against the pre-Christian statue known as *Groac'h er goard* or *Groac'h ar Goard*, to obtain a cure. This old seven-foot high granite statue, better known as the *Venus of Quinipily*, represents a naked woman with "indecent forms" and could be a vestige of the cult of Venus or Isis.

Guajona

The *Guajona* (Cantabrian *Gwa'hona*; Spanish: *Gwa'xona*) or *Lumia* is a creature in Cantabrian folklore, resembling an ugly disfigured woman. It is thought to resemble one of the many forms of witches and *Hags* of medieval Europe. Guajona is an augmentative of *Guaja*, present also in the neighboring Asturian mythology as *Guaxa* (see below). The origin of *Guaja* or *Guaxa* could be in classical Arabic وحش *Wahsh*, meaning "beast". Folklore is often specific about their feeding habits. She is covered from head to toe in an old thin black cloak, her hands and feet are gnarled bird legs, her face is yellow and consumed by rough and hairy warts, her eyes are tiny and bright as stars and she has an aquiline nose. Her mouth contains a single black razor sharp tooth that extends to under her chin and is used to suck blood. The creature is nocturnal. It is unknown where she is meant to sleep during the day although it is suspected to be hiding underground. Guajona invades homes without getting noticed and walks silently toward healthy young children to suck their blood in their sleep by sticking her tooth into their veins. She does not kill them, but leaves them almost bloodless, so when they wake up in the morning they will be very tired, pale and disoriented. Guajona also attacks adults. This is one of the few myths or legends about vampiric beings that exist in Spain, along with the *Conde Estruch*. The Conde Estruch, however, (in Catalan *Comte Estruc*) is a character in a 1991 novel, entitled *Estruch*, written by Salvador Sainz and has been mistakenly believed to be part of Catalan folklore, including him in the usual legends of Catalonia as a 12th century vampirized Catalan nobleman named Guifred.

Guaxa

The *Guaxa* is a type of Asturian *Vampire* that especially attacks children, on whom it feeds. To avoid attacks, they must be protected by an amulet or be exorcised. The Guaxa is described as a dry, wrinkled old woman,

with eyes in whose depths seem to shine sparks of hellfire. She attacks children at night, but she also preys on robust young men and beautiful strong girls, always when they are asleep. With its one tooth, it penetrates an artery and enjoys sucking blood from it. There is no way to prevent her arrival, for she will reach every place where she is able to pass a breath of air. She usually doesn't kill, but in case of children hinders their development. However it was believed that when a child suddenly disappeared, it was killed. In such a rare – and of course very suspicious and disputable – case, the conclusion: "*Se lo comió la Guaxa*" (Eaten by the Guaxa) was made.

There were several remedies against a Guaxa. One of them was to administer a preparation made with a maceration of deer antler fragments and a small amount of silver to which "alicornio" was added, which had rested for nine days in some water. What is meant by alicornio is uncertain, as it could be a fragment of the tooth of a male narwal, or more likely larkspur *(delphinium)* which is however extremely poisonous. Then – and this could be considered as an alternative treatment – the patient could also be measured with a strong black thread. This thread was then used to make an improvised rosary, with nine small knots and one larger one. This was hung around his neck, and a small bag containing ten grams of wheat for the Guaxa-victim, who had to wear it on its body for several days. After this, the victim had to lead a new, active and quiet life, stepping barefoot in the dew of the fields every morning, and finally it had to kill the Guaxa by a knife in the chest.

Harpy (1582) by Melchior Lorch (1526-1583)

H

Hadas

Hadas (*Fates* in Catalan, *Fades* in Galician-Portuguese) are the Hispanicized Roman *Fatas* (feminine plural of *Fatum*). The Fatum in Roman times were personifications of destiny. Hadas, however, has changed in meaning and became more akin to the *Anjanas* or is now also used as a general word to describe all sorts of mythological beings, not only *Duendes* but also *gres*, *Sirenas* (Mermaids) and others, similar to the British *Fairies*.

Hamadryad

A *Hamadryad* (ancient Greek: Ἁμαδρυάδες, Romanized: *Hamadryádes*) is the Greek term for a spirit that lives in trees. *Tree-spirits* were also very important among the Germanic and Celtic peoples. The Hamadryad is a particular type of *Dryad* which, in turn, is a particular type of *Nymph*. Hamadryads are born bonded to a certain tree. Some maintain that a Hamadryad is the tree itself, with a normal Dryad being simply the indwelling entity or spirit, of the tree. If the tree dies, the Hamadryad associated with it dies as well. For this reason, both Dryads and gods would punish mortals who harmed trees. In medieval Germany in some regions, a person who for the wrong reasons cut a tree, was literally put to death by having their belly slit open after which their bowels were wrapped around a tree. The miracle of the Findhorn project, which baffled scientists all over the globe, has proven that the spirits of trees and plants are real entities with which a unique communication is possible. The *Deipnosophistae of Athenaeus* lists eight Hamadryads, the daughters of *Oxylus* and *Hamadryas* and gives the name of the tree they are linked to:

- *Karya* (walnut or hazelnut)
- *Balanos* (oak)
- *Kraneia* (dogwood)
- *Morea* (mulberry)
- *Aigeiros* (black poplar)
- *Ptelea* (elm)
- *Ampelos* (vines, especially vitis)
- *Syke* (fig)

Other known Hamadryads are: *Atlanteia*, *Phoebe*, *Chrysopeleia*, *Byblis*, *Dryope*, the *Heliades* and the *Hesperides*. *Atlanteia* or *Atlantia* was a Hamadryad Nymph who consorted with King Danaus of Libya and was perhaps the mother of some of the *Danaïdes*: *Hippodamia*, *Rhodia*, *Cleopatra*, *Asteria*, *Hippodamia*, *Glauce*, *Hippomedusa*, *Gorge*, *Iphimedusa*, and *Rhode*. Perhaps, all this came about because the Hamadryad *Phoebe* also consorted Danaus.

The Tree-Nymph *Chrysopéleia* (ancient Greek Χρυσοπέλεια Chrysopéleia, from χρυσός chrysós, "gold" and πέλεια péleia, "wild dove" lived in an oak tree. When a torrent once threatened to sweep away the oak tree in which she lived, *Arkas*, the son of Zeus, came to her rescue. He diverted the water and protected the tree with a dam. Out of gratitude she slept with him and had with him the sons *Elatos* and *Apheides*. There are several versions of the story of *Byblis*. *Antoninus Liberalis* portrays Byblis as overcome with unanswered – incestuous – love for her brother *Caunus*. After he leaves, she rejects all the proposals of numerous suitors and attempts to commit suicide by jumping off a cliff. However she is saved by Hamadryads, who cause her to fall asleep and transform her into a fellow Nymph.

Dryope (ancient Greek: Δρυόπη, derived from δρῦς *drys*, "oak"; *dryope* "woodpecker") is the daughter of *Dryops* (oak-man), king of *Oeta* – or of *Eurytus* (and hence half-sister to *Iole*). She is sometimes thought of as one of the Pleiades and therefore a Nymph. Dryope mothered Amphissus, conceived by Apollo who had mated with Dryope in the shape of a snake. According to Antoninus Liberalis, the Hamadryads, who had always been friends of Dryope, finally turned her into one of them. In Ovid's version, Dryope accidentally turned into a black poplar after picking a red blossom from a lotus tree, while formerly the Nymph Lotis who, when fleeing from Priapus, had been changed into that tree.

The *Heliades* were the sisters of *Phaëthon*, who died after attempting to drive his father's chariot (the sun) across the sky. He was unable to control the horses and fell to his death (according to most accounts, *Zeus* struck his chariot with a thunderbolt to save the Earth from being set afire). The Heliades grieved for four months and the gods turned them into poplar trees and their tears into amber. According to some sources, their tears (amber) fell into the river Eridanus, in which Phaethon had fallen. According to Hyginus, the Heliades were turned to poplar trees because they yoked the chariot for their brother without their father *Helios*' permission.

The *Hesperides* (ancient Greek: Ἑσπερίδες) are the Nymphs of evening and golden light of sunsets, who were the *Daughters of the Evening* or *nymphs of the West*. They were also called the *Atlantides* (ancient Greek: Ἀτλαντίδες, Romanized: Atlantídes) because of their reputed father, the *Titan Atlas*. The Hesperides tended a tree with golden apples in a beautiful garden. The name means: originating from *Hesperos* (evening). Hesperos, or *Vesper* in Latin, is the origin of the name *Hesperus*, the *evening star* (i.e. the planet *Venus*) as well as having a shared root with the English word "west".

In Greek Mythology, the *Meliádes* or *Meliai* (ancient Greek Μελιάδες, from μελία *melía*, "ash tree", hence also *Ash-Nymphs;* Latin: *Meliae*), also called *Melic* or *Melian Nymphs,* who live in ash trees. They are often commonly associated with the *Dryads* as Tree-Nymphs or *Hamadryads*. They were created, according to Hesiod's *Theogony*, from the blood that fell on *Gaia* when the *Titan Kronos* emasculated his father *Uranos*. Besides the Meliádes, the *giants* and the vengeance-goddesses, the *Erinyes*, were also created in this way. In Hesiod's *Works and Days*, the ash trees, perhaps meaning the Melian Nymphs, are said to have been the progenitors of the generation of men belonging to Hesiod's Bronze Age. The Meliai were nurses of the infant Zeus in the Cretan Dikti mountains, according to the 3rd century BC poet Callimachus, *Hymn to Zeus*, where they fed him on the milk of the goat *Amalthea*, and honey.

Hárpyia

In Greek and Roman mythology, a *Hárpyia* or *Harpy* (raging storm; pl.: *Harpies*; Ancient Greek: ἅρπυια, Romanized: *Hárpyia*) is a winged hybrid creature of Greek mythology in bird form, with a female head and a personification of storm winds. The Harpies are the daughters of the *Sea-Titan Thaumas* and the *Oceanid* Electra. Their number is undetermined, but never more than two Harpies are named at the same time. Some of these names are:

- *Aello* – Ἀελλώ; (storm wind, whirl, wind-bride).
- *Okypete* – Ὠκυπέτη; pl. ὠκυπέτης ōkypétēs; (fast flying), from ὠκύς ōkýs (fast), and πέτομαι pétomai, (I fly: the fast-winged).
- *Podarge, Podargo* – Ποδάργη Podárgē; (the swift-footed). She is the

mother of the horses of Achilles.
- *Kelaino, Celaeno* – κελαινός kelainos (poetic); (dark, ominous: the dark one), first mentioned in the *Aeneid* of the Roman poet Virgil.

The sister of the Harpies is *Iris*, goddess of the rainbow, wife of *Zephir*, the west wind. In the earlier tales of Greek mythology they are described as beautiful women with curly hair and bird wings – later they are ugly light-haired demons. The Harpies dwell in a cave in Crete and must carry souls of the dead to Tartarus at the behest of Zeus, or kill people who arouse his wrath. The Harpies are described as swift as the wind and invulnerable.

Herensuge

Herensuge is a gigantic demonic snake, a variant of a dragon, and one of the most important creatures in Basque mythology. It flies through the air and is usually represented with one or seven large heads. The only difference with the traditional fire-eating dragon is that the Pyrenean snakes – like Herensuge – die from the inner fire that consumes them. Its names may vary, but the permanence of the suffix *suge* (snake) is sufficient to indicate its nature. We find the names of *Erensugue* (the pronunciation *-sugue* is transcribed with or without "u"), *Erensuge, Lerensuge, Herainsuge, Errensuge, Hensuge, Edensugue, Edeinsuge, Edaansuge, Igensuge, Iraunsuge.* Herensuge has, in popular tradition, replaced another snake, *Sugaar*, or *Sugoi*. It is not known exactly what *(H)eren* means, but according to the Bascologist Michel Morvan it must mean "male" as *-ar* in Sugaar.

Origins and legends

During the creation of the Earth, Herensuge mates with *Sugaar* (here, not as the husband of Mari but a "snake goddess"), who then gives birth to the Sun and the Moon. Herensuge then swallows the whole Earth and spits it out again. Within ten days, he swallowed all of Creation to regurgitate it in the flames. Then, having accomplished these tasks, he falls asleep. Herensuge was believed to dwell in the caves of Azalegui or Ertzagania, on the Ahuski mountain, in the Saint-Michel-in-Excelsis abyss on Mount Aralar, and many other Basque mountainous areas. With his powerful breath, he would suck in the herds that passed within his reach, and even the accompanying shepherds, and swallow them. An offspring of the Herensuge-legend deals with the giant snake of Lake

Isaby, in Lavedan, and other Pyrenean places. In some Basque tales, he is said to be the protector of the Basajaunak. In several tales, the giant fire snake crosses the sky and crashes into the ocean: a seven-headed Herensuge for example flies in a terrible noise to *Itxasgorrietas* (the Red Seas of the Setting Sun). In another legend, the son of the castle of Çaro managed to poison Herensuge, who, setting fire to the building, also flew towards the sea – cutting down part of the forest of the Arbailles in the process. In Saint-Michel-in-Excelsis – in the service of christening the Basques – it is the guardian-archangel himself who kills this kind of dragon/snake, now equaled to the Devil. Herensuge is thought to be sleeping now. It is said that, the day Herensuge wakes up, he will destroy the whole world in flames and blood.

Herrauscorritsehe

Herrauscorritsehe is a Basque god and daemon from the region of Tardets/Atharratze (Soule/Xiberoa-Zuberoa). On a hill known as "de la Madeleine" there is a chapel named "Herrauscorritsehe". In the days of the Old Religion the site of de la Madeleine was a very important sacred place. The chapel is built on a former center of worship. A votive inscription, written in Latin in honor of the Basque deity, is embedded in a wall of the chapel. The chapel is now dedicated to Saint Magdalene, who, according to legend, took refuge here in the 14th century. Pilgrims meet there twice a year: on the Sunday before Palm Sunday and on July 22, the feast of Saint Magdalene. Several hypotheses have been put forth about the meaning of the name Herrauscorritsehe, as *God of Red Dust* (according to Bishop de Saint-Pierre) or *God of Red Lightning* (Dr. Urutibehety) – (*Heraus*: what comes down from the sky, lightning; *corritse*: red). This is the generally accepted interpretation, particularly because of the need for shepherds to ensure the benevolence of a deity linked to storms, equivalent to Jupiter.

Hippocampus

The *Hippocampus* or *Hippocamp*, also *Hippokampos* (pl.: *Hippocampi* or *Hippocamps*), Ancient Greek: ἱππόκαμπος, from ἵππος (horse) and κάμπος (sea monster) – often called a "sea-horse" in English – is a water-creature, shared by Phoenician, Etruscan, Pictish, Roman and Greek mythology, though its name has a Greek origin. The Hippocampus has typically been depicted as having the upper body of a horse with the lower body of a fish. Its appearance has a lot in common with a certain type of *Water-horse* or *fresh water-spirits* of the British Isles and the island range up to Iceland.

Hodei

In Basque mythology, *Hodei, Odei* or *Odai* (Basque: Cloud) was an *Irelu* who caused thunder, lightning and storms who also appears in the shape of a storm cloud. He frightened the peasants by spoiling their crops with his lightning. According to the Basques: When you hear thunder, you say: *"Odeiak jo"* (the thunderer has struck). When you hear loud thunder, you say: *"Odei asarrea"* (the angry thunder). When dense clouds are seen: *"Odeia dator"* (the storm cloud is coming). When the thunder is coming: *"Odei dago"* (there is a storm in the air). In these expressions, which are especially used in the rural areas, the main meanings of the word Odei clearly appear to be: thunder, Irelu of the storm or of the stormy cloud. He was the substitute of the ancient god *Ortzi* or *Urtzi,* and occasionally appears in legends as the evil son of Mari, chief of the Ireluak.

People try to control Odei with magical procedures, or they turn to God to ward of the damage he is capable of. In Saint-Esteben (Labort), blessed candles are lit, laurel branches are burned in the house or an axe is placed on the threshold of the front door of the house, with the edge facing upwards, to conjure him and appease his fury. In Gesalibar/Arrasate (Guipuscoa), Odei is called *Odeiaixe,* a wind or thunder-wind from the east that brings gusts. It is also said that Odeiaixe can pass without discharging rain or hail, as long as the north wind does not get in its way. But when the north wind, *Urdalatx,* arrives with its battery of clouds making them run on the flanks of Odeiaixe, the fusion of the two winds causes a strong storm of rain or hail. This becomes even more violent if a third wind, *Naparraixe,* intervenes by surging from the side of Muru, a mountain that is to the southeast of Gesalibar.

Hombre de las Narices

El Hombre de las Narices (in Catalan: *Home dels Nassos*; "Man with Noses") is a folkloric character whose tradition is kept alive in Catalonia, but also in other parts of Spain such as Aragon, La Rioja, Navarre, Álava, Burgos, Majorca, etc. El Home dels Nassos has as many noses (in other places also eyes or ears) as there are days in the year (i.e. each day that passes he loses a nose and grows a new one). He can only be seen on December 31. According to folklorist Joan Amades, el Hombre de las Narices seems to be a degeneration of a mythical character who symbolized the course of the year. The character is said to live in the base of a tree – in Catalan, *l'Arbre dels Nassos* (the Tree of Noses) – which Amades believes is the origin of this myth. El Hombre de las Narices is dressed in the leaves of twelve different trees, in four colors. According to Amades, this character may have been inspired by Janus, the Roman god of two faces.

Adults explained to children that on the last day of the year el Hombre de las Narices emerges, who imagined this bizarre character with 365 noses on his face, without realizing that on December 31 he has only one nose left. There were also those who told their children they saw him reflected in the water gutters. Nowadays, in some towns or villages a parade is organized with a man with a big head who represents el Hombre de las Narices. In the smaller villages it was said that he appeared in church to drink from the holy water basin. In Barcelona, the custom was to find him at noon on December 31 in the Plaça del Palau, in front of the Llotja, on an elevation so that everyone could see how he covered the 365 noses he was supposed to have all over his body with dozens of sheets, because they did not fit on his face. In several other places you will find local variations on the ritual.

Houzier

The *Houzier* was a small, semi-aquatic, mud throwing *Farfadet*, who lived along the streams in the commune of La Hardoye. This little *Waterman* could easily hide; in the summer in the high grass, and in the winter he would lock himself in a hole. Mischievous, his great joy was to splash and cover passersby with mud, especially the young girls when they wore pretty dresses. Folklore has it that for a long time, in La Hardoye, it was no longer safe walking along the streams.

Hupeur or Hueur

The *Hupeur* or *Hueur* is a demonic night bird from French folklore that nests near ponds and marshes. When night falls, it cries out in a human voice to attract wanderers. If someone makes the mistake of answering, the bird starts telling all kinds of stories to lure its victim into the mud and mire of a swamp. Then the demon transforms into a shape in which it can easily drown its victim. When finished it resumes its original bird guise and looks for another victim. His call would be irresistible, and perceptible even to sleepers, who could not help but get up to look for the source.

Hutzêran

In the folklore of the French speaking canton of Vaud in Switserland, the Hutzêran is a howling *Elf* who overturns branches and causes leaves to swirl. This malignant, green-clad forest creature is said to be of massive proportions. According to Paul Sébillot, its name comes from the Hutsi dialect *hucher*, which means "to call out loud."

Hyades

In Greek mythology, the *Hyades* (ancient Greek: Ὑάδες, Romanized: *Hyádes*, popularly called "rain-makers" or "rainy ones"; from ὕω, hýō, "I fall as rain", or from ὗς, hŷs, "swine") are a sisterhood of *Nymphs* that bring rain. In most stories, the Hyades were the daughters of *Atlas* (by either *Pleione* or *Aethra*, one of the *Oceanides*) and sisters of *Hyas*, although one version mentiones Hyas and *Boeotia* as their parents. The Hyades are sisters to the *Pleiades* and the *Hesperides*. The main myth concerning them provides an etiology for their weepy raininess: Hyas was killed in a hunting accident and the Hyades wept from grief. They were then changed into a cluster of stars, the Hyades, set in the head of Taurus.

I

Iditu

Iditu or *Idittu* is a nocturnal *Irelu* in Basque folklore. This creature is also known as *Iditxu*, *Irel*, *Irel-suzko*, *Ireltsu*, *Ieltxu* and *Iratxo*. It is known in most of Biscay. In some cases it appears in human form, but it is also known to appear as a donkey, a black sheep, a pig, as a bird spitting fire through its beak and a burning flame in the dark nightly sky. Though basically not evil inclined, by showing himself unexpectedly, he scares people. Following an Iditu, driven by curiosity or for another reason, is not without risk, as the demon tends to lead his followers through dangerous ravines, precipices and other high-risk places. Ditches and caves are the natural home of this creature.

Ihizi

Ihizi is a nature-spirit that may have survived from the Paleolithic period. He is a protecting *Irelu* of Basque folklore, shaped as a red bull, or other animal, and subordinate to goddess Mari. This nature-spirit especially guards the caves of Mari in Oxabia and Austokieta, which is why he has also been called *Austoki* or *Oxabi*. In the mountains of Lizartza, he was seen wrapped in a fiery garment, moving from one place to another. This Irelu has been ordered to punish men who commit evil deeds, using his horns of fire, and threatening the people who do not respect the wild nature of the Pyrenees. Ihizi literally means "hunting" in ordinary Basque. Game is called *ehiza*. Hence the term *ihizi* in Basque mythology or folklore usually means "wild animal". This Irelu usually appears as a red bull (Zezengorri) in the caves of Ostibarre (Camou) in Zuberoa (Soule), among other places. In the caves of Austokieta and Ubedi he takes the form of a fire bull. In the shape of a cow Ihizi appears in Leize (Sare) and in Labourd; as a white horse in the caves of Lexarrigibel (Alçay) in Soule; as a black mare in the cave of Obanzun (Berastegi), and in the form of a goat in the caves of Akelarre in Zugarramurdi (Navarre). Finally Ihizi can also be seen as a white goat in a cave in Villafranca, as a sheep in the caves of Okina and Aketegi or as a red pig in Marizulo d'Amezketa. Alhough wild in nature, Ihizi may only operate in the service of Mari. One legend tells that the Irelu once escaped from a cave and terrified the people around

Hupeur (2022) by Benjamin Adamah

him, without the permission of Mari. As reaction the goddess hung a bell on Ihizi's neck, so that Mari could always hear him when he was active.

Incubus / Succubus

Incubus (pl. *Incubi* or *Incuben* – from Latin: *incubare* for "to lie on top", "to hatch" or "incubate"), is the name given in mythology to a male, often sexual dreams causing nocturnal demon, *forest-spirit* or *Sylvan.* It mates with sleeping women, with or without them noticing, or – according to the *Malleus Maleficarum* – is deliberately attracted by women, lifting their skirts in the middle of a field. In addition, the Incubus was considered a representative of Satan, who was responsible for dragging souls of sinners to hell with them after their death. The female counterpart is called a *Succubus* (also *Sukkubus*, *Succuba* or *Sukkuba*, pl.: *Succubi*, from Latin: *succumbere* 'to lie under'). A Succubus preys on sleeping men to steal their seed and sexual energy. Although the Incubi and Succubi phenomenon was very prevalent in the Middle Ages and Renaissance – especially because of the *Malleus Maleficarum*, which contains extensive, inquisition-filtered, information on the subject – even today people still encounter this entity. The general consensus about the Incubus and Succubus is that it is one and the same creature, able to manifest itself in both male and female form, depending on the gender of its victim, to feed on orgasmic energy. The creature has overlap with creatures as the *Alp*, *Mare*, *Moor*, *Nightmare*-type, certain vampiric beings, and even some *forest* and *field-spirits* of whom some are known for sexual intrusions as well. The difference is that the Incubus/Succubus is only preying on sexual energy, not intended to harm its "donor", which in rare cases makes even long term relationships possible. Some nightly sexual encounters are mistakenly attributed to the Incubus/Succubus, but are actually real people who are skilled in projecting their etheric double to act sexually on people they visit at night. A link between the *Faun* or *Satyr* or *Nymph* and the Incubus/Succubus has been made by Sinistrari of Ameno, in his book *Demoniality.*

Modern reports

Modern reports of Incubi and Succubi have been growing rapidly since out of body-experiences (OBE) and astral traveling got more serious attention on specialized internet-forums and new books on the subject. Ever since the publication of Robert A. Monroe's *Journeys of the Body* in

1971, the interest in consciously projecting the energy-body or making astral journeys has increased dramatically. The biggest boost came with the work *Astral Dynamics*, of the Australian metaphysicist Robert Bruce, followed by *New Energy Ways* and *Mastering Astral Projection, 90-day guide to out of body experience.* Bruce set up an extensive forum via www.astralpulse.com in which people participate with mostly serious discussions, questions and frank exchange of experiences. In relation to the Incubus or Succubus, you come across these kinds of entries:

> *"I have been visited twice by an Incubus/Succubus in the past. Both times after intensive trance/energy work, perhaps the most intensive thing I have ever done. The first time I was scared and didn't know what was going on. I cut off the experience and that's exactly why I was very curious the second time and let it happen in its course. The creature manifested itself as a handsome girl. I was partly in a trance and didn't fight against anything'[...] 'I've had quite a bit of good sex in my life, but nothing even came close to what I had the night before".*

Although horror films transform the image of an irresistible sex partner into a gruesome demon according to the 'Lamia formula', you will never find anything demon-like within serious research circles. Neither the Medieval nor recent stories explicitly depict an Incubus or Succubus as a destructive evil being. Robert Bruce regards the creature as a unique class of *astral wildlife*. According to Bruce, Incubi are actually very beautiful to see and not terrifying at all. They look like a cellular organism, a bit like an amoeba. Seen clearly or with astral vision, while they manifest themselves close to the physical dimension, their real form is an oval of about 18 inches to 3 feet (± 40-90 cm) and they seem to consist of a kind of clear jelly. Inside the body, hundreds of small speckles of light shine in all kinds of colors. At one end there is an internal structure that looks a bit like a red daisy. This seems to be the back end. The Incubus pulsates with a dense red glow when it moves. It moves fast and with fits and starts, just like many other creatures from the astral fauna move when they are observed with astral vision.

Incubus-type entities usually attack quickly and with great force. Their victim is usually asleep, but not always. Sometimes they attack someone in their sleep, sometimes when someone is awake, but relaxed. During the first type of attack, the Incubus attaches itself directly to the genital energy-center and very quickly causes a forced orgasm. The second type of attack works with the telepathic and hypnotic transmission of sexual dreams or illusions, along with the stimulation of the genital center. When someone wakes up during the attack, the Incubus will often create the illusion of a beautiful human figure that sits on top of the victim like an Alp and performs all kinds of sexual acts. The end result is always the same; an orgasm that is many times more intense than the victim experiences normally. This is due to the direct stimulation of the second chakra.

Incubi and Succubi during the Middle Ages and Renaissance

In the Middle Ages and Renaissance, the Incubi and Succubi were thought of as a major problem by ecclesiastical authorities, such as Pope Innocent VIII. In his *Summis Desiderantes Affectibus* from 1484 he wrote:

> *"Many people of both sexes, not thinking of their own salvation and straying from the Catholic faith, have surrendered themselves to devils, Incubi, Succubi. Such devils hinder men in performing the sexual act and women in receiving..."*

The Catholic opinion leaders' ban on sex with Incubi and Succubi regularly led to hysterical excesses and extremely violent political actions. One group that opposed the church taboos were of course the "witches". A term that should be used with caution here, because there were periods in which almost every woman in a region was demonized and persecuted as a witch by the inquisitors. In his book *The Discoverie of Witchcraft* from 1584, Reginald Scot gives a number of examples of the role that Incubi and Succubi played in sexual satisfaction. Thus we read on page 43:

> *"Howbeit M. Mal [Malleus Maleficarum], proceedeth, affirming that all witches take their beginning from such filthie actions, wherin the divell, in likenes of a prettie wench, lieth prostitute as Succubus to the man, and reteining his nature and seede, conveieth it unto the witch, to whome he delivereth it as Incubus."*

A little further on (page 43-44), Scot refers again to the *Malleus Maleficarum* and we read how excited women, who had pulled up their dresses till above their bellybuttons, walked into the woods and fields and twisted their bodies lustfully to get sexually satisfied by a "black fog" of the length and size of an adult man.:

"For proofe hereof James Sprenger and Institor affirme, that manie times witches are seene in the fields, and woods, prostituting themselves uncovered and naked up to the navill, wagging and mooving their members in everie part, according to the disposition of one being about that act of concupiscence, and yet nothing seene of the beholders upon hir; saving that after such a convenient time as is required about such a peece of worke, a blacke vapor of the length and bignesse of a man, hath beene seene as it were to depart from hir, and to ascend from that place."

A striking detail is that the taste of the Incubi is similar to that of the average construction worker. Blondes were particularly popular (page 45): *"But here the inquisitors note maie not be fogotten, to wit: that Maides having yellow haire are most molested with this spirit"*. Whether or not they whistled at these girls is not known. However, their sense of humor cannot be denied, although one Bishop Sylvanus had very different ideas about this (page 45):

"You shall read in the legend, how in the night time Incubus came to a ladies bed side, and made hot loove unto hir: whereat she being offended, cried out so lowd, that companie came and found him under hir bed in the likenesse of the holie bishop Sylvanus, which holie man was much defamed therebie, untill at the length of this infamie was purged by the confession of a divell made at S.Jeroms toombe".

Addictions to Incubi or Succubi

Cases of copulation with Incubi or Succubi occur very frequently, through all times and all over the world. There are many common denominators, especially the orgasm that is much more intense than in normal intercourse. The reports of Incubi and Succibi encounters of the Renaissance period are very accurate and well documented. They often show great similarities with reports that can be found on contemporary internet forums on paranormal subjects, although in other cases they appear to be filtered by Inquisitional interrogations. Witch judge Pierre de Lancre (1553-1631) received from the young witch Marguerite de Sare, the 'confession' that she and the witches in Labourd copulated with an Incubus in the shape of a billy goat, which had a member the size of a mule, using her whole arm as a measure of length to illustrate this. De Lancre then quotes a report by inquisitor Bogue, who wrote that the witches in Franche-Comté got off with a penis no bigger or thicker than a finger and wrote very ironically that Satan apparently took better care of the witches in Labourd than of those in the Franche-Comté region.

There are serious reports from men and women who are addicted to a Succubus or Incubus and have long-term relationships with it. Even under the threat of violence or imprisonment, people often do not want to give up their astral sex partner. The rumor that sex with a Succubus/Incubus is much more satisfying than ordinary sex, starts with Pico della Mirandola's story of a man who has a relationship with his Succubus for forty years and said that he would rather die in prison than give her up. In his *Les Incubus* (1897), Delassus cites an exorcism held in 1643, in which a 20 year-old girl had to be freed from an Incubus. The arrival of the Incubus was always accompanied by a sudden delirious state of excitement, in which she threw herself on her bed and was unable to concentrate on God. Exorcisms failed because, according to the priest, the girl did not want to lose her Incubus at all. In the *Compendium Maleficarum* (1608) by Francesco Maria Guazzo, a handsome young man asks the Bishop of Aberdeen to deliver him from a Succubus, which has been visiting him for months and *"is more beautiful than any woman he has ever seen"*. The most remarkable historical anecdote however reports of an Italian brothel in Bologna, where a number of Succubi were exploited. The operator was actually sentenced to death for this offense in 1468. Pious people with an aversion to such illegal sexual adventures could protect themselves against Incubi and Succubi by carrying a red peony, a peony root, a piece of red coral or a red jasper or pebble with them.

Inguma or Mauma

Inguma or *Mauma* in Baigorri, is an *Alp*-type *Irelu* of Basque folklore. It brings nocturnal visits to people's homes and squeezes the throats of people while they are asleep, making it difficult for the victims to breathe, and causing unspeakable anxiety. The Irelu *Aideko* is similar to Inguma, but he is also blamed for all diseases whose natural causes are unknown. Its victims can only be saved by burning rooster feathers. To avoid the effects of this Irelu, many small formulas were said aloud in which Mary or Jesus were invoked for protection. In Arrasate (Mondragón) *Amandre Santa Ines* was worshiped against the attacks of the Inguma. In Espelette and Sara, they sing a little rhyme to prevent the Alp from appearing. God and Maria are evoked for protection, and the Inguma is ordered not to appear until all of their friends, the stars in the sky, grass on the ground and the sand on the shore are counted. This apotropaic formula uses the same logic as the scattering of poppy seeds on or in the grave of a Vampire in eastern Europe, who could not leave the place until all the seeds were counted:

"Inguma, enauk hire izu
Jainkoa eta Andre Maria
hartzentiak lagun;
zeruan izar, lurrean belar, kostan hare
haiek denak zenbatu arte
etzadiela niganat ager."

Intxisua

Intxisua (pl. *Intxisuak*; also *Intxisu, Intxiso, Intxixu, Intxitxu, Intxusi, Itxiso*) is an *Irelu* from Basque folklore and a character from the Oiartzun carnival, who could be an *Iratxo* or a *Sorgina* (witch). This Irelu preferably lives in desolate wild places or in mountain caves, shunning people. In the town of Ataun (Gipuzkoa), Intxisua is said to have originally been a male witch or warlock, while in the town of Oiartzun (Gipuzkoa), he was an *Iratxo* who easily hid or escaped from the caves of Arditurri. Very difficult to encounter, not only because of his shyness, but also because of his wild nature. According to belief, the Intxisuak were less than four feet / 1.20 meter tall, thin, dark-skinned, bearded, and with a very hairy body. Some say that they were like Goblins and had great strength, but it seems that they only had that strength at night. According to folk-belief, Intxisuak, Sorginak, etc. were buried under the local *cromlechs* (prehistoric standing stones) in the area. Some etymologists believe the word Intxisua comes from the Spanish word *hechizo* (spell, incantation). Others state that the name Intxisua is similar to other anthroponyms for the words *Leltxu* or *Iratxo,* and therefore of Basque origin. It was customary, that when a dog began to bark in the middle of the night without any explanation, people said that the Intxisua was doing his thing. If a child did something mischievous or would not obey, the expression *"Intxisua baino bihurriagoa zara"* (You are more mischievous than an Intxisua) was often used. A strange story tells of a forester from Oiartzun who found an Intxisua in a cave. In his words, the creature was half human and half-cow. In Arditurri a mysterious creature was found by miners, of which was reported that *"it was a man but also a woman"*.

Some of the miners tried to talk to it in Basque, Spanish and even French, but didn't succeed in communicating with it. Over time the creature lost weight and eventually it died.

Inuus

In ancient Roman religion – according to Maurus Servius Honoratus – *Inuus* was used both to denote *Faunus* or *Pan* as the god of sexual intercourse, or as that aspect (daemon) of the god that embodied sexual intercourse. He wrote that Inuus is an epithet of Faunus, named from his habit of intercourse with animals, based on the etymology of *ineundum*, (a going in, penetration), from *inire* (to enter), in the sexual sense. Other names for the god were *Fatuus* and *Fatuclus*. Walter Friedrich Otto (1874-1958) a German classical philologist particularly known for his work on the meaning and legacy of Greek religion and mythology, disputed the traditional etymology and derived Inuus instead from *in-avos*, "friendly, beneficial" (*aveo*, "to be eager for, desire"), for the being's fructifying power. Livy is the sole source for identifying Inuus as the form of Faunus for whom the *Lupercalia* was celebrated: *"naked young men would run around, venerating Lycaean Pan, whom the Romans then called Inuus, with antics and lewd behavior."* Although Ovid does not name Inuus in his treatment of the Lupercalia, he may allude to his sexual action in explaining the mythological background of the festival.

Ipotx

In Basque folklore the *Ipotxak* (pl.) or *Nanoak* are a race of *dwarves* or dwarfish *Ireluak*, like the *Iratxoak* and *Gnomoak* (Gnomes).

Iratxoak

Iratxoak (sing.: Iratxo) are the *Imps* or *Goblins* of Basque mythology and ancient Biscayan folklore. Usually benevolent, they help with farming labors in the night, if given presents of food. Its prefix *Ira* is said to come from the Basque word *Iratz* and is formed by the suffix *txo*, which indicates "smallness". Another theory has it that the name seems to be directly associated with ferns (*ira*, in Basque), of which it is a diminutive. According to an old Basque belief, Iratxoak are born from the seeds of ferns on St. John's Night. It is well known that ferns do not produce seeds, but according to this belief, they do grow on that magical night. Other names for these creatures are *Irel*, *Irelu*, *Ireltsu*, *Ieltxu*, *Idittu*, *Iritxu*, *Irelsuzko* and *Iruztargi*. The beliefs in this character are widespread in the Basque Country and Navarre, as well as in the French Basque Country. Nowadays it is used, as in many other cases, as a masculin name, although this is not very widespread. It seems to be confused with the feminine version, *Iratxe* or *Iratze*, although etymologically it has nothing to do with it. *Galtxagorriak* are a specific kind of Iratxo. Their name means "red-pants". These creatures, especially well-known in Bizkaia, appear at night, and apart from their appearance as a woman or a child, they may appear like a donkey, a black ram, a pig, or a bird with a fiery tongue. Although they have a habit of appearing suddenly, in order to frighten people, they are not evil. Wells and caverns are the usual abodes of these jokers. There is also an Iratxothat, an underground spirit, who will abduct anyone that bothers him. His strange footprints were found by shepherds at the entrance of the caves of Armontaitz and Malkorburu. Legend has it that if you climb the mountain called Ubedi you may hear his song, mingled with the sound of the wind.

Irelu

In Basque folklore the word *Irelu* (pl. *Ireluak*) is in most cases used as a generic term for all kinds of supernatural creatures, mostly nature-spirits, demons or daemons that are often connected to the goddess Mari. As a blanket term Irelu is used in the same way the Spanish use the term *Duende*, the British, Irish and Scottish people use *Fairy*, the German speaking people use *Elben*, etc. Nevertheless, there is the difference that some Ireluak are not self-contained beings but specific, sometimes local, manifestations or materializations of the goddess Mari.

Ireltxu

Ireltxu (pl.: *Ireltzuak*; also: *Ireltso*, *Ireltxo*) is an *Iratxo* from the folklore of Biscay. Ireltzuak sometimes look like birds or people blowing fire from their beaks or mouths; in other tales they are horses or cats; but for the most this creature was seen in the shape of a small and repugnant pig, which at sunset came out of the depths with its companions, to walk the old road between Bermeo and Mundaka, in search of travelers to devour. A legend assures that they were exterminated definitively by the local people of Bermeo.

J

Janara

The *Janara* is an entity of southern Italian folklore that is a hybrid between a lonely, aggressive solitary witch with a bitter character from the Benevento area, and an *Alp* or *Succubus*. Most likely, she was a witch projecting her etheric double. The name may derive from *Dianara*, which is "priestess of Diana", or from the Latin *ianua*, meaning "door". It was before the door that a bag of salt, grain or a broom was placed. When she wanted to enter a room, the Janara could do nothing but count the grains or branches of the broom. She would linger until sunrise, the light of which was deadly to her. The same was done for protection of the mares in the stable. The Janara would go out at night and sneak into the stables to get a mare and ride through the night. She would also have the habit of braiding the manes of the kidnapped young mare to leave a mark of her presence. It sometimes happened that the mare, exhausted by the long ride, could not bear the enormous effort she had undergone and died of fatigue. The feeling of suffocation that sometimes occurs during sleep was also attributed to the Janara, it was thought that the Janara liked to jump on sleeping people to suffocate them, especially young men. It was also said that children who suddenly showed physical deformities had been pulled through the tripod, used in the fireplace to support the kettle, by her. Of such a child it was said: *"La Janara ll'è passato dinto 'u trepète"* (The Janara has passed him through the tripod). No doubt, that of course this has camouflaged many cases of child abuse by family members, in order to keep a decent social profile.

Janas or Gianas

The *Janas* or *Gianas* are the *Fairies* or *Little People* of the Sardinian tradition. They are also known as *Giannèddas*, *Nanos*, *Mergianas*, *Birghines*, or *Le Faddi*. It is said that they lived in the Domus de Gianas, or the prehistoric tombs carved into the rock. Depending on local folklore, very different features are attributed to the Janas. Male and female Janas are almost indistinguishable, except for the fact that the women may have very long breasts that they throw over their shoulders. In Aritzo, the Janas are said to be nearly one foot (25 centimeters) tall; shy little creatures who hid from humans. According to most Sardinian legends, their nature was benevolent and the Janas wove beautiful fabrics using gold looms. But in some parts of the island, there are myths describing the Janas as evil witches. Some accounts even state that they were *vampiric* beings who lured in human men, murdered them, and later gave birth to half-human children. They sometimes appear as nocturnal *washer-women* and some believed they were souls of women who died in childbirth. The Giana or Jana is cognate with the *Anjana* of Spain, *Zana* of Romania/Albania and *Xana* of Asturia, and possibly linked to the goddess *Diana*. Other details are reminiscent of the *Fates*.

Jaunagorri

Jaunagorri, Yaunagorri or Yona-Gorri, literally means the "Red *(gorri)* Lord *(jauna)*" in Basque. He is a mysterious *mountain Irelu* and his usual residence is located at the top of the peak of Anie (2504 m), in Basque Ahuñamendi, in the Pyrenees, where he is said to possess a wonderful garden producing fruits that would give immortality. But the bold ones who try to climb the mountain are repelled by terrible storms, or hail storms triggered by the Red Lord. According to José Miguel Barandiaran (*Mythologie Basque*, 1989), some inhabitants of Lescun saw in Jaunagorri a representation of the goddess *Mari*, always in relation to the storms that this character could cause. The inhabitants of Lescun, who see storms and lightning forming on Mount Anie, look at it as the dwelling place of their Yona-Gorri, the being dressed in the color of fire. They look with a worried eye at any stranger who goes to this mountain, because Yona-Gorri gets irritated by these indiscreet visits, and takes revenge by throwing storms on the plain. In some tales, Jaunagorri is a character somewhat related to the Devil, whose attempts are thwarted by Saint-Pierre.

Jean de l'Ours

Jean de l'Ours is a mythical hybrid being, half human, half animal, and like the ancient Greek *Thereus*, born of a woman and a bear, and endowed with a superhuman strength that allows him to overcome various trials. He is also known as *Juan Artz, Xan de l'Ours, Joan de l'Ós, Ivachko-Ourseau* and *Ivanko-Ourseau*. The richness of the tale comes first of all from this double nature and the tug-of-war it implies. The progressive folklorization of its different versions has tended to attenuate this fundamentally dual and ambiguous nature of the character, torn between his animal, wild, pagan or even satanic nature, and his humanity – aspiring to the spiritual and to religion, to make him a kind "teddy bear", a positive hero. In old versions, John the Bear terrifies people with his ugliness and does evil without wanting to, by his excessive strength. Throughout the Pyrenees, as in other countries and in several languages, we find the story of a hairy child born from the mating of a bear and a woman. This story reflects the mythological role played by the bear, which is linked to fertility in Europe and elsewhere. Dagmar Fink mentions that in Arles-sur-Tech, on Candlemas Day, a man dressed as a bear hunts down a young girl named Rosetta, and leads her into his "cave". Folklorist Arnold van Gennep reports several of these spring fertilization rituals in his *Manuel de folklore Français*, pointing out that the bear costume is unique to the Pyrenees, and that the bear is an essential character of carnival and festivals in Vallespir. Basque folklore sometimes equates Jean de l'Ours with *Basajaun* or *Baxajaun* (the wild Lord of the Forest, pl.: Basajaunak), a strong, hairy and wild mythical figure, also found in the Pyrenees, most often in the Irati forest.

Jentilak or Gentiles

The *Jentilak* (sing.: *Jentil*, *Gentiles* in French), are a race of giants. This word, meaning *gentile*, from Latin *gentilis*, was used to refer to pre-Christian civilizations. In the Basque tradition, the Jentilak (and *Mairuak* in other versions) are the builders of the megaliths, dolmens and cromlechs of the Basque Country. These monuments are called *jentil-baratza* (garden of the gentiles), *jentil-arria* (stone of the gentiles), etc. while the caves that honor the creature are known as *jentilzulo* or *jentilkoba*. Like the *Basajaun*, *Tartalo* and other Basque "Yeti-like creatures", the Jentilak inhabit this gray zone between myth and cryptozoology. Within this context a Jentil is a hairy giant which stands more than 12 feet tall and weighs about 1600 pounds. The Jentilak were believed to have lived alongside the Basque people. They were so tall and strong that they could *"walk in the sea and threw rocks from one mountain to another"*. Many Basque locations have names that remind one of the rock throwing Jentilak. Within this context the term *jentilarri* is used to designate certain cliffs that, according to certain legends, occupy the current sites for having been thrown from distant places by the Jentilak. Such are the ravines of Urdiola (Arrankudiaga), thrown to that place by the Jentilak who bowled between the mountain of the same name and

Arakaldo Castle; the ravine of Markola (Karrantza) which, when thrown by a Jentil, crushed a man and his team of oxen; the so-called Aitzbiribil (in Mutriku), thrown by the Jentilak from Santakruzmendi which is above Ondarroa; that of Amil (in Mutriku), thrown by the Jentilak from Mount Arno; that of Osunako-erreka (in Soraluze), thrown by a Jentilak from the summit of Atxolin, and so on. This throwing of stones has led to several tales and explanations for ancient stone buildings and large isolated rocks. Even the Basque ball game, *pilota*, is ascribed to these stone-throwers. The tradition lives on in the Basque power games of stone lifting and throwing.

Just as in some folktales the Basajaunak were taught the first technical skills, before the humans made them their own, the Jentilak were said to have invented metallurgy, to grow the first wheat, and to teach humans how to run a farm. However, they were unwilling to civilize completely and move to the valleys from the mountains, ushering a certain unwillingness to progress. Finally they disappeared into the earth under a dolmen in the Arratzaren valley in Navarra, when a portentous luminous cloud – perhaps a star – appeared, said to have heralded the birth of Christ (Kixmi) and the end of the Jentil-age. Other stories say the Jentil threw themselves from a mountain. Only *Olentzero* remained, a giant who as a kind of Santa Claus brings gifts to Basque children for Christmas, and who is reproduced as straw dolls.

Jetins

Jetins (from *jeter*, "to throw"; also *J'tins*, *J'tuns*, or *Crions*) are tiny *Lutins* native to the seaside caves of Brittany and close related to the *Fions*. Despite their size – ranging from thumb-sized to 1.5 feet tall – they are incredibly strong, capable of lifting and tossing huge boulders with ease. The Jetins are said to be common in the rocks and caves along the coast of Ille-et-Vilaine and on the island of Guernsey. Those from the banks of de la Rance are reputed to come out of their holes every evening to amuse themselves in the countryside, in particular by playing tricks such as entangling the horses' manes, making the pigs run away and opening the hen houses. The Jetins are, however, generous by nature, and will gladly give bread, bacon or sausages to anyone who asks. One should not try to keep one of their knives. They are also notorious for their habit of kidnapping beautiful babies to substitute them for their old and wrinkled looking *changelings*.

Juancaballos

Juancaballos are Andalusian creatures who, according to legends, lived in Sierra Mágina (Jaén), Andalusia. They are described as a being half man, half horse (very similar to a *Centaur*) and were endowed with great strength, ferocity and cunning. The *Juancaballos* were very difficult to see because they hid in secret caves and caverns, such as the hills of Huelma and Sierra del Natin; and it is said that they would attack a passerby when they were hungry. They have been known for many centuries. In folklore there are some accounts of terrified men who survived their attack.

K

Kallikantzaros

The *Kallikantzaros* (Greek: καλικάντζαρος, pl. καλικάντζαροι *Kallikantzaroi*; Bulgarian: караконджул; Serbian: караконџула / *Karakondžula*; modern Greek plural: *Callikantzari*) is a malevolent *Goblin* in Southeast European and Anatolian mythology and folklore. Stories about the Kallikantzaros or its equivalents can be found in Greece, Bulgaria, Serbia, Albania, Bosnia and Cyprus. The term "kallikantzaros" is speculated to be derived from the Greek *kalos-kentauros* (beautiful centaur), although this theory has been met with many objections. A second theory proposes that the word comes from Turkish *Kara-kondjolos* (Werewolf, Vampire), from kara (pure) and koncolos (bloodsucker, Werewolf). Kallikantzaroi are believed to dwell underground but come to the surface during the twelve days of Christmas, from 25 December to 6 January (from the winter solstice for a fortnight, during which time the sun ceases its seasonal movement). One particularity that set the Kallikantzaroi apart from other Goblins or creatures in folklore was its appearance on Earth for only twelve days each year. Their short stay on Earth, as well as the fact that they were not considered purely malevolent creatures but rather "impish" and stupid, led to a number of theories about their creation. In folk-mythology it was told that Kallikantzaroi stay underground, sawing at the trunk of the world tree so that it will collapse, along with the Earth. However, when they are about to saw the final part, Christmas dawns and they are able to come to the surface. Then they temporally forget the tree and come to bring trouble to mortals, until on Epiphany (January 6) the sun starts moving again, and they must return underground to continue their sawing – as during their absence the world tree heals itself, so they must start working all over again.

There is no standard description of the appearance of Kallikantzaroi; there are regional variations as to how their appearance is described:
- with some animal parts, such as hairy bodies, horse legs, or boar tusks;
- enormous;
- diminutive;
- as humanoid, of small size with a horrible odor;
- predominantly male, often with protruding sexual characteristics;
- tall, black and hairy, with burning red eyes, goats' or donkeys' ears, monkeys' arms, tongues that hang out and heads that are huge;
- mostly blind, speaking with a lisp while they love to eat frogs, worms, and other small creatures.

Nonetheless, the most common belief is that they are small, black creatures, humanoid, apart from their long black tails, and are said to resemble little black devils. In Greek, the term Kallikantzaros is also used as a general term to describe a number of other short, ugly and usually mischievous beings in folklore.

Protection against Kallikantzaroi

Kallikantzaroi are believed to be creatures of the night. According to folklore, there were many ways people could protect themselves during the days when the Kallikantzaroi were on the loose. One such method was to leave a colander on their doorstep to trick the visiting Kallikantzaros. It was believed that since it could not count above two – three was believed to be a holy number, and by pronouncing it, the Kallikantzaros would supposedly kill itself – the Kallikantzaros would sit at the doorstep all night, counting each hole of the colander, until the sun rose and it was forced to hide. It is an annual tradition in some regions to throw *loukoumades* (a donut-like dessert filled with syrup) and sausages on your roof, and sing a specific song. It is believed that once this is done, the Kallikantzaroi will eat these and leave, returning to their work underground. Another supposed method of protection from Kallikantzaroi was to leave the fire in the fireplace burning all night, so that they could not enter through it. In some areas, people would burn the Yule log for the duration of the twelve days. In other areas, people would throw foul-smelling shoes into the fire, as the stench was believed to repel the Kallikantzaroi, forcing them to stay away. Additional ways to keep them away included marking one's door with a black cross on Christmas Eve and burning incense. According to legend, any child born during the twelve days of Christmas was in danger of transforming into a Kallikantzaroi during each Christmas season, starting in adulthood. The antidote to prevent this transformation was to bind the baby in tresses of garlic or straw, or to singe the child's toenails. According to another folk-belief anyone born on a Saturday could see and talk with the Kallikantzaroi.

Karnabo

The *Karnabo* or *Carnabot* is found on the Rocroi plateau, near Regniowez in France. It is a creature of Ardennes folklore, a *Bogey*, comparable to the *Mahwot* but with a more restricted distribution. It was born from the union of a Gypsy-sorcerer and a 67 year old female *Ghoul*. The Karnabo has an almost human head but has a trunk-like nose with which it makes a shrill whistling sound, yellow basilisk eyes and a dark and rough skin like the walls of the abandoned, sealed-off slate quarry where it lives. The horrible nasal whistling of the Karnabo is enough to paralyze or asphyxiate anyone foolish enough to wander within range of the quarry. Livestock are killed outright. In contrast to this destructive behavior, the Karnabo learned from his father how to cure paronychia (cuticle infection) by chanting certain magical phrases. The creature is said to work its curative powers on Good Fridays.

Katakhanás

Once upon a time the village of Kalikráti, in the district of Sfakiá (southwest Crete), was haunted by a *Katakhanás*, and people did not know what sort of man he was or where he came from. This Katakhanás destroyed children and many times even full grown men; and desolated both their village and many others. A special feature of the Katakhanás was that he was believed to feed himself with human livers. Finally a local man, who was highly regarded during his lifetime, with an arch build over his grave near church was dug up, looking still like a fresh corpse, as if he had just been buried the day before. The locals then gathered wood and burned the body completely to ashes, taking care that even the nail of one of his little fingers that afterwards was found in the ashes of the Vampire was also burned. A full report on this vampiric being was published in an article entitled *Pashley's travels to Crete* by Robert Pashley (Fellow of Trinity College Cambridge), in The *Monthly Review*, May-August issue, 1837.

Kères

In Greek mythology, according to Hesiod in the *Theogony*, the *Kères* (Κῆρες, sing. *Kèr* (Κήρ / *Kèr*), are the daughters of *Nyx*, belonging to the family of *Furies*. But in the same passage, a few lines apart, the poet makes the Kères the sisters of *Thanatos*. Still others saw them as the sisters of the *Moires* (Μοίρες, "Fates"). The Kères are present in the *Iliad*, where Homer shows them as *Fates* that determine the fate and destiny of the hero, to whom they appeared offering him a choice, on which depended the beneficial or evil outcome of his journey or personified the kind of life and death of the hero. Thus the origin of the Kères is confused since Antiquity, and the authors lean on an oral tradition of practical cults. The theological aspect is secondary. The Greek word κήρ (kèr) means "death" or "doom" and appears as a proper noun in the singular and plural as Κήρ and Κῆρες to refer to divinities. Homer uses Κῆρες in the phrase κήρες θανάτοιο, (Keres of death). By extension the word may mean "plague, disease" and in prose "blemish or defect". The relative verb κεραΐζω or κείρω means "ravage or plunder". Sometimes in Homer the words κήρ and moira have similar meanings. The older meaning was probably "destruction of the dead", and Hesychius of Alexandria relates the word to the verb κηραινειν "decay".

Mathias Egeler suggests a connection exists between the Kères and the *Valkyries* of Norse mythology. Both deities are war-spirits that fly over battlefields during conflicts and choose those to be slain. The difference is that Valkyries are benevolent deities in contrast to the malevolence of the Kères, perhaps due to the different outlook of the two cultures towards war. The word *valkyrie* derives from Old Norse *valkyrja* (pl.: *valkyrjur*), which is composed of two words; the noun *valr* (referring to the slain on the battlefield) and the verb *kjósa* (meaning "to choose"). Together, they mean "chooser of the slain". The Greek word "Ker", as illustrated above, etymologically hints to doom, destruction and death. Related in Irish mythology to the Kèr is *Badb,* meaning "crow", a war goddess or daemon who takes the form of a crow, and is thus sometimes known as *Badb Catha* (Battle Crow). She is known to cause fear and confusion among the soldiers and to move the tide of battle to her favored side. Badb Catha may also appear prior to a battle to foreshadow the extent of the carnage to come, or to predict the death of a notable person. She would sometimes do this through wailing cries, leading to comparisons with the *Bean-sídhe* (See *Bean-sídhe* under *Banshee* in *Spirit Beings in European Folklore – Compendium 1).*

Appearence

The Kères are infernal daemons, who haunted the battlefields like *Vampires* to drink the blood of the dying, to seize the dying and to lead the souls of the dead to the underworld. They bring misfortune and destruction and taint all those they touch, causing blindness, rapid old age and death. They are depicted as hideous, with sharp nails and shoulders covered with a long cloak reddened by the blood of the bodies they carry away. They were described as dark beings with claws and gnashing teeth and with a thirst for human blood. A description of the Kères can be found in the *Shield of Heracles* (Ancient Greek: *Ἀσπὶς Ἡρακλέους,* Aspis Hērakleous), an archaic Greek epic poem that was attributed to Hesiod:

> *"The black Dooms gnashing their white teeth, grim-eyed, fierce, bloody, terrifying, fought over the men who were dying for they were all longing to drink dark blood. As soon as they caught a man who had fallen or one newly wounded, one of them clasped her great claws around him and his soul went down to Hades, to chilly Tartarus. And when they had satisfied their hearts with human blood, they would throw that one behind them and rush back again into the battle and the tumult."*

Cult

Every year in Athens the *Anthesterion* was celebrated. The Anthesteria was one of the four Athenian festivals in honor of *Dionysus*. It was held each year from the 11th to the 13th of the month of Anthesterion (a month of the ancient Greek calendar), around the time of the January or February full moon. The festivities took place over three days, the last day of the festival was devoted to the souls of the dead. The first day was called *Pithoigia*, the second was called *Choes*, the third and last day was

Korrigans (1843) illustration taken from *Le Magasin Pittoresque*

the *Chytroi*, (literally: pots). The sacrifice made to the chthonian Hermes was then practiced, using a pot filled with cooked porridge. At the end of the day, the souls of the dead were cast out with the formula, θὺραζε Κᾶρες, οὑκέτ' Ανθεστὴρια (At the door, the Kères; no more Anthesterias).

Kobalos

The *Kobalos* (pl.: *Kobaloi*; Ancient Greek: Κόβαλος, pl.: Κόβαλοι) was a sprite from Greek mythology, a mischievous creature, fond of tricking and frightening mortals. In Greek myths the Kobaloi are depicted as impudent, thieving, droll, idle, mischievous, dwarfish *Gnomes* and also as funny, little tricky *Elves* of a phallic nature (Robert Brown, *The Greek Dionysiak Myth vol. 2* – 1923). The term Kobalos also means "impudent knave, arrant rogue" in ancient Greek, and individuals with these characteristics were thought to invoke Kobaloi spirits. Depictions of Kobaloi are common in ancient Greek art. The Kobaloi were companions of Dionysus and could shapeshift as Dionysus in the guise of *Choroimanes-Aiolomorphos*. The Kobaloi are related to two other Greek sprites: the *Kabeiroi* (*pygmies* with large phalluses) and the *Kerkopes* (mischievous forest creatures who lived in Thermopylae, or on Euboea). The word entered Latin as *cobalus*, then possibly entered French as *gobelin*. From this, the English *Goblin* and Welsh *Coblyn* may be derived.

Korrigan

The *Korrigan* is a *Lutin* from the folklore of Brittany. The *korr* in Korrigan etymologically refers to *dwarf*, while modern Cornish uses the word *korrik* (pl. *korrigow*) to refer to a *Gnome* or *sprite*. Benevolent or malevolent, depending on the case, he can show extreme generosity or horrible vengeance. The Breton language knows a very large number of words to designate the little people, and, it is common to distinguish them by their habitat. Pierre Dubois sums up *Kornikaneds les bois*, the *Korils*, *Courils*, *Corrics*, *Kriores*, *Kéréores* and *Kannerez noz les landes*, the *Poulpiquets les vaux*, the *Teuz les prés*, the *Boléguéans les tumuli*, the *Hoseguéannets les cercles de pierres*, the *Boudics*, *Boudiguets* and *Bouffon noz les ferme*. But Brittany also knows *Farfadets*, *Duz*, *Korrigs*, *Kerrighed*, *Komaudons*, *Korandons*, *Kormandons*, *Kérions*, *Ozégans*, *Fomiquets* or even *Chorriquets*. Over time, all of these once distinct little creatures have come to be referred to under the single name of Korrigan.

The appearance of Korrigans is varied. They can be endowed with magnificent hair and luminous red eyes, with the help of which they are supposed to bewitch mortals, or they can be described as small, black and hairy, wearing flat hats with velvet ribbons, the girls wearing purple bonnets. Dubois describes them as horned dwarfs one to two cubits high, with goat feet, iron hooves and cat claws. Folklore most often situates them in caves, tumuli or even in dolmens. Like the *Nains*, these smaller beings inhabit abandoned Druidical monuments or dwell beneath the foundations of ancient castles. Carnac is sometimes alluded to in Breton as *Ty C'harriquet* (the House of the Gorics), the country-folk in this district holding the belief that its megalithic monuments were reared by these manikins, whom they describe as between two and three feet high, but exceedingly strong. Korrigans also haunt the springs, fountains or moors of the Breton country. The witches' circles that can sometimes be found on the meadows or in the undergrowth are also attributed to them. It is said that they make a circle there to dance at nightfall. To the mortal who disturbs them, they sometimes propose challenges which, if they are successfully executed, give the right to a wish (which is generally the case for good men) but which can, in case of a failure, turn into death traps leading straight to Hell or to an underground prison with no hope of deliverance. On the night of October 31, they are active near the dolmens, ready to drag their victims into the underworld to avenge the misdeeds of the living. This tradition links them to the Celtic Halloween, originally the festival of Samhain.

L

Lamia

Lamia (Ancient Greek Λάμια / *Lámia;* latinized pl. *Lamiae*; also *Sybaris* (Σύβαρις / *Súbaris*), was originally a name borne by several female characters in Greek mythology. After late antiquity, it is associated primarily with one of these characters, who transforms into a monstrous creature under varying circumstances. John Cuthbert Lawson, M.A. – in *Modern Greek Folklore and Ancient Greek Religion – A Study in Survivals,* 1910 – wrote of the Lamiae, that they are:

> *"...hideous monsters, shaped as gigantic and coarse-looking women for the most part, but, with strange deformities of the lower limbs such as Aristophanes attributed to a kindred being, the Empusa. Their feet are dissimilar and may be more than two in number; one is often of bronze, while others resemble those of animals—ox, ass, or goat. Tradition relates that one of these monsters was once shot by a peasant at Koropíon, a village in Attica, and was found to measure three fathoms in length; and her loathsome nature was attested by the fact that, when her body was thrown out in a desert plain, no grass would grow where her blood had dripped. The chief characteristics of the Lamiae, apart from their thirst for blood, are their uncleanliness, their gluttony, and their stupidity."*

The Lamiae later become a mythological species of monstrous creatures of at least partly feminine appearance that prey especially on young men, and also profit sexually from them. When a Lamia is embarrassed, or her identity has been discovered, she instantly turns into her snake form to kill the women around her, and take the young men. In ancient "Bestiaria" the Lamia is represented as having the head and breasts of a woman, and the body of a four-footed animal with flowing tail, the hind feet having divided hoofs. Lamias are mentioned in particular in novels by Greek and Latin authors: Apuleius alludes to them in his *Metamorphoses* and Philostratus includes in his *Life of Apollonius of Tyana* an episode in which Apollonius unmasks a Lamia disguised as a young and beautiful Corinthian woman who was busy seducing one of his friends with the help of powerful spells of illusions.

Lamina

The *Lamina, Lamiña* or *Lamia* (pl.: *Lamiak* or *Laminak*; also *Amilamiak*) is a *Siren*- or *Nereid*-like nature-spirit or *Irelu* in Basque mythology and must not be confused with the *Lamia* of the ancient Greeks. The term "Lamia" (indet. form *lami*, pl. *lamiak*) is frequently used in the Spanish Basque Country. The female Laminak are usually found at the river shore combing their hair with a golden comb, and charming men. Mythology in coastal areas includes the *Itsaslamiak*, a variety of Laminak who live in the sea and have fish-like tails, similar to a *Mermaid*. The appearance of the Laminak varies a lot according to the regions or localities where the report comes from, or according to the role that is attributed to them in the story. Sometimes their appearance is not of interest in the narrative and is not described. However, two main competing trends can be identified. Either the Laminak are represented as young women. Resembling a mortal, often of great beauty, the Lamina is never completely human. She can be distinguished by the shape of her feet (goose feet, hen feet, goat feet) or by the coppery color of her skin. It is agreed that she has long hair that reaches down to her waist. In the coastal regions, she is represented as a Mermaid. Or, in the other version, the Laminak take on the appearance of very small men. Some descriptions make them extremely hairy, sometimes even having hairy faces. In some legends, their building skills are highlighted and they are all called *Guillen* (Guillaume). There are also intermediate variants, as small men with webbed feet, small women comparable to the *Fairies* of the European domain, or even more singular characteristics are sometimes attributed to them: according to Azkue, in Igorre the Laminak light up through the mouth. In Zeanuri and Elantxobe in Bizkaia, they are small women with a single eye in the middle of the forehead (like the *Tartaro*). In Berriz, they are thought to have no hair except for some hair on the back of the neck. In addition, some local legends depict the Laminak using a particular language made up of onomatopoeia (the formation of a word from a sound associated with it, e.g. cuckoo, sizzle) and expressions that are specific to them.

Yes is no & no is yes

The attitude of the Laminak towards humans is ambiguous and can vary from the best to the worst, from great sympathy (shelter offered and spontaneous donations) to strong malignity (abduction of young girls), passing through intermediate attitudes of justified revenge, pacts or exchanges of services. A very strange feature of the Laminak is that they express the duty of truth within the community through the theme of "no" (*eza* in Basque), the concept of negation. Perhaps because they live by negation, Laminak often express the opposite of what they mean, as the following legend shows. A Lamina had accepted a human girl that was looking for a job as a servant. She gave her the task of breaking dishes, beating children and smearing their faces. The girl did the opposite. Satisfied, the Lamina offered her a choice of a bag of coal or gold as her reward. The girl chose the coal and got the gold.

Mostly nocturnal creatures, the Laminak live underground, in caves or near springs and streams. The stories and tales about the Laminak form an important part of the corpus of Basque legends. Even many toponyms are related to Lamiak or Laminak, including Lamikiz (Markina), Laminaputzu (in Zeanuri), Lamitegi (in Bedaio), Lamirain (in Arano), Lamusin (in Sare), Lamiñosin (in Ataun). The creatures are described as helping those who give them presents by providing them with help at work. For example, if a farmer were to leave food for them at the river shore, they would eat it at night and in exchange finish ploughing his field. In some places, bridges were believed to have been built at night by Laminak: Ebrain (Bidarray, Lower Navarre), Azalain (Andoain, Gipuzkoa), Urkulu (Leintz-Gatzaga, Gipuzkoa), Liginaga-Astüe (Labourd). According to local Basque beliefs the Laminak had to leave the river site, if the bridge that they were building at night was left unfinished at cockcrow. It was also believed that the Laminak had left a river when a stone in the bridge was missing. Other beliefs claim that most Laminak disappeared when men built small churches in the forest. Laminak are also believed to dwell at the other side of the rainbow, where they are combing their hair. It is said that when the sunlight strikes their hair, the rainbow appears.

Belief in the existence of Laminak

It is interesting to note how several legends – regardless of the 19th or 20th century – refer to the Laminak as belonging to a recent but gone past. Their disappearance is explained either by the industrial era (for example, the development of arms factories in the city of Eibar) or by the advances of Christianization; the Laminak would have disappeared from the surrounding area because of the processions of the Rogations, or the sound of the church bells, or the construction of a hermitage or a chapel.

However, in 1972, Barandiarán reported that until relatively recently, some people still believed in the existence of Laminaks. These beliefs took the form of a compromise, summarized in two Basque proverbs: *"Everything with a name must exist"* and *"One must not believe that they exist; it must not be said that they do not exist"*. The Laminak was offered food, corn cakes, bits of ham, glasses of cider, left in the kitchen in the evening, milk or curd terrine that the shepherds placed in certain caves, or food that the farmers placed at the edge of their fields as a form of propitiation.

Lampádes

In Greek mythology, *Lampádes* (ancient Greek Λαμπάδες) are chthonic *Nymphs* of the underworld. They accompany the goddess *Hecate*. They are associated with the *Mysteries of Eleusis*. Their name is supposed to originate from the word "lamp" – the Lampades indeed carried luminous torches. The Roman name of the Lampádes is *Avernales nymphae* (Infernal Nymphs). The Lampádes are the companions of Hecate, the Greek goddess of witchcraft and crossroads, and they are a gift from *Zeus* for Hecate's loyalty during the *Titanomachy*. They carry torches and accompany Hecate in her nightly travels and hauntings. Some stories tell how the light of the torches of the Lampádes has the power to drive one to madness. The Lampádes were probably the daughters of various gods of the underworld, *daimôns*, *river-gods* of the Greek underworld or *Nyx*. They also serve as handmaidens to other goddesses of Hades (underworld), such as Persephone / Proserpina. They loved to play tricks on people. Some even say that they lead travelers to their death. Others say that they helped people.

Lares

The *Lares* (Latin *Lares*; sing. *Lar*) are the patron gods or guardian spirits of certain places and families in Roman religion. The *Lares Familiares* – along with the *Penates* – were the guardian spirits of the family, symbolized the household, and were equated with the deified souls of their deceased ancestors. They were worshiped at all family festivals and accompanied the family when it moved away. The cult probably dates back to prehistoric home burials. The comedy poet Plautus lets himself characterize a Lar as follows:

"I am the Lar Familiares of the house from which you have seen me step. This house I have owned and cherished for many years, already for the father and grandfather of the one who now inhabits it."

The *Lares Loci*, on the other hand, were the guardian spirits of a particular place. In a small sanctuary, the Lararium, the Lares Loci of the place were represented by one or more serpents, and worshiped. Lares Loci were stationary, that is, they did not move with the inhabitants of a house. *Lares Publici* were the guardian spirits of entire towns. In central Italy they were also called *Lares Compitales* in towns, and *Lares Paganales* in villages. Lares were also guardian spirits of public places and crossroads. In ancient Rome, at each crossroads there was a shrine dedicated to them.

Lares were male and very procreative. Their female partners were the *Virae*. The worship of the Lares and Penates was banned on November 8, 392 AD. On this date, Theodosius I outlawed all non-Christian rituals, and ordered large-scale persecution of the non-Christians. Together with Tychon, Epiphanius organized this persecution on Cyprus, destroying most of the temples on the island, and killing thousands of non-Christians. It is assumed by some folklorists that the Lares and Penates were at the basis of some later medieval *household spirit*-traditions in Europe.

Lehen

In Basque legends the *Lehen* is a giant sea snake, and regarded as an *Irelu* connected to the sea and coastline. Sometimes the Lehen was confused with the *dragon*, but they were different creatures. Giant sea-snakes are reported all over the world, either in a mythical-folkloric setting or a cryptozoological one.

Lemures

The *Lemures* were shades or spirits of the restless or malignant dead in Roman religion, and are probably cognate with an extended sense of *Larvae* – from Latin: *larva* (mask) – as disturbing or frightening.
The distinction between Lemures and Larvae is unclear, possibly the former being older but gradually receding more into the background in favor of the latter. The determination of Larvae as evil per se or due to neglect of the cult, of Lemures as the freshly departed good spirits of the

dead and of *Manes* as neutral, which is attested from the 2nd century AD onward, is an afterthought. This conception is not valid over the entire period of Roman antiquity, the valuations changing from author to author. Both Larvae and Lemures seem to have been mostly, and moreover originally, menacing ghosts. Lemures, haunted the graves like ghosts, either because they were unable to find rest in the grave due to a failure in their burial, or because they had led a criminal life. They were considered to be spirits of terrifying appearance, which confused people's minds. Popular belief connected them with the death of Remus – and because of the very common confusion of *L* and *R* in the Roman language – Lemures was considered to be the same word as *Remures*. Remus' spirit would not have let Romulus rest until he had reconciled him by founding a separate feast, the *Lemuria*. This feast was celebrated over three nights, 9, 11 and 13 May, and seems originally to have been nothing more than a general festival in honor of the dead, like the *Feralia* in February. The only difference was that, with the Feralia, the dead were offered sacrifices on their graves, while with the Lemuria, they were regarded as spirits wandering about at night, seeking their former homes. Thus, the ceremonies necessary to put them to rest were performed in their own homes. Black beans were sprinkled around the house by the pater familias, therefore freeing the inhabitants of the house, as it were, from the evil spirits (an apotropaic act). The day of the feast of the Lemures was a day of evil omen. The temples were closed and the undertaking of important things, especially marriages, was avoided on that day.

Gradually, the belief in the Lemures passed into a belief in ghosts. They were believed to be able to make the living insane, and even tease and torment the dead in the underworld. Their appearance was imagined to be completely emaciated or skeletal, and the goddess Mania was no longer called the mother of the Laren, but changed into the mother or grandmother of the Larvae and Lemures. In Roman and Etruscan mythology, *Mania* (or *Manea*) was a goddess of the dead, chaos and insanity. She, along with *Mantus*, ruled the underworld. She was said to be the mother of ghosts, the undead, and other spirits of the night, as well as the *Lares* and the Manes. Her name links her to the Manes, *Mana Genita*, and *Manius*. Both the Greek and Latin *Mania* derive from (Proto-Indo-European) *men-* (to think). Cognates include Ancient Greek *ménos* (mind, thought) and Avestan *mainyu* (spirit). In shamanistic traditions all over the world, forms of insanity or mental disorder are basically attributed to possession by spirits of the dead or other entities, whereby patients are cured by exorcism. In Goethe's *Faust. Der Tragödie zweiter Teil, Act 5*, the spirits of the dead are summoned by Mephistopheles to bury Faust:

"Herbei, herbei! Herein, herein!
Ihr schlotternden Lemuren,
Aus Bändern, Sehnen und Gebein
Geflickte Halbnaturen."

(Come, come! Come in, come in!
You slithering Lemurs,
Of ligaments, sinews and bones
Patched half-natures)

Lenghelo

The *Lenghelo*, also called *Lenghero*, *Lenghelu* or familiarly *Lengheletto*, is an *Elf* or spirit present in the popular tradition of the Castelli Romani. In many regions of Southern Italy this magical figure is known under the name of *Farfaro*, while it is known by other names in the various regions of Italy. According to legend, the creature has a long slender body, hence the name Lenghelo, meaning "long" or "elongated". A mischievous but not evil spirit, it can be observed in various situations: it walks on the wooden stairs, or it hides in the basement. It disturbs with jokes those that do not respect their relatives, or simply those that do not like him, literally jumping on their bellies during their sleep. In addition, he hides or breaks small objects in the house, but can also find money or give winning numbers in the lottery. According to a popular tradition, the shelter of the Lenghelo would be inside Palazzo Sforza-Cesarini in Genzano di Roma, but the most widespread belief, at least in the past, was that every family had one. The Lenghelo appears in the typical expression in Marinese dialect *"Te ballo sopp'a panza comm'u Lenghelu!"* (I dance on your belly like the Lenghelo). In addition, in the Tombola Marinese the number 63 is associated with the Lenghelu.

Leuce or Leuke

In Greco-Roman mythology, *Leuce*, also spelled *Leuke*, (ancient Greek: Λεύκη, "White", specifically "White Poplar") was a *Nymph* and a daughter of the *Titan Oceanus*. *Hades* fell in love with her and abducted her to the underworld. She lived out the span of her life in his realm, and when she died, the god turned her into a white poplar which he placed in the *Elysian Fields*. To celebrate his return from the underworld, the hero Heracles crowned himself with a branch of this tree. The white poplar was also sacred to *Persephone*, for whom Leuce seems to be a doublet or epithet, as a goddess of regeneration. Robert Graves used the myth of Leuce in developing his poetic theories of mythology. Graves, for instance, holds that the back of the poplar leaf was turned white by the sweat of Herakles. In *The White Goddess*, he names the *white poplar* as one of the "three trees of resurrection", along with *alder* and *cypress*.

Limnades

In Greek mythology, the *Limnades* – or *Lyumnads*, *Lymnads* or *Limnatides* – were the *Naiads* or *Water-Nymphs* of lakes and stagnant waters. They were able to read the souls of men and took the form of a loved one in order to devour them. These characters, feeding on ambrosia, had the power to always remain beautiful and young. Although occupying a lower rank in the divine hierarchy, they were however admitted on Mount Olympus and were venerated by the mortals. Literature left us more detailed data of some of the Limnades:

- The *Astacides* (αἱ Ἀστακίδες) were the *Naiads* of Lake Astakos (Astacus) in Bithynia (northern Anatolia).
- *Bolbe* (Βόλβη), Nymph of a Thessalian lake of the same name, also classed as an *Oceanid* due to her parentage (daughter of *Oceanus* and *Tethys*).
- The *Limneas* were most likely Nymphs of pools and/or swamps. But *Limnaee* (Λιμναία) was also the daughter of the Indian river god Ganges, and one of the reputed mothers of Athis.
- *Pallas* (Παλλάς).
- *Tritonis* (Τριτονίς), Nymph of the homonymous salt-water lake in Libya, mother of *Nasamon* and *Caphaurus* (or *Cephalion*) by *Amphithemis*, and, according to an archaic version of the myth, also of *Athena* by *Poseidon*.

Lamina (2010) by Morburre (licensed under the Creative Commons Attribution-Share Alike 3.0)

Linchetto

The *Linchetto* is a devilish *Imp* or *Alp*-like *Folletto* present in the popular tradition of the province of Lucca, both in Lucchesia, Versilia and Garfagnana. He is often identified as the same creature as the *Buffardello.* In some lore he is described as more evil, in others as merely a nasty prankster. According to the *Vocabolario lucchese* of Idelfonso Nieri, the Linchetto is a spirit that is not bad but mischievous, that goes at night, enters rooms, uncovers (sleeping) people, upsets, transforms objects that are there and laughs at his own pranks. The name derives from the Latin *Incubus*, via *Lincubetto, Lincuetto.* According to the Italianist Felice Del Beccaro, the Linchetto could in fact be a relic of the sylvan god *Faun* who in his aspect of *Incubus* frightened people and tormented them with bad dreams and apparitions. Differently from the Buffardello, in almost all cases, the Linchetto is described as a being that has nothing human about it: it is thought to be an animal, similar to the dog or the cat, or a bird, or to be a hybrid of different species (mouse, bird and man). Although many say it is invisible, it is also described as a black beast wrapped in a cloud of fire.

Tales about the Linchetto were recorded in 1984-1987 by Oscar Guidi in the municipalities of Careggine, Castelnuovo di Garfagnana (but only in the hamlet of Cerretoli), Fabbriche di Vallico, Gallicano, Molazzana (only one person, in Brucciano), San Romano in Garfagnana, Colognora di Pescaglia, Vagli Sotto and Vergemoli. The Linchetto would live in the countryside or on the outskirts of towns and was once seen near a metato (chestnut dryer). Near Fabbriche di Vallico a stream is named after the Folletto: the *Borellin del Linchetto.* Like the Buffardello, the Linchetto bothers people while they are sleeping by throwing the sheets in the air and by climbing on or beating on the chest in such a way as to make breathing difficult. At night he can cause quarrels, especially during a wedding night, when he attacks the groom pinching and spanking him with accompanying sneers. A remedy to avoid disturbances during the wedding night could be to have the Linchetto carry letters to faraway places, but this is a rather sterile attempt, because he completes his mission in a very short time, after which he returns to his usual mischief; a much more effective remedy is instead to order him to straighten a curly pubic hair of the bride, an undertaking that for the Linchetto seems to be difficult; to discourage him further and make him disappear permanently, the bride can also order him to straighten all the hairs before sunrise.

The Linchetto harasses cows, tiring them and making them paw, and he amuses himself in inextricably intertwining the tails of horses and cows; in the case of horses the tail and mane thus twisted must not be untied otherwise the animal loses its good qualities. In the case of cows, it happens that the Linchetto takes one in sympathy and gives it food by taking it away from the others, just as he takes a cow in dislike and takes away her food. He also throws her dung in the air and can make her sick until she dies. Other mischief consists of knocking at the door at night, hiding or stealing objects, slapping the girls, undoing the braids of the girls' hair, kidnapping children, hiding in the vats during the grape harvest. According to the 19th century ethnographer Giovanni Giannini, the Linchetto is however usually affectionate with children, caressing and cradling them, while in contrast it cannot stand old women, which combines all kinds of spite and that had earned him the nickname of *Caccavecchia* or *Carcavecchia*. According to Giannini, to make the Linchetto definitely run away, it is necessary to adopt a method very similar to the one used for the Buffardello: it is enough to eat bread and cheese, do one's own needs and pronounce the following formula in the face of the Linchetto: "*Mangio e caco questo pane e questo cacetto*" (I eat and shit this bread and this little turd).

Lobo hechizado

The *Lobo hechizado*, also known as *Lobo hechoízo* or *Lobo hechicero* refers to a kind of *Werewolf*, typical of the Castilian folklore. It was sometimes depicted as a crouching person with the appearance of a rabid dog that came down from the thicket of the mountains and sierras, walking on all fours, but with notable changes, like the excessive growth of nails, canines and abundant, long hair all over his body. But in other versions, the metamorphoses from man to wolf was less radical than in most classical European Werewolf-versions, resulting in a "*being between human and animal, with big ears*".

Longana

In Italian folklore the *Longana* (or depending on the place, as in Oltrepiave and Auronzo: *Anguana*) is a female aquatic creature, typical of the regions of Cadore and Comelico (especially Lozzo di Cadore). A Longana is depicted as a beautiful and very intelligent woman, looking like a *Satyra* (female *Satyr*) with the legs of a goat, and linked to the *Sylvan spirits*, with extraordinary abilities to predict natural events. According to tradition, these creatures usually live in groups in caves or rocky ravines that take their name from the local toponymy: in Vallesella there is a ravine called "Bùs de le Longane" and in Lozzo a rock called "Sass de le Longane". The Longanas practiced rituals of purification in nocturnal baths and could also intimately connect with humans. In one Domeggese legend, the founder of the locally well-known Da Deppo family, falls in love with a Longana and marries her, on the condition that he never remembers her origins. After prosperous years, the man insults her by calling her *piè di capra* (goat's foot) after which the Longana disappears in the woods, leaving her husband and their children abruptly behind.

Loup-garou

Loup-garou is a term that occurs in the 11th century in Old French under the forms *Leus warous* (wolf-man) in the *Chanson de Mainet* and *Warous* (Norman-Picardian forms). Further, also in the 12th century, the forms *Garwaf*, *Garvalf*, *Garval* occur, derived from Frankish *Wariwulf* or *Werwolf* (wolf-man), a word reconstructed from Middle Dutch *Warwulf* with the same meaning. The Norman dialect also uses the term *varou*, from a probably Old Norman *Warouf* – see, for example, Mount Varouf on Guernsey. Loup-garou became the most commonly used term for *Werewolf* in French and – in addition to its use in France – is also used in French Canada, in Louisiana, and in some of the Francophone Caribbean islands. For a very comprehensive piece on the Werewolf see *Spirit Beings in European Folklore – Compendium 2*. For a variety of Werewolf-species, many of which are fused to the Vampire phenomenon, see *Spirit Beings in European Folklore – Compendium 3* which deals with Slavic folklore.

Lutin

The word *Lutin* (also *Luiton*; female: *Lutine*) is originally used for a dwarfish, nocturnal and humanoid creature, originating from the folklore of some regions in the northwest of France (especially Normandy, Berry and Picardy). The Ardennes and Wallonia have their *Nuton,* and Brittany has its *Korrigans*, while in the Alps, the name *Servan* is used. The word *Lutin* is specific to the Romance languages, and especially to France. Hundreds of small creatures, with different names, can be designated as Lutins, now a generic term for the population of small, dwarfish, *Goblin*-like creatures in France. No solid consensus has been created so far concerning the etymology of Lutin, which is still at drift between a derivative from *Neptune* and the term *lutiner* (linked to his assumed fondness for women). As early as the 11th and 12th centuries, the Lutin appears in tales and chronicles – already endowed with the peculiarities that are still known in our time. For centuries, peasants have passed on rituals aimed at attracting its good graces or, on the contrary, at banishing the creature from their homes. Salt, for example, is considered disgusting to them, and they are believed to look for ways to avoid stepping on it when it is spilled on the ground.

In addition to his small size, the Lutin is known for his mischievousness, his gift of metamorphosis and invisibility, his obsession with women, controlling the weather, shaving the house-owner's beard before he wakes up on Sunday and his habit of taking care of human homes, especially stables. Angry or resentful Lutins may trouble the homeowner constantly with any number of minor annoyances, such as dulling the scythe or filling the shoes with pebbles. The ability to metamorphose and change size is one of the most typical characteristics of Lutins in the folk-stories about them. They can also take on the appearance of animals, or even change into objects. Their animal metamorphoses are varied, including especially the horse and the frog, then the cat and the snake. Traces of household-spirits worshiped in the form of snakes have been present since ancient times in Europe, the animals sharing a common trait with the Lutins, which is the reputation for loving milk. In some stories the Lutin also has the ability to change humans into animals, particularly equidae. In the nineteenth century, a Lutin from Lorraine is said to have transformed a farmer into a donkey. A number of texts, including *Les Évangiles des Quenouilles*, link the *Will-o'-the-wisp* to the Lutin, as the latter also sometimes appears in the form of a small light. The Lutin traveled with the French colonists to the Canadian province of Quebec, where the spirit usually appears in the form of a pet animal, especially as a furry white cat.

M

Mahwotte

According to the folklore of the Ardennes, there lived a strange nocturnal creature at the bottom of the Maas (Meuse River). It moved underwater from one end of the river to the other, from Revin to Liège. Depending on the country, it was called the *Mawhotte* in Belgium and *Mahwot* in France. The Mahwot was as big as a calf and shaped like a lizard and its very rare appearances were a harbinger of misfortune. There are however no records of his appearance since July 1870, and it is unclear whether the Mahwot belongs to the spirit world or to cryptozoology.

Maide

In Basque folklore, *Maide* is an *Irelu* of sleep. It is a nocturnal entity who descends through the chimney into the kitchens to receive the offerings that are placed there before going to bed. Its attributed features however vary according to region; in some places it is a mountain genius. In general *Maideak* (plural) are benevolent Ireluak. In some places they behave as typical *household-spirits*, looking after the farm while the family rests, and getting angry if they don't see the house tidy – a feature of household-spirits, that is typical all over Europe. In Mendive, Maide is called *Saindi Maindi* or *Sainte Maide,* in Zenarruza *Autzek* and in Domintxainen *Etxajaun*. In Soule, this Irelu is credited with the construction of the cromlechs and in Mendive with the construction of the dolmens of the region, thus sharing this feature with the heavyweights of Basque folklore like the *Jentilak*, *Mairuak*, *Basajaunak* etc. We hear however more often that these constructions are the work of the Maides' companions, the *Lamiñak,* and to make it even more complex: in Oiartzun (Guipuscoa) the *Intxixu* are regarded as the builders of the cromlechs, which are said to be their cemeteries. The cromlech is called here *Mairubaratza* i. e. "Mairu's cemetery" (literally Mairu's garden).

Mairi

Mairi (pl. *Mairiak*) is the name given to a male supernatural being, the local *Mairu*, in Lower Navarre. According to popular belief, he is endowed with colossal forces. For some people, he is a humanoid creature who lived in the Basque Country a very long time ago. He is hardly known by that name outside this region. The Mairiak carried, with their bare hands, huge boulders from the Arradoi mountain to the place where castles, dolmens and other structures were built. Large stone slabs, such as those covering *Mairietxe* (Mairi's house), or the dolmen of Gaxteenia in Mendive, Armiaga in Behorlegi (Lower Navarre/Bere-Nafarroa), were transported by a Mairi. The large slab of Mendive, located on the hillock of Gaxteenia, must have been transported here from Mount Armiaga or Urtxuri: these are the nearest places where this type of red rock can be extracted. It is said that a Mairi carried them on his head. The themes of this legend are widespread in a large part of the Basque Country, some even beyond. One of the *Laminak* (locally regarded as the female version of the Mairi and Mairu or *Maide*) who lived in Lezao, in a cave in Entzia, carried on her head the large stones of the Arrizala dolmen, near Agurain (Araba/Alava), while spinning with her spindle and her cattail. In the Mendi countryside it was believed that a Mairi would meet a Laminak once a week *"to have fun"*.

Mairu

The *Mairu* (pl. *Mairuak*), also called *Intxisu(ak)* in the Bidasoa valley or *Maideak*, *Mairiak*, *Saindi Maidi* in Basse-Navarre, are giants, building dolmens in the mythology of the Basque Country. They are often associated with the *Laminak* or *Lamiak*. The Mairu are credited with the construction of certain dolmens and cromlechs, such as those of Ibañeta in Zugarramurdi (Navarre), of Oiartzun (Guipuscoa) and of Buluntza (municipality of Aincille in the Pyrénées-Atlantiques). In Mendive (Basse-Navarre), these constructions are attributed to the female companions of the Mairu, the Laminak. In Oiartzun, they are called *Intxitxu* and it is said that these constructions are the cemeteries of these creatures. Thus, the name of *Mairubaratza* (garden, or cemetery of the Mairu) linked to *Maide*, *Mainde*, *Mayor* and *Mairu* may have a common origin with Intxitxu, a male *Ireluak* corresponding to the Laminak and *Sorginak* (witches). In Oiartzun there is a cave of which the name varies from *Maidazulo* (Hole of Maida) to *Intxitxu*, *Mairi* or *Mairu*. Characters with this name are found in various legends of Lower Navarre, Labourd and eastern Gipuzkoa, with the same characteristics. In other areas of the Basque Country, these giants are associated with other names: *Mairi*,

Maru, *Mooru*, *Moro*, *Jentil*, *Maide*, *Lamina* or *Sorgin* – not the strange fusion here of witch (Sorgin) with giant.

The idea that the Megalithic buildings were not built by the ancestors of the local people, but by "others" may have its origins in a migration of people that took place long ago. In some areas of Atlantic Europe people believed in the arrival of "people from the South" who knew the science of building Megalithic Monuments. The presence of genetic chromosomes in the male DNA (haplogroup E1b1b1), of isolated minorities of the European population (including the Basques) along the European Atlantic coast up to Scotland, and in female DNA up to the Scandinavian countries, seems to confirm the arrival – many centuries if not millennia ago – of Mediterranean navigators of North African origin, where this genetic type is more frequent among the population. The Basque and Gaelic languages contain traces of Berber borrowings, still unexplained, since neither language comes from the same linguistic family.

Mairu-beso

There are legends in which the dried arm, or an arm bone of Mairu appears, with mysterious virtues. Its name is *Mairu-beso* (or Mairu's arm), more specifically a bone from the arm of the unbaptized dead child. In the stories, the protagonist uses this bone as a torch at night and sometimes to lull to sleep the inhabitants of the house where the torch is lit. This rather gruesome legend is known, at least, in the region of San Juan Pie de Puerto (French: Saint-Jean-Pied-de-Port – Lower Navarre). There, Mairu is still today a term to designate *"the one who is not baptized"* and therefore is not Christian: thus they mention Mairu-beso when they mean the arm of an unbaptized child or an adult who has died without being baptized. When unbaptized children died, they were buried in the surroundings of their own house or in the orchard next to it. The stories in which individuals use human bones for lighting at night can also be seen in other places such as Ataun (Guipúzcoa) and Meñaca (Vizcaya).

Name variations

It is possible that the name of the Basque goddess *Mari* owes its origin to the Christian *María*. But another origin cannot be ruled out either; it could be related to *Mairi*, *Maide* and *Maindi*, with which other legendary characters of the mythology of the Basque Country are designated. The term "mairi" is found in the oriental dialects. The *Mairi* (Mairu in unified

Basque) is the builder of dolmens; the *Maide* (and possibly the variant *Mairü* in Zuberoa) is an *Irelu* of the mountains, of the male sex, a builder of the cromlechs, while the corresponding Ireluak of the female sex are the *Lamiñak* or *Lamias,* who are in charge of the fountains, rivers and caves. Possibly related to the Mairu are the *Saindu-maindiak,* the souls of ancestors that at night visit their old homes, according to beliefs of the region of Mendive. The name *Maya* seems to be related to *Suga(a)r,* who is the consort of goddess *Mari.*

The term *Mairu* is still quite widespread, especially in names of localities or locations:

- *Mairumendia* or "Mountains of Mairu" (in Artajona, Navarre, near Manurga (Alava); now *Marinundia,* according to Jimeno Jurio.
- *Mairubide* or "Mairu road" (near Manurga, Alava).
- *Mairuelegorreta* or "Dry lands of Mairu" (Gorbea caves).
- *Mairuburueta* or "Peaks or Extremities of Mairu" (term of Acosta, Álava).
- *Mairubaratz* or "Orchard or Cemetery of Mairu" (Oyarzun's cromlechs).
- *Mairuillarri* or "Grave of Mairu" (cromlechs of Zugarramurdi, Navarra).
- *Mailarreta* or *Mairuilarrieta* or "Pedregal of Mairu", (a place of cromlechs on the mountain Otsondo-Mondarrain, Navarra).
- *Mairuetxe* or "House of Mairu" (standing stones of the Buluntsa mountain, dolmen of Mendive (Basse-Navarre) and in the region of Okabe (Soule)).
- *Mairu-artxan/Mairu archan* or "Blackthorn or Plum tree of Mairu".
- *Mairu-ilhar* and *Mai-ilar* or "Heather or Heath of Mairu", or "Vetch of Mairu".
- *Mairukeri* or "Shelter of Mairu", or "Wild behavior of Mairu".

Maju

Maju is an underground *Irelu* or god who, when leaving his cave, unites with *Mari.* It is during their embrace that a storm starts to develop, which will discharge itself with hailstorms. Maju is usually a pseudonym for the god *Suga(a)r* or *Sugoi.*

Mazapegul (date unknown) Bertarelli Collection in Milan

Malabron

In French folklore, the *Malabron* – mentioned in a medieval song by Gaufrey and Huon de Bordeaux – is a hunchbacked type of *Lutin* that swims faster than a salmon. By putting on a special skin he can assume the shape of a fish at will. He can also transform himself into a horse or ox or make himself invisible with a magical cloak. He has a fearsome appearance, is covered in fur, has red eyes and sharp teeth. The Malabron does not seem to have originated in any Celtic tradition.

Mamur

The *Mamurrak* (plural) are small *Ireluak* of Basque mythology. They are like insects but have the appearance of tiny men, who, according to some, wear red pants. These naughty creatures are known by other local names: *Galtzagorriak*, *Famerijaleak* in the forests in Kortezubi, *Beharreztanak* in Orozco, *Aidetikakoak* in Saran, *Patuak* or *Patuek* in Ibarruri, *Zaingorriak* in Ordizia, *Ximelgorriak* in Abadiño, etc. Outside the Basque Country, we can also find similar creatures in the Pyrenees. In Catalonia, for example, they are called *Minairons* and *Diablorins*. According to legend they can be captured the night before Saint John's Day (June 24, preceded by Saint John's Eve or Saint John's Night on June 23) by placing an open pin box on a bush. A legend of Zarautz (Guipuscoa) claims that in the past Mamurrak were sold in a shop in Bayonne (Labourd) for an ounce of gold.

The Mamurrak function in the same way as the Catalan *Minairons*; when they are released from a vase or box, they come out and start circling around their owners' heads asking them over and over again, "*What do you want us to do?*". They then very quickly carry out the requested work, however improbable it may be. Some people who perform wonders or extraordinary works, such as diviners, wizards or certain healers, are believed to own Mamurrak. There are a lot of Basque folktales about these creatures, almost all of them are about the miraculous advantages they bring to their owners, related to work, transportation or bets. It was believed the goddess Mari created the Mamurrak to help men to perform their duties.

Manes

Manes, from the Latin *d(i)i manes* (m.), in Roman religion (especially in imperial times) are the spirits of the dead, including some environmental spirits. These are usually hostile to the Romans, being the ancestors of their enemies. Therefore, they were made lenient with various sacrifices (including goats) and rites, as well as being called *Divi Manes* or *Dii Manes*, 'good gods' (usually abbreviated as D-M on tomb inscriptions). If these sacrifices and rites were not performed, the Di Manes could become *Larvae* or *Lemures*, respectively, which had a threatening character. In some instances, the Di Manes were also equated with the *Di Parentes* (the deceased ancestors), who ascended from the underworld on their holy days and awaited appropriate atonement sacrifices. For this purpose, people went to the *lapis manalis*, a stone that covered a pit in which a sacrificial animal was deposited and the Di Manes were appeased.

Manona

In Asturian folklore *Manona* or *la Mano Negra* (the Black Hand) and *el Pesadiellu* are usually identified with the same character. It is an invisible and evil being, whose manifestation consists of an immense weight, suffocation or oppression that this "something" exerts on some people, just like the *Alps* or other variables of the *Nightmare*-type. Whoever suffers from it, feels an extreme pressure in the body, and must resort to prayers to get rid of it. Sometimes Manona takes the form of a flying, hairy hand. Though often regarded as the same entity as the Manona, the Pesadiellu usually manifests itself outdoors instead of indoors, and can also take the form of a very shaggy black dog. This type of Pesadiellu in the form of a dog is reminiscent of the *Grim* and the *Black Dog* of Anglo-Saxon folklore.

Marabbecca

The *Marabbecca* is a legendary creature in Sicilian and Maltese folklore. In Malta it is known as *Il-Belliegha*. This creature (whose name is likely Arabic) lives in wells and water reservoirs, and was probably invented by Sicilian parents to prevent their children from playing near dangerous wells. The Marabbecca's are said to have long limbs, which they can stretch unnaturally far, to pull a victim into their well, and they are also believed to turn any water they touch into a foul smelling poisonous substance.

People will fall ill or die if they drink from this water. They sometimes change location by swimming through sewers, rivers or channels.

Mari

Mari, also: *Anbotoko Mari, Anbotoko Dama, Lezekoandrea, Loana-gorri, Maddi* or *Murumendiko Dama* is a mother goddess in Basque mythology. She is a female deity and witch-goddess, who represents many nature forces, and a *daemon* with many forms in with she can manifest herself, including several male creatures like a red bull *(Zezen gorri)* or black billy goat *(Akerbeltz)*. In Aragonese mythology she is known under the name of *Mariuena*. A general feature of the ancient Basque religion is that – in strong contrast to the Indo-European and especially the Abrahamitic religions, with their *transcendental* and *patriarchal* interpretation of God or the divine – the Basque religion *perceives* the divine primarily as something *immanent* in nature and daily life. The distinction between heaven and earth is mostly resolved into nature as a divine totality. This implies that there is also no hard division between gods and "lower" beings such as the many kinds of *Ireluak*, since many of these can exist both independently as nature-demons, and as a temporary manifestation or even materialization of, usually, the goddess Mari. In all European pre-Christian religions we find the experience and interpretations of – and connection to – the divine, similarly constructed in beliefs that root in immanence instead of transcendence. To emphasize her immanence, Mari even lives underground, usually in a cave in the high mountains (compare to *Demeter*), where she and her husband *Sugaar* or *Maju* meet every Friday to design storms that will bring fertility (and sometimes damage) to the land and the people. It is said that Mari is served by a *Sorginak*-court called Akelarre (meadow of the billy goat). These nightly gatherings of witches' took place on Fridays. With Sugaar Mari has two sons: the perverse and evil *Mikelatz* (or *Mikelats)* and the kind and civilized *Atarrabi* (or *Atagorri)*.

Mari is the lady of the Earth and meteors. She has mastery over the weather forces and the interior of the Earth. Her missions include punishing lies, theft and pride. From her come the goods of the earth and the water of the springs. With men she behaves in a tyrannical way, or quite the contrary, she falls in love with one of them, showing herself as a docile and hardworking woman, but always with the aim of imparting justice by means of the rule that she absolutely does not tolerate any kind of lie. If you lie, Mari takes away everything she gave you. She also foretells storms and determines the weather. In some legends Mari "drinks men's lives" and makes them unhappy, thus acting in the way of a *Mare* or *Succubus*, although these stories of a vampiric Mari are possibly the result of an erroneous replacement of Mari by *Mare*, within a Christian campaign to demonize the gods of the Basques.

There is a lot of confusion about the origin of the word Mari. For some, it is just the transposition of the baptismal name of Jesus' mother, Mary, but others prefer to believe that it is a modification of *emari* (gift) or *amari* (to the mother). It is difficult to believe that such an important deity, the only god really known to the Basques before Christianity (with her husband *Sugaar*), has a name derived from a Christian icon. The Basques were not converted to Christianity until the 16th century and worshiped natural forces such as the sun, moon, and the spirits of air, water, mountains, forests, etc., which often took on human forms. Some current beliefs may date back to Paleolithic times. Mari is the most significant mythical figure in Basque traditions, being the Lady of all telluric *Ireluak*. This goddess is therefore neutral, balancing the powers of Mother Earth or *Amalur*. Most of the mythical beings in the Basque Country are of the "chthonic" or "telluric" type because they refer to the earth, the subterranean world or the hells.

Core-appearance

Mari, personification of Mother Earth, is the queen of nature and of all the elements that compose it. She is generally presented with the body and face of a woman, elegantly dressed, generally in green (compare the Jewish archangel *Haniel*, whose color is also green and represents the wild pure beauty and forces of nature). She may also appear in the hybrid form of a tree and a woman with the legs of a goat and the claws of a bird of prey, or as a woman of fire, a flaming rainbow or a horse dragging clouds. In the appearance of a woman, she appears with abundant blonde hair that she cares for, in the sun, with a golden comb.

Anboto's abode

Of the many dwellings that Mari has, the main one is in the Anboto, a (1,331 m or 4,367 ft) limestone mountain of the Western Basque Country, the highest peak of the Urkiola range and not far from the Urkiola mountain pass between Durango and Vitoria-Gasteiz. The so-called *Mariurrika kobea* or *Mariren kobia* is located, just below the summit of this mountain. Its entrance is located in the impressive verticality of the east wall, that forms with the west of the Azkilar the impressive channel of Artaungo Sakona. The cave has a large high entrance, which opens to a corridor into a room illuminated by an opening to the abyss. This "window" is visible from below, while the entrance is hidden, because it is located in a chamber of the rock. At its side falls a squirt of water, (drops in summer) which must be drunk if one wants the request made to the goddess to become a reality. From the illuminated room there is another corridor towards the interior of the mountain. Above it there is a natural formation reminiscent of the face of a woman in whom some see the face of Mari. This corridor ends in a 75 yards / 70 meters deep chasm. On the right, passing through a small opening, you reach another minor chasm. To reach Mariurrika Kobea, you have to climb up to the Aguindi-pass, which is made up of the cover of the Anboto and the spur of Fraile Atxa, and from there follow the small path to the east that leads, under the summit, to the vertical wall in which the cavity is located. When you reach the edge of it, a natural tunnel allows you to access the cliff.

Marraco

The *Marraco* (Catalan: *Lo Marraco*) is a dragon or fearsome creature in the folklore of the city of Lleida. It possessed a mouth wide enough to swallow a human being whole. The Marraco had the function of *Bogey* and stories about the creature were supposed to frighten children and prevent mischief or disobedient behavior. It has been claimed that the term Marraco is derived from a Basque word for "dragon," but linguistically no consensus has been reached on this.

Maru

In Basque folklore *Maru* are legendary mountain creatures. In Ataun, this name refers to some *Ireluak* living in the caves of the mountain called Maumendi (Maru Mountain). They were feared by the locals because they sometimes confined local people who took the risk to look for their herds on this mountain, or entered their territory for any other reason. The Maru were believed to steal cattle. There are two caves in Ataun called Mauzulo (Maru's hole).

Mateo Txistu

In the folklore of the Basque Country, *Mateo Txistu* is a tragic ghostly hunter, surrounded by his barking dogs. In the area of Tolosa, although others say that it happened in Ataun and others in Oiartzun, there lived a priest who was in charge of a small parish a long time ago. His occupations were not many, apart from the normal ones of his position – masses, baptisms and funerals – so he had enough free time to devote to his favorite hobby: hunting. One day the Devil decided to test the priest and paid him a visit in the guise of a distinguished gentleman. Mateo Txistu however immediately recognized the true character of his visitor and abruptly asked him:

"What do you want, wicked man?
"Me? Nothing!", answered the Devil, confused.
"Then... why are you here?"

And laughing, Mateo Txistu whistled to his dogs, picked up his shotgun and disappeared from the Devil's sight into a nearby forest. The Devil was furious that he had made a fool of himself, since a village priest had recognized him. So he made a plan to take revenge. On a Sunday, in the middle of mass, a beautiful white hare peeked its nose through the door of the sacristy where the priest's dogs were waiting for its owner. As soon as they saw the hare, the dogs perked up their ears and began barking furiously. Mateo interrupted the mass for a moment and glanced into the sacristy to see what the fuss was about. He did not think twice, when he spotted the white hare. He left the mass, left the astonished parishioners, took his shotgun and went out with the dogs in pursuit of the hare that had escaped across the field. Mateo Txistu never returned. However, since that day, many have heard him whistling to his dogs, others have heard the sad barking, and when the moon is full, the silhouettes of the priest, his dogs and the hare in their eternal wandering can then be seen with clarity moving across the nocturnal sky.

Apart from Mateo Txistu, under which name he is especially known in Ataun, he is called *Juanito Txistularia* (little Jean who plays the flute) in Zerain, *Martin Abade* (Martin the Abbot) in Gelazibar, *Errege Xalomon* (King Solomon) in Saint-Esteben, *Salomon Apaiza* (Solomon priest) in Oiartzun and *Prixki Juan* in Usurbil.

Mazapégul

The *Mazapégul* is an *Imp* of Italian mythology, belonging to the folkloric tradition of Romagna, in particular of the Forlì Apennines. The creatures form a small family of nocturnal *Goblins*, related to the *Incubi*, and composed of several tribes, such as *Mazapedar*, *Mazapégul*, *Mazapigur*, and *Calcarel*. In the *Romagnolo-Italian dictionary* of Mattioli the Mazapégul is defined as a *"Spirit that was superstitiously believed to turn into a man to lie with women"*. Luciano De Nardis gives a more detailed description:

> *"He would be between the cat and the monkey. Small, of gray hair ... he wears a red cap on his head. For the rest he has no clothes whatsoever... The amorous passion is its exclusive manifestation* (La Piè, 1924 n°2) *...Mazapégul impersonates sensuality, erotic passion. And he is its most remote symbol. ... He comes from the eras of the bestial conjugations."* (La Piè, 1927 n°3)

The appearance of the Mazapégul is often depicted as part rabbit, cat and monkey. The spirit enters rooms at night as light as the wind, turns from one piece of furniture to another and ends up in bed, where he lays on the belly of a beautiful woman because he falls in love with her eyes and hair and sighs: *"Ad bëll òcc! Ad bëll cavéll!"* (What beautiful eyes! What beautiful hair!). If she responds affectionately submissive to him, he makes her stockings, tidies her rooms, and does other helpful work, but if she mocks him, or worse, has preferred her boyfriend or husband to him, he shakes her, beats her, bites her, scratches her, squeezes her flesh, dishevels her hair or tangles her work, hides the most disparate objects, cuts up her clothes, etc. When he enters the house, he leaves his cap on the edge of the water well in the courtyard. In order to be saved from his passionate insistence it is enough that someone hurries to the well and throws the red woolen cap into the water. Women who are harassed by the creature can also get rid of the inconvenience by eating a piece of bread at night while pretending to pee on themselves. The Mazapégul is so offended that he doesn't show up anymore, but not so much because of the outrage he has suffered, but because he considers his protégé a very unclean person. Similarly, she can visit the toilet and eat bread and cheese, while defecating at the same time. The following night the Mazapégul appears to the young woman irritated and scandalized and says to her: "*Bruta troja, vaca, t'megn et pess et fe la caca!*" (Ugly bitch, cow, eat and piss and make the poop!). And having said that, he flies away never to be seen again.

Mazaròl

The *Mazaròl* is a character typical of the folklore of the Dolomites. Generally, he has the features of an old man of sturdy build, dressed in red, with a large hat and a black cape. His character is usually benevolent, but gruff and wild, being also touchy and vindictive towards those who betray his trust (he hid disobedient children under his cloak). Whoever put his/her foot on a footprint left by him, was forced by the power of a spell to follow his footprints until one reached his cave; there this person was forced to drink the milk of a black goat that made him or her immediately forget everything about the Mazaròl.

Mazzamurello

The *Mazzamurello* (or *Mazzamauriello*, *Mazzamëriéllë* in Ascolano, *Mazzamuriéllë* in Neapolitan, *Mazzamureddu* in Sicilian) is a dwarfish mountain spirit of the folkloric tradition of most of the central-southern regions of Italy. He is sometimes considered the Italian version of the Welsh *Robin Goodfellow*, or *Pwca*. The main characteristic of the Mazzamurello is the production of noises inside houses to manifest its presence to the inhabitants. In fact, the etymology of the name is popularly derived from the terms *mazza* (blow) and *murello* (wall), to indicate its habit of beating against the walls of a house to manifest itself. However this may be an inaccuracy as another etymology derives the name from *ammazza Mori*, where *amazza* (kill) combined with *Mori* (Saracens) gives "kill the Saracens". In any case, according to the popular tradition, the presence of a Mazzamurello in the house indicates either the proximity of a treasure, an imminent danger for one of the inhabitants or (more often) a message from a dear deceased trying to communicate with the living. Especially in the territory of the Sibillini mountains, the Mazzamurelli are traditionally considered as messengers between the ordinary world and the enchanted world, that is between the earthly world and the world of the afterlife.

Meiga

Meiga is the name given in Galicia – and in neighboring areas of León and Asturias – to the witch or sorceress whose task is to *megar* or to *enmeigar* (to do good). She is capable of undoing the evil spells and the evil eye of the Bruxas. According to anthropologist Carmelo Lisón

Tolosana, the Meiga should not be confused with the Bruxa, whose mission is to do evil to people and animals, for which she establishes a pact with the Devil. However this depiction of the Bruxa is highly controversial. Unlike other types of witches or witchy creatures in European lore the Meira and Bruxa are human.

Melinoë

Melinoë (ancient Greek: Μηλινόη) is a chthonic *Nymph* or goddess invoked in one of the *Orphic Hymns* and represented as a bringer of nightmares and madness. The name also appears on a metal tablet in association with Persephone. The hymns are of uncertain date but were probably composed in the 2nd or 3rd century AD. In the hymn, Melinoë has characteristics that seem similar to *Hecate* and the *Erinyes*, and the name is sometimes thought to be an epithet of Hecate. The terms in which Melinoë is described are typical of moon goddesses in Greek poetry. Melinoë may derive from the Greek *mēlinos* (μήλινος), "having the color of quince", from *mēlon* (μῆλον), "tree fruit". The fruit's yellowish-green color symbolized the pallor of illness or death for the Greeks. Following is the translation by Apostolos Athanassakis and Benjamin M. Wolkow, of the *Hymn to Melinoë*:

> *"I call upon Melinoe, saffron-cloaked nymph of the earth,*
> *whom revered Persephone bore by the mouth of the Kokytos river*
> *upon the sacred bed of Kronian Zeus.*
> *In the guise of Plouton Zeus and tricked Persephone and through wiley plots bedded her;*
> *a two-bodied specter sprang forth from Persephone's fury.*
> *This specter drives mortals to madness with her airy apparitions*
> *as she appears in weird shapes and strange forms,*
> *now plain to the eye, now shadowy, now shining in the darkness—*
> *all this in unnerving attacks in the gloom of night.*
> *O goddess, O queen of those below, I beseech you*
> *to banish the soul's frenzy to the ends of the earth,*
> *show to the initiates a kindly and holy face."*

Melinoë is the daughter of *Persephone* and was fathered by *Hades* or *Zeus*. Hades (the central fire) and Zeus the (luminescent air) were, at times, syncretized with each other. The Orphics in particular believed that Zeus and Hades were the same deity and portrayed them as such. The translation of the Orphic *Hymn to Melinoë* by Thomas Taylor (1887) has given rise to a conception of Melinoë as half-black, half-white, representing the duality of the heavenly Zeus and the infernal Hades. The *Hymn* also references this by mentioning that Persephone was impregnated upon the bed of *Zeus Kronion* in the underworld by the underworld river *Cocytus,* Zeus taking on the form of *Plouton* before impregnating Persephone. Melinoë is then born at the mouth of the Cocytus, one of the rivers of the underworld, where *Hermes* in his underworld aspect as psychopomp was stationed. In the Orphic tradition, the Cocytus is one of four underworld rivers. Melinoë is at least partially syncretized with Persephone herself and also with Hecate. Melinoë is described in the invocation of the Orphic Hymn as κροκόπεπλος *(krokopeplos)*, "clad in saffron", an epithet in ancient Greek poetry for moon goddesses. In the hymns, only two goddesses are described as krokopeplos; Melinoë and Hecate. Melinoë's connections to Hecate and Hermes suggest that she exercised her power in the realm of the soul's passage, and in that function may be compared to the torchbearer *Eubouleos* in the mysteries. According to the hymn, she brings night terrors to mortals by manifesting in strange forms.

Melinoë on a magical bronze triangle

Melinoë appears on a bronze tablet (3rd century AD) for use in a kind of private magical ritual. The use of bronze was probably intended to drive away evil spirits and to protect the practitioner. The construction of the tablet suggests that it was used for divination. It is triangular in shape, with a hole in the center, presumably for suspending it over a surface. The content of the triangular tablet reiterates triplicity. It depicts three crowned goddesses, each with her head pointing at an angle and her feet pointing toward the center. The name of the goddess appears above their heads: *Dione* (ΔΙΟΝΗ), *Phoebe* (ΦΟΙΒΙΗ), and the obscure *Nyche* (ΝΥΧΙΗ). "Amibousa", a word referring to the phases of the moon, is written under each goddess's feet. Densely inscribed spells frame each goddess: the inscriptions around Dione and Nyche are *voces magicae*, incantatory syllables (magic words) that are mostly untranslatable. Melinoë appears in a triple invocation that is part of the inscription around Phoebe: *O Persephone, O Melinoë, O Leucophryne*. Esoteric symbols are inscribed on the edges of the triangle.

Mélusine

Mélusine (also *Merlusigne, Melusina; Merlusse* in Vosges; *Merluisaine* in Champagne) is a figure of European folklore, a female spirit of fresh water in a holy well or river. She is usually depicted as a woman who is a serpent or fish from the waist down (much like a *Mermaid* or a *Lamia*). She is also sometimes illustrated with wings, two tails, or both. Her legends are especially connected with the northern and western areas of France, Luxembourg, and the Low Countries. The French littré suggests the Latin *melus*, meaning "melodious, pleasant". The core of the legend is that Melusine marries a knight under the condition of a special viewing taboo, according to which he should not see her in her true form: that of a *water-spirit*, usually with a snake's body. Melusine becomes the source of his prestige and wealth until the knight breaks the taboo.

The oldest traditions of the Mélusine-legends date back to the 12th century. Possible origins can already be found in pre-Christian sagas of the Hellenic, Celtic as well as Near Eastern cultures. As a historical-genealogical story the Mélusine-legend goes back to the Lusignan family from the French region of Poitou. In the course of time the texts have changed. Early on, Melusine appeared as a demoness, but in the courtly novels of the Middle Ages she became more and more Christianized as the ancestress of certain families. Since modern times, the elements of the family story have disappeared, and more emphasis was placed on the tragic love affair. Until the 20th century, Melusine was one of the most popular stories in European cultures. Adaptations exist in many European languages. However, since the 20th century it has lost its presence.

Mikelats

Mikelats is an evil *Irelu* of Basque folklore, and one of *Mari's* two sons. With his mother, Mikelats shapes storms and hail showers that destroy crops and frighten herds. In a legend distorted by Christian politics he and his brother *Atarrabi* (also called *Axular*), who is his opposite and a symbol of moral good, studied at the *Devil's school*. At the end of their education, the *Devil*, as a payment, kept Mikelats in his service. Mikelats wanted to destroy the wheat fields of Sare of which his brother had become the priest. To counter his plan of destruction, Atarrabi opposed him with prayer and saved his people's crops.

Minairons

The *Minairons* (sing.: *Minairó*) are very small and hard-working creatures, typical of the folklore of the Pyrenean area of northwest Catalonia, and especially of Pallars. Of certain houses that had become very rich, it was believed that they had a canutillo (small basket) with Minairons, and in one of these baskets there could be hundreds of them. When the canutillo was opened, the Minairons would come out and say: "*¿qué haremos, qué diremos?*" (what shall we do, what shall we say?) – and if the person who had opened the basket did not order them to do some work immediately, they would kill him; but if he ordered them to do something (whatever it was) they would very quickly complete their task. According to folk belief the stones in many of the mountain quarries had been formed by the Minairons obeying the order of their owner when the latter, by forgetfulness or accident, had opened the quarry in the middle of the mountain. The desperate master, faced with the threat of having these tiny beings surrounding him saying: "*¿qué haremos, qué diremos?*" ordered them to simply gather all the stones from the surrounding area at a specific point. It was not until the job was finished, done at great speed, that he could order them to go back inside the canutillo. The Minairons were in this strange symbiosis dependent on their owner, because if too much time passed without orders from their master, they would fall ill and die.

Mirokutana

Mirokutana is a nocturnal *Irelu* of Basque folklore, that looks like a dog or wolf, according to the legends in Oiartzun (Gipuzkoa). He is also described as a lycanthrope or *Werewolf* and an anthropomorphic god that lives in Peñas de Aya since ancient times.

Monuca

The *Monuca* is a legendary animal from Cantabrian folklore. It is born every eleven years in the spring, from the crossbreeding of a wild cat and a rámila (stone marten), to which it bears a great resemblance. Blind and colorless at birth, it is born in a cave. It then wanders through the bush until it regains its sight, after which it returns to its den to kill its mother, sucking her blood and gouging out her eyes. From then on it takes refuge near rivers, until it acquires its peculiar coloring; its head is white like sheep's wool, while its body is red, blue and black, with a purple tail. It feeds in the

Melusine (1870) illustration by Emile Bayard (1837-1891) for Paul Christian's *Histoire de la Magie*

meadows on grasshoppers and turtledoves that it hunts, as well as on the blood it sucks from lambs and children. When it reaches the age of five, its size prevents it from running or climbing trees, so it ends up being hunted by the wildcat. The Monuca usually ends its days by falling off a cliff or being hunted by a wild animal. Monucas love men, so a man who catches one and takes it home is lucky for life. They loathe women, however, and scratch their faces trying to gouge out their eyes, as they did their mother's.

Mora

La Mora is described by Greek philologist Nikolaos G. Politis as a hybrid between a rich and very powerful *Lamia* and a *Pesadilla* (Spanish for *Nightmare*). The creature walks alone at night and when she encounters sleeping men on her way she sits on their chest and crushes them. And she is so heavy that he whom she crushes groans like an ox. But if the man is not asleep and sees her and takes away her hat (fez), she will give him whatever he asks her, provided he returns the hat. La Mora comes from *Mare*, *Mahr*, *Moor*, etc. synonyms for Nightmare, *Alp*).

Morgens or Marie-Morganes

Morgens, *Morgans*, *Mari-Morgans* or to use the Breton term *Marie Morgane*, are – eternally young – Welsh and Breton *water-sprites* that lure and drown men. The name may derive from *Mori-genos* or *Mori-gena*, meaning "sea-born". The name has also been rendered as *Muri-gena* or *Murigen* and may also be cognate with the Irish *Muirgen*, the alternate name of *Lí Ban*, a princess who was transformed into a *Mermaid* when her city was flooded. The Cornish term for a Mermaid is usually *Morvoren*. In Breton, *mor* means "sea" and *ganet* means "born". According to François-Marie Luzel in *Notes de Voyage* (1873), the *Morgan* are called *Morganed* in the plural, and their wives are the *Morganezed* (*Morganez* in the singular, and *Morgane* in French)

Welsh and English legend

The oldest occurrence of the name is in Geoffrey of Monmouth's *Vita Merlini* (The Life of Merlin), where the ruler of Avalon is referred to as *Morgen*. As such, the origin of *Morgan le Fay* may be connected to these Breton myths. English folklorist Ruth Tongue collected several tales with the term "sea-morgan", as in *The Sea Morgan and the Conger Eels* and *The*

Sea-Morgan's Baby, attributed to western Somerset, in which a fisherman adopts an infant Morgan, who grows up to return to the ocean. *Sea-morgan* is a direct translation of the Breton *Mari-morgan.* A parallel tale comes from Brittany, where the child is called a Mary Morgan.

Breton legend

In Brittany, the formation Marie-Morgan or Mary-Morgan is common. The French folklorist, painter, and writer Paul Sébillot (1843-1918) compared the Mari Morgan to *Sirènes* (the French term for Mermaids), who lured sailors with their hypnotic voices and sat in the water to comb their hair seductively. They were believed to live near coasts, at cave entrances and at the mouths of rivers, with some held to still inhabit a cave near Crozon. The Marie-Morgans, who were well-versed in evil spells, would drag young men underwater and the men would never be seen again. In some versions, however, Marie-Morgans carried kidnapped sailors to underwater palaces of mother-of-pearl and crystal, and married them. The Morgens were also blamed for heavy flooding that destroyed crops or villages.

The Morganès of L'île d'Ouessant

The oral tradition of L'île d'Ouessant has preserved a story of a *Morganès* who was frequently seen along the shores. It was written down by François-Marie Luzel in 1873. This story is interesting because in the occult tradition it is widely believed that nature-spirits often help good people and approach them in a friendly way, while they can be dangerous to those who violate their ethics or natural habitat.

Two young girls from the island of L'île d'Ouessant, were looking for shells one day at the seaside, and saw a Morganès who was drying her treasures in the sun, spread out on two beautiful white tablecloths. The two curious little girls came up to her without being seen and the Morganès, surprised to see that the young girls were kind, gentle and wise, gave them each a treasure and told them not to look at it until they returned to their parents. One of the girls was too eager to not look at what she thought were wonderful treasures, so she opened her tablecloth and found only horse manure. The other little girl went home and opened her treasure in front of her parents' eyes: precious stones, pearls and gold, with rich fabrics. The family became rich and built a beautiful house. According to the legend, their descendants still live on the L'île d'Ouessant and are rich, thanks to the treasure of the Morganès.

Mormo

Mormo (Greek: Μορμώ, Μορμών, Mormō) or *Mormon* was a female spirit in Greek folklore, used by mothers and nurses in Greece as a *Bogey* to frighten children in order to keep them from misbehaving. The term *Mormolyce* (μορμολύκη; pl. *Mormolykeia* μορμολύκεια), also spelt *Mormolyceum* (μορμολυκεῖον *Mormolukeîon*), is considered equivalent. The plural form *Mormones* means "fearful ones" or "hideous one(s)", and is related to an array of words that signify "fright". The variant Mormolyce translates to "terrible wolves", with the stem -lykeios meaning "of a wolf". According to one source (*Scholios to Aristides*, Dindorf, p. 41), the original Mormo was a woman of Corinth, who ate her children and then flew away.

Mormo or Moromolyce has been described as a female specter, phantom, or ghost by modern commentators (William Smith, Steven M. Stannish, Christine M. Doran). Mormolyce was one of several names given to the female phasma (phantom) in Philostratus' *Life of Apollonius of Tyana*. According to one scholar (*Scholios to Theocritus Idylls* 15.40) *Mormo* and *Gello* were aliases for *Lamia*, who he describes as the queen of the *Laestrygonians*, a race of man-eating giants. A Mormo or a Lamia may also be associated with the *Empusa*, a phantom sent by the goddess Hekate.

Moro Mussa

In Valencian and Catalan folklore, *El Moro Mussa* is a terrifying, snake-wrapped, phantom that carries a black cat, and especially serves as a *Bogey*. In Alicante, he is known as *El Moro* or *El Morusso*. In villages in La Ribera, such as Albalat de la Ribera, he is known as *El Moro Mus*. According to legend, El Moro Mussa was once a prince of Balansiya who lost his dominions after the conquest of James I of Aragon. In revenge, he hunted down children. In Valldigna, people protected themselves from El Moro Mussa through magic. In the folk belief of Catalonia El Moro Mussa once was a prince from the region of Montserrat who, when he fled, left a treasure behind in the cave of Salnitre. His daughter, according to legend, still watches over that cave.

Mourioche

In Breton folklore the *Mourioche* can be a stealing, malicious shape-shifting demon, horned and hunchbacked, and sometimes dressed as a jester. It usually transforms itself in some animal shape it chooses, and exhibits behavioral features of the ghostly British-Celtic *Water-horses*. In default appearance he is like a year-old foal. Other shapes are those of a pig, cow, or sheep, often with a pair of muscular arms. It has the power of invisibility, which is very useful for playing tricks. It usually lives in the woods, but moves closer to the warmth of houses in the winter-season. Nobody knows exactly where Mourioche came from. Some say that it once was a Breton man or a woman, versed in the dark arts, who sold his or her soul for a magical ointment. Other accounts simply describe the *Mourioche* as a *Werewolf* without control of its actions. It is possible that Mourioche has always haunted Brittany along the coastlines of Côtes-d'Armor and around Jugon-les-Lacs. At night, it preys on nocturnal travelers. Sometimes he is a horse standing by the side of the road, waiting for riders. Its spine stretches as more and more people get on, then he gallops right into the lake, his laugh echoing in the darkness. At other times it wrestles with passers-by, throwing its victims into muddy ditches. Like the Flemish *Kludde* or German *Aufhocker*, it will jump onto men's back and force them to carry its body, which gets heavier and heavier, until they drop of exhaustion. It will follow people along the road, changing shape every time they turn to look at him, and making a sound like tearing canvas. There is also a legend in which Mourioche appears as a monster, a kind of *Bogey-Werewolf* hybrid, who, in the eleventh century, lived in the pond of the Castle of Beauchêne, in Langrolay, and fed on children that had the misfortune to be outside after dark. Noisy or mischievous children were silenced with the words: *"Be good, now, the Mourioche is coming!"* It was killed in an epic battle by Jehan, the young Lord of Beauchêne. This legend is reported by Jules Haize, who specifies that *La Mourioche* is also used to denote the *White Lady* who appears on the Ebihens tower, opposite Saint-Jacut.

Fausserole

The *Fausserole* of Saint-Cast is very similar, and may be another – and feminine – form of Mourioche. She likes to appear as a white beast, a dog or a calf, and has no qualms about tossing clergy around, as the rector of Saint-Cast found out.

Mouros

The *Mouros* or *Moros* (female: *Mouras*) are characters from the Galician, Asturian, Leonese and Portuguese folklore. The Latin term *maurus* (derived from the Galician *mouro*) according to philologist Isodoro Millán comes from the Celtic *mrvos* related to the Indo-European term *mr-tuos*, which leads us to the Latin *mortuus*. Hence the idea that the Mouros were a died out race of the past. For others, their name is related to the Galician *ouro* because of their relation to the shiny metal gold (the Old Galician and Old Portuguese *ouro*, comes from the Latin *aurum*, from Proto-Italic *auzom*, from Proto-Indo-European *hé-hus-o-* "glow"). According to the Spanish Galicians, the Mouros were creatures that lived underground in lairs and tunnels under the earth, where – depending on the area – they were dedicated to the extraction of gold. Their realm was called *Mourama,* a magical place where the Mouros and Mouras live under the earth in Portugal and Galicia. Mourama is the otherworld, the world of the dead to which everything returns. It may be compared to the Fairyland. The Mouros worked in gold smithing and in some cases were dark-skinned, as if they were people alien to the Galician land, while they had a reputation as sorcerers. On the other hand they were sometimes depicted as redheads with white complexions. They are the same as humans except that they live underground, are wealthy, have magical powers or live under some kind of enchantment. They usually appear to people alone, proposing them tests of courage, or they conduct businesses or exchanges with humans, that were paid for in gold, except if they would tell others the origin of their wealth, in which case the gold was instantly converted into worthless stones or charcoal. Just like many *mountain spirits* the Mouros were regarded as guardians of fabulous treasures, which constituted the origin of the wealth of several families. Like the *Mairu* of Basque mythology were believed to have built the *dolmens* or *harrespil* – the origin of the *castros*, the *mámoas* (tumuli or burial mounds) and other structures of ancient origin were attributed to the Mouros. It was also said that the race had lived in the past in Galicia and fought constantly against different peoples such as Romans, Visigoths, French, etc., until most of them were expelled.

In Galicia it was believed the Mouros lived in a very similar way to the Galician peasant people, since these people knew no other way of life. They buried their dead and honored them, they listened to masses of their cult and had their own Mouros priests. In addition, they liked to eat meat, drink wine and dance at night, besides being very given – especially the female Mouras – to try to seduce the peasants. They also used to make deals with the villagers by which these had to periodically deliver something to the Mouros (usually milk, wine or some goods that the Mouros did not have) and a good price was paid for these goods, again on condition of total discretion regarding the pact. The word *mouros* appears in several Galician place names, usually indicating the presence of castros, burial mounds, Roman mines or any kind of ancient ruins.

In Asturian mythology

In Asturia Mouros or Moros are more often seen as a race of magical beings that lived in Asturia since the beginning of time, where for unknown reasons they were forced to live underground, exercising the trade of mining, metallurgy or goldsmithing. They are also seen as the builders of dolmens and castros, and due to their way of life they have obtained great treasures that are protected by bewitchments or spells. They rarely go outside except to collect food, and only come out at dusk or at night, or on special days such as the night of San Juan (June 23). They do not usually mix with humans, except in rare chance encounters.

Moura encantada – the female Mouros

According to José Leite de Vasconcelos, the *Moura encantada* (enchanted female Mouro) are *"beings compelled by an occult power to live on a certain state of siege as if they were numb or asleep, insofar as a particular circumstance does not break their spell"*. The state of occult enchantment of the Moura is generally caused by a male figure, her father, or some other enchanted Mouro, that left her to guard his treasures. It are usually the Mouros that have the power to enchant the Mouras. In legends, the Mouras may appear alone, accompanied by other Mouras, or by a male being, a Mouro, that may be her father, a beloved person or a brother. To break the spell of the Moura she may ask a human for a kiss, a cake or bread with no salt, milk, the pronunciation of a certain word, or realization of some chore like not looking at something hidden. To fail means not to free the Moura and causes to *dobrar o encanto* (double the spell), lose the treasure or lose the beloved Moura. The legends where bread is asked may be related to the old traditions of offering food to the dead. According to ancient lore, Mouras are the souls of young maidens who were left guarding the treasures that the males, Mouros encantados (enchanted Mouros) hid before heading to Mourama. The enchanted

Moura often appears singing and combing her beautiful long golden or black hair with a golden comb, and promises to give treasures to anyone who sets her free by breaking her spell. (In Galicia, though, they are more commonly redheads.) She is believed to be dangerously seductive and able to shape-shift. Mouras encantadas appear as guardians of the pathways into the earth and of the liminal frontiers where it was believed that the supernatural could manifest itself. These places could be castles, caves, bridges, wells, fountains or rivers. José Leite de Vasconcelos considered the possibility that the Mouras encantadas may have assimilated the characteristics of local deities, such as *Nymphs* and other nature-spirits. Consiglieri Pedroso referred to the Mouras encantadas as "feminine water genies". The tales of the Mouras are part of a wider lore of the Mouros encantados, where they sometimes appear as *giants* or warriors, which in contrast also include the *Mourinhos* or *Maruxinhos*, a very small *Elf*-like people who live under the ground.

The phenomenon of the Mouras encantadas is generally thought to be of pre-Roman, Indo-European Celtic origin, as they are related to other Indo-European, and especially Celtic, female water-divinities. Almost every Portuguese or Galician town has a tale of a Moura encantada. There are also general specific species of Mouras:

- *Pedra-Mouras* are Mouras encantadas who dwell inside stones. It was believed that whoever sat on one of these stones would become enchanted, or, that if any enchanted stone was taken to a house, all the animals in the house would die. It was also believed that the Pedras-Mouras hid enchanted treasures inside them. There are several legends where the Mouras lives inside the stones. This Moura is also described as traveling to Mourama while sitting on a stone that can float in the air or over water. It was not uncommon among the people of pre-Roman Iberian Peninsula to believe that the souls of the dead dwell in certain rocks.
- *Princesa Moura* appears as a snake with long blond hair.
- *Moura-Fiandeira* is a spinning maiden or nocturnal weaver, who carries stones on her head to build the hill forts while she spins the yarns with a distaff that she carries at her waist. Mouras encantadas were believed to be the builders of the Paleolithic hill forts, the dolmens, and the megaliths. They are believed to still live there. The ancient coins found on the hill forts were called *medalha das Mouras* (medals of the Mouros). The Pedra Formosa found on Citânia de Briteiros was,

according to folklore, brought to this place by a Moura who carried it on her head while she was spinning with a spindle.

- *Animal shaped Mouras.* In some tales, the enchanted Moura is a shapeshifter who takes the form of a snake: *Moura-Serpente;* or cobra: *Moura-Cobra*; sometimes of a dog: *Moura-Cão*; a goat: *Moura-Cabra*; or horse: *Moura-Cavalo.* Moura-Serpente may have wings and can appear as half woman/half animal and likes to be offered milk. The fountain is one of the places where Mouras Serpentes appear frequently, and magical properties are attributed to their waters as the *Fonte da Moura encantada.* It is also a popular custom to say to those that marry in foreign lands drank from the fountain *(bebeu da fonte)*, as an allusion to the legends where young men were enchanted by the Mouras and fell in love with them.
- *Moura-Mãe* (Mother-Moura) takes the form of a charming pregnant young lady. The person who finds a midwife to help her giving birth is later rewarded by the Moura.
- *Moura-Velha* is an old woman. The legends where a Moura appears in the shape of an old woman are however rare.
- *Moura-Lavadeira* is a washerwoman which is only seen putting white clothes out in the sun, contrary to the *Lavandières* who wash blood-stained clothes.
- *Frades* are Mouras encantadas who appear like friars dressed in white. Frades are like white stone pillars.

The gold of the Mouras may appear in various forms: figs, coal, skirts, hanks of yarn, animals or tools. There are several ways to obtain this gold: it may be offered by the Moura encantada as a reward, it can be stolen, or found. Frequently the gold is inside a vase, hidden inside buried pots, or other receptacles, which has raised the question that this could be related to funerary urns. It was believed that on San Juan's Day the Mouras appeared with their treasures and that this was an opportunity to break their enchantment. In some legends it is on this day that the Moura encantada spreads figs, or a hank of yarn on a large rock, in the moonlight, or in other versions in the sun. These legends are possibly related with the popular tradition of, in some regions, the harvesting of the *figo lampo* (a type of white figs that were offered as a gift on San Juan's day). This day marks the date of the summer solstice, its reference is perhaps reminiscent of some pagan sun-worship or spring time deity, referenced as *São João o Verde* (St. John the Green One).

Muladona

In Catalan folklore, a *Muladona* or *Donamula* (Mule-woman or Woman-mule) is a female mule with a human woman's head. Her manes are like a woman's hair and her face, while still appearing to be like that of an animal, is nevertheless also obviously human. It is always represented with the four legs of a mule, and in addition, the animal is always represented with breasts, to underline that it is female. Legend has it that a young woman was cursed by the townspeople for being irreverent and irreligious, which turned her into this creature. She is said to wander the mountains, especially at night, joining mule trains. It is thought that the mules are frightened by her presence, stampede, and may even run into ravines in panic. The muleteers used to feed their mules a small Muladona-shaped piece of bread, in the belief that this would stop the animals from being frightened and allow them to ignore the creature if she would appear. In addition, they would repeatedly count the number of mules in the mule train, in order to discover in time if the Muladona had joined their animals, and prevent her from causing havoc.

Munaciello

The *Munaciello* or *Monaciello*, ("little monk" in Neapolitan) is a legendary spirit of Neapolitan folklore. A spirit of both benevolent and mischievous nature, he is usually depicted as a deformed little boy or a person of short stature, dressed in the habit of a monk, with a broad brimmed hat and silver buckles on his shoes. According one hypothesis, reported among others by Matilde Serao in her *Leggende Napoletane* (Neapolitan Legends – 1881), the Munaciello legend originated in a character that really existed in the 15th century. In another legend, the Munaciello was once the *pozzaro*, the city's ancient manager of the water wells, who was able (because of his small stature) to enter houses through the channels that were used to lower the bucket. Since their clients often refused to pay the pozzari, they took revenge by entering the homes of the Lords and stole precious objects as a compensation. The same precious objects were then sometimes given by the pozzari to their mistresses, whose home the managers of the wells also entered through the bucket-channels. And so the legend emerged that the Munaciello sometimes steals, and sometimes gives. There is also a third hypothesis, which describes the Munaciello as a small demon, mischievous because he is bad, even when he leaves coins (in that case, the money would be a bait for the living to lure them to his side).

Muladona, 18th century illustration

N

Naiads

In Greek mythology, the *Naiads* (Ancient Greek: Ναϊάδες, *Naïades*, from the verb νάω, to flow) are *Water Nymphs*, and probably daughters of the *Potamids*, the river gods. They personified and, according to the Greeks, guarded all rivers, lakes, swamps, fountains and springs. The Naiads are primarily related to fresh water, although there are overlaps with the (salt water) *Oceanids*. The Naiads were divided in five main categories: the *Crinaeae* ruled fountains, the *Eleionomae* lived in swamps, the *Limnades* in lakes, the *Pegaeae* lived in springs and the *Potamides* had their habitat in rivers.

Nain

In the last century the description of *Nain* became a sort of blanket term for the many French types of dwarfish *Fairies,* perhaps because etymologically Nain simply means "small". In the Romance space, the term *dwarf* is derived from the Latin *nanus*, itself forged from the Greek νάνος (*nanos*), meaning "small" (compare nanoparticle). Lewis Spence was however very specific in defining the creature, when he published his *Legends and Romances of Brittany* in 1917. In his definition the Nain

> *"is a figure fearsomely Celtic in its hideousness, resembling the gargoyles which peer down upon the traveller from the carven 'top-hamper' of so many Breton churches. Black and menacing of countenance, these demon-folk are armed with feline claws, and their feet end in hoofs like those of a satyr. Their dark elflocks, their small, gleaming eyes, red as carbuncles, and their harsh, cracked voices are all dilated upon with fear by those who have met them upon lonely heaths or unfrequented roads. They haunt the ancient dolmens built by a vanished race, and at night, by the pale star-light, they dance around these ruined tombs...//"*

According to Spence, the Monday, Tuesday, Wednesday, Thursday and Friday were celebrated days of the Nain and the names were sung while dancing. In contrast, they shunned the Saturdays and Sundays; those being the days people were protected from Fairy-influence. Bad luck attached itself to the human who chanced to behold the midnight festivities of the Nains, and if someone entered the charmed circle and danced along with them, the death of this person was certain to ensue before the year was out. Wednesday was the Nains' high-day, or rather high-night, and their great *Nuit Festale* always took place on the first Wednesday in May. That they should have possessed a fixed festival at such a period, full of religious significance for most primitive peoples, suggests that they must at one time have been held in considerable esteem. But although the Nains, while best known for their innocent habit of dancing to the repetition of the names of the days of the week, they also have a less innocent side to their characters. They are forgers of false money, which they fabricate in the recesses of caverns. The Nains were also regarded as the originators of a mysterious alphabet, the letters of which are engraved on several of the megalithic monuments of Morbihan, and especially those of Gavr'inis. He or she who is able to decipher this magic script, will – according to tradition – be able to tell where hidden treasures are to be found in any part of the country. Sorcery hung about the Nains like a garment and much of their magic power was employed for evil purposes, which is why many Bretons feared them.

Napaeae

In Greek mythology, the *Napaeae* (Ancient Greek: ναπαῖαι, from νάπη, a wooded valley) were a type of *Nymphs* that lived in forested valleys, glens or small caves. The Napaeae were shy but cheerful *Dryads* (thus connected to trees), and kept the hunting goddess Artemis company.

Negret

A *Negret* in Eastern Catalan folklore, especially those of Majorca, is a small, dark-skinned *sprite* who, if touched with a burning candle by a mortal, instantly turns into a trove of coins. The word is the diminutive of the Catalan *negre* (black).

Nereids

In Greek mythology, the *Nereids* (ancient Greek: Νηρεΐδες *Nēreídes*; sing. Νηρεΐς *Nēreís*; Latin *Nēreis, Nēreides*) are the daughters of the sea-god *Nereus* and *Doris*, an *Oceanid*. These *Sea-Nymphs* are believed to have blue hair. They, along with the *Tritons*, accompany the sea god Poseidon and they are helpful to sailors during severe storms. Each Nymph represents a facet of sea life, such as waves, coasts and beaches and/or skills of seafarers, such as strength, speed, skill, etc. They live with their father in a silver cave at the bottom of the Aegean Sea. Unofficially, *Thetis* was their leader. In another version the queen of the sea is *Amphitrite*, who has the same parents as Thetis. It is often assumed that their number was fifty, but nowhere is there a complete list of them, and according to Plato their number was hundred. In many ancient Greek depictions, the Nereids ride on the backs of dolphins or *Hippocamps* (*sea-spirits* with the head of a horse and the body of a fish).

Nicole

The *Nicole* is a spirit of relatively modern creation, who tormented the fishermen of the Bay of Saint-Brieuc and Saint-Malo. Just as they were about to draw in their nets, this mischievous spirit leaped around them, freeing the fish, or raising a boat's anchor so that it would drift onto a sand-bank. The spirit could also divide the cable that holds the anchor to the vessel and cause endless trouble. The Nicole received its name from an officer who commanded a battalion of fishermen conscripts, and who from his intense severity and general reputation as a whipmaster obtained a bad reputation among the seafaring population.

Nitus

The *Nitus* are male miniature *demons* of Catalan folklore, small as grains of dust, impossible to describe because of their smallness, that enter through the ear of the person to reach the brain. They do not kill, but they do leave their victim without memory and make him/her feel like sleeping. It is for this reason that anyone who is very sleepy or has a bad memory is asked if they have a Nitus. *Las Falugas* are their female equivalent.

Nuberos

The *Nuberos/us*, *Nubleros*, *Ñuberus*, *Nubeiros* or *Renuveros* are *Duendes*, present in Asturian, Cantabrian, Galician and northern León mythology to whom is attributed the ability to control the weather, especially clouds and rainfall. They are generally considered to be evil beings. Their appearance varies according to the region, but they are almost always described as anthropomorphic, male, aged, extremely ugly, dark-skinned, with large mouth and ears and a bushy beard. Their sunken eyes glow like red embers. They usually wear a fur suit and a wide-brimmed black hat. The Nuberos are very similar to the *Entiznáu* of Extremaduran mythology, although the latter differs from the former in its enormous size.

In Asturian folklore

In Asturian villages it is common to ring bells in order to exorcise Nuberu. There is also an Asturian saying about scary-looking places that refers to the malevolent character attributed to him: *"Tien cara de nuberu"* (has the face of a Nuberu). The Nuberu controls the weather at will and amuses himself triggering storms and gales, striking animals with streaks of lightning and ruining the harvests with hailstorms. He will not hesitate to use lightning as a weapon if he is attacked or bothered. Among the people of Cantabria and Asturias, he is feared for the damage he causes in villages. Nights of rainfall and storms are attributed to him. For this reason locals light up candles during the dark hours and ring bells to scare him away. Fishermen fear the Nuberu, because they blame him for the strong northwestern winds of the Cantabrian Sea, which forces them to return hurriedly to port. In Asturias, another of the names traditionally given to the Nuberu is *Xuan Cabritu*. According to the story, he lives with his wife and children on top of a mountain in a city covered with clouds, and when he comes out of there it is to unload storms and downpours on the people. Some authors place his house in the summits between Asturias and León, in a house made of mud.

In Cantabrian folklore

In Cantabrian mythology, Nuberos are often a multitude of little creatures, not a single one. They are described as small, chubby and mischievous, with devilish grins in their demonic faces and little black wings, always riding on dark rain-clouds. They aren't as evil as the Asturian Nuberu, but are still powerful and inconsiderate, and take great joy in causing misery and destroying the property of humans. They are blamed of the fierce, rainy storms that unleash during the night, damaging the rooftops of houses. That is why during the hours of darkness the villagers light candles and ring bells to scare them away.

However, the Cantabrians that fear the Nuberus the most, are usually not the house owners but the sailors. Unlike the *Ventolines*, the fishermen fear the Nuberos because they blame them for the terrible and unpredictable *galernas* (sudden storms) of the Cantabrian Sea and the Bay of Biscay, which make them hurry back to port, where their worried family and friends are waiting for them.

In Galician folklore

In Southern Galicia, the Nubeiros have the appearance of a small man, with a body covered with hair and a long, twisted tail. They ride on large clouds and are responsible for summer storms and many other ravages. To avoid their mischief, the locals ring the bells or call on the parish priest to conjure them away. In other parts of Galicia the Nubeiro is one big man covered in wolf or goat skins, and associated with storms, lighting, fog, and to a lesser extent, avalanches. He is missing one eye, so his aim is less than perfect. He comes out in the mornings from his smithy to ride the skies, causing storms and throwing lightning rods and returns at midnight with a few snakes and lizards. Sometimes he comes down to earth to see the result of his exploits, or to ask for asylum in a house or hut after losing a cloud.

In Castilian folklore

Due to its condition of being frontier land, Castilian myths are particularly eclectic and resemble those of the region they border closest to, creating a mix of the aforementioned narratives with heavy elements of the *Entiznau* of Extremadura. Castilians don't consider Nuberos as evil as the other regions do, and tend to welcome the rain they bring during the fall, but they do blame as their most evil aspects the lightning and fires caused by summer storms. To prevent the disasters these creatures cause, tradition recommends burning dry grass in the right seasons to make sure that the little demons have no target to hit.

Nuton

The *Nuton* (or *Nûton*) is a small creature, a kind of *Goblin* of the French Ardennes and Wallonia. It lives in caves and is very close to the French *Lutin* or *Lûton* and the Dutch and Flemish *Kabouter*. In Celles, not far from Dinant, there is a votive stone dedicated to a popular divinity named "NVTTO" of which it is the only known evocation.

This inscription triggered the hypothesis that the Nutons in the Belgian Ardennes are linked to the mythology of the Gallo-Roman period. On the side of Malmedy (East of Belgium) one finds the trace of very old toponymies with its Trô from Dûhons (Hole of the Duhons), whose etymology comes from the *Duses*. Moreover, in the carnival of Malmedy (Cwarmê), one finds a character named *Sotê* which is more than likely the local Nuton.

The Nuton shares the same origin as the *Goblin*, but according to local folklore, caves, caverns and subterranean tunnels form the main part of its habitat, just like many *Kobold*-like creatures of the Germanic world who dwell underground or in mines or inside mountains. It was once customary for the local people of the Ardennes to leave damaged objects for the Nuton in the evening, along with some food, and traditionally they were found repaired in the morning – as in the Grimm's tales. Although the Nuton is rarely differentiated from the French *Elf*, folklorist Pierre Dubois also insists on the fact that the *Elves* form "a race of their own", not to be confused with the Nutons, whose habitat and legends are different.

The Nutons speak little, and when they do they usually deliver unpleasant messages, so much so, that "Nuton" has become a synonym for "misanthrope" and "taciturn". Their spells are particularly feared in the Ardennes. A well-known story tells of a Wallonian farmer mowing his wheat to bring it in before the storm, when he sees the Nuton from his home helping him by carrying one ear at a time. Annoyed by what he considers to be useless help, he ignores him. The Nuton comes out of his silence, and gives him this curse: *"Ear by ear, I have enriched you, sheaf by sheaf I will ruin you"*. This is quoted by both Albert Doppagne and Pierre Dubois. In the rest of the story, the Wallonian peasant loses all his possessions and ends up ruined. In the 1970s, Albert Doppagne became interested in these creatures and collected the testimony of a 60 year-old Wallonian woman who claimed to have seen Nutons running on the windowsill of her house. Where popular beliefs have largely receded, expressions linked to Nutons remained, generally to designate misanthropy or, in Warmifontaine, greed. The quinces of Comblain-au-Pont are called *Apples of Nutons*. Towers and *Holes of Nutons* are still visible in Belgian toponyms, as well as *Étrons de Nuton*; blocks of pyrite in the Entre-Sambre-et-Meuse.

Nymph

A *Nymph* (ancient Greek Νύμφη *nýmphē:* bride, young woman, veiled; Latinized: *nympha*) is a semi-generic term for female nature demons in Greek and Roman mythology, often bound to a particular place or plant species. Nymphs belongs to the chthonic demons and appears very often – as well as their stalkers, the *Satyrs*, *Pans*, *Panisks* and other creatures of the same kind – in the retinue of *Dionysos* (god of wine and extasy). A Nymph is a graceful girl, who in the religious representations of the Greeks was a personification of the life and restless activity which prevails in nature. The work of Nymphs therefore extends across the whole of nature. She can reveal herself both in the murmur of springs and streams, and in the germination of plant life, in the forests and on fields and meadows. She is a tender, lovely maiden, who, though generally friendly to men, yet takes no pleasure in the proximity of human habitations and the noisy daily occupations of them, but withdraws timidly into the solitude of the forest and of the mountains, which provokes quiet contemplation and sweet dreaming. There she lives a cheerful, cozy life in caves and mountain crevices, which she inhabits. According to the older conception of the Nymphs, they are counted among the immortal gods, since, among other things, they participate in the meetings of the gods and enjoy divine worship from men. Immortality is also their portion and they are as free in their actions as the gods above them in rank and dignity. Later, however, especially in regard to a section of the Nymphs, the *Dryads*, the idea arose that their lives were connected with those of the tree in which they sat, and that, for example, a violent destruction of that tree would also result in their death. In the same way the Nymphs of springs and wells died when the water source dried up. Hesiod also names the *Maenads* or *Bacchae* as Nymphs, although they are for the most part simple humans. The Greek Nymphs were later assimilated with the various Roman deities of fountains, springs and rivers. The Nymphs are distinguished according to the different parts of nature in which they lived and worked:

• Water-Nymphs or Hydriads

The Nymphs of the waters or *Hydriads*, to which are also included the *Oceanids* and the *Nereids* (both Nymphs of the sea), are especially the Nymphs of those waters, which are found on the earth, the streams and springs, which bore the general name of *Naiads*. They were the daughters of the river gods or *Potamids*. Different types of Naiads are: *Crinaeae*,

Eleionomae, *Limnades* and *Pegaeae*. They are the beneficent feeders of the plants, whom they provide with whatever they need to live. Through the plants they also feed the herds and thus the people. For this reason they enjoyed special veneration and altars were erected to them at the springs inhabited by them. In several legends it is said that children of the gods were entrusted to them for their education (for example Dionysos). Like the Sea-Nymphs, they have the gift of prophecy, and like them they are friends of song and poetry, as is particularly the case with the *Muses*, who were originally nothing but Spring-Nymphs. Among the Naiads are the fifty Daniads (punished to carry water for murdering their 50 husbands on their wedding night). The Sea-Nymphs are often daughters of important sea gods such as *Nereus* and *Oceanos*. For example, the Oceanids are the three thousand children of Okeanos and Thetys. They were associated with salt water, although there are overlaps with the Naiads. Sometimes the Naiads are considered a group of Oceanids. A total of fifty Nereids are said to exist. These Sea-Nymphs were the daughters of the ancient sea god Nereus.

• **Oreads**

The *Oreads* are the Nymphs of the mountains, but are sometimes considered the protectors of one entire mountain, to which the *Napaeae*, the Nymphs of the valleys and gorges, are also included. The Oreads were a very scattered genus of Nymphs, who also bear separate names after different mountain regions. They were the daughters of the five *Hekaterids*. They were mainly the companions of *Artemis*, with whom they performed farewell dances and looked forward to the hunt. The Boeotian Nymph *Echo* was one of the Oreads, who became known especially for her sad fate. She has been the subject of poetry and many representations of her have been made in the visual arts.

• **Dryads or Hamadryads**

The Dryads or Hamadryads are Forest-Nymphs. Dryads (at least the Hamadryads) live in the trees and die with them, because they are correlated to "soul" and "life force" of the tree. These Nymphs do not possess immortality, although in an oak tree, for example – if they are so lucky – they can of course live up to several centuries. A Dryad punishes those who cause damage to her tree. These Nymphs are primarily classified as a different species. Although the Hamadryads sometimes refer to the entire group of Dryads, it is generally assumed that they are the protectors of the oak tree. The *Meliae* are the protectresses of the ash tree, born from the blood of Uranus after he was castrated. The most famous of these Nymphs is *Melia*. The Epimeliads are also called *Meliads*, not to be confused with the Meliae. These are the Nymphs of the fruit trees. The *Alseids* were the Nymphs of small groups of trees in general, just like the Auloniads, which other sources say protect the valleys. Alseid is derived from the Greek word alsea, meaning "grove". Some *Daphniads* protect the laurel, while others focus on other rarer tree species.

• Other Nymphs

The *Anthousa* are the rather unknown Nymphs of the flowers. The *Aurae* are the Nymphs of the breeze, and probably daughters of the *Anemoi*, or four winds; *Boreas* (North wind), *Notos* (South wind), *Euros* (East wind) and *Zephyros* (West wind). The *Lampads* carry torches, to light the path of their mistress *Hekate*. The ancient Greeks believed that these Nymphs were also responsible for the visions of mortals. Hesiods' *Maenads* or *Bacchae* accompany Dionysos, the god of wine and extasy. They wear long robes and animal skins, and perform wild dances. Their food consists of raw meat, which they tear off their victims with their bare hands. Some Maenads are Oreads, others Naiads or others Nymphs, but mortal women can also become Maenads. The *Limoniads* are the Nymphs of flowers, meadows and fields. The *Hesperids* guard the Tree with the Golden Apples in the land of Hesperia. If you eat from these apples, you become immortal.

Worship

The worship of the Nymphs in Greece was of very ancient date. Temples they never had, but people dedicated to them dens and caves, erected their altars at springs, and built to them in larger cities so-called *nymphae*, i.e. richly decorated fountains with colonnades. Goats and lambs were offered to them; for libations they took milk and oil, but never wine. As local goddesses, they were also named after the corresponding regions; for example, the *Peliads* are the Nymphs of the Pelion mountain range. The Nymph *Noris* is linked to the Middle Franconian city of Nuremberg. One of the most famous Oreads was *Echo*, the Nymph of Mount Helikon. The goddess *Hera* deprived her of speech, leaving her only the ability to repeat the last words addressed to her. A Tree-Nymph is *Eurydice*, the wife of *Orpheus*. The Greek Nymphs are believed to have exerted a strong influence on the evolution of female nature-spirits and water-spirits in the Balkan and Easter Europe.

Napaea (1564) by Cornelis Cort (1533-1578) after Frans Floris I

NAPÆA
is inuentor
-6-
·H· cock excudebat
FACILES VENERAE NAPÆAS. VIRG.

O

Oceanides

In Greek mythology, the *Oceanides*, or *Oceanines* (from the ancient Greek Ὠκεανίδες / *Ōkeanídes*, pl. of Ὠκεανίς, *Ōkeanís*), are aquatic but not marine *Nymphs* (unlike the *Nereids*), mainly attached to the course of their father Ocean. They are sometimes considered the Nymphs of the inaccessible sea bed. They accompany their mother, *Tethys*, while crowned with flowers. According to Hesiod, they are the daughters of *Oceanos* and Tethys, three thousand in number; their role is symmetrical to that of their brothers, the river gods, of whom there are also three thousand. Each one was the guardian of a river or lake, in short of a particular water point (this also included the waters of the underground world, for example the Styx). Another of their divine prerogatives consisted in watching over the childhood of young boys, a function received from the hand of *Zeus* and which they carried out in the company of their brothers, and of *Apollo*. In the earliest traditions, notably in the works of Hesiod, Aeschylus and in the Homeric Hymns, the Oceanides have the rank of goddesses in their own right and constitute a group clearly distinct from the *Naiads*, who are generally regarded as the daughters of the river gods or of "rainy" Zeus, and who enjoy an unusually long, but not eternal, existence.

Ogre

An *Ogre* (feminine: *Ogress*) is a legendary monster usually depicted as a large, hideous, man-like being that eats ordinary human beings, especially infants and children. Ogres frequently feature in mythology and folklore and appear in many classic works of literature, most often associated in fairy tales and legends with a taste for infants. In mythology, Ogres are often depicted as inhumanly large, tall, and having a disproportionately large head, abundant hair, unusually colored skin, a voracious appetite, and a strong body. Ogres are closely linked with *giants* and with human cannibals in mythology. In both folklore and fiction, Giants are often given ogrish traits (such as the giants in "Jack and the Beanstalk" and the *Jötnar* of Norse mythology); while Ogres may be given giant-like traits.

Orcus

The word *Ogre* is most likely derived from the Etruscan god *Orcus*, who fed on human flesh. Orcus was a god of the underworld, punisher of broken oaths in Etruscan and Roman mythology. As with Hades, the name of the god was also used for the underworld itself. In the later tradition, he was conflated with *Dis Pater*. A temple to Orcus may once have existed on the Palatine Hill in Rome. It is likely that he was transliterated from the Greek daemon *Horkos*, the personification of oaths and a son of *Eris*. The origins of Orcus, depicted as a monstrous figure, may have rooted in Etruscan religion. The so-called *Tomb of Orcus*, an Etruscan site at Tarquinia, is a misnomer, resulting from its first discoverers mistaking a hairy, bearded giant for Orcus; it actually depicts a *Cyclops*. The Romans sometimes conflated Orcus with other gods such as Pluto, Hades, and Dis Pater, all gods of the land of the dead. The name Orcus seems to have been given to the malicious and punishing side of the ruler of the underworld, as the god who tormented evildoers in their afterlife. Like the name Hades, Orcus could mean both the land of the dead itself, as well as its ruling deity. In the charitable interpretation of such a place, it was believed to be an abode for purification of the souls of the deceased.

Orcus was chiefly worshiped in rural areas; he had no official cult in the cities. This remoteness allowed for him to survive in the countryside long after the more prevalent gods had ceased to be worshiped. He survived as a folk figure into the Middle Ages, and aspects of his worship were transmuted into the *Wild Man*-festivals held in rural parts of Europe through modern times. Indeed, much of what is known about the celebrations associated with Orcus come from medieval sources. From Orcus' association with death and the underworld, his name came to be used for demons and other underworld monsters, particularly in Italian where *Orco* refers to a kind of monster found in fairy tales that feeds on human flesh. The French word *Ogre* (appearing first in Charles Perrault's fairy tales) may have come from variant forms of this word, *Orgo* or *Ogro*; in any case, the French *Ogre* and the Italian *Orco* are exactly the same sort of creature.

Ogres in the earliest literature

Its earliest attestation is in Chrétien de Troyes' late 12th-century verse romance *Perceval ou le Conte du Graal*, which contains the lines:

"Et s'est escrit que il ert ancore
que toz li reaumes de Logres,
qui jadis fu la terre as ogres,
ert destruite par cele lance."

(And it is written that he will come again,
to all the realms of Logres,
which was formerly land of ogres,
and destroy them with that lance.)

The Ogres in this rhyme may refer to the Ogres who were, in the pseudohistorical work *History of the Kings of Britain* by Geoffrey of Monmouth, the inhabitants of Britain, prior to human settlement. The Italian author Giambattista Basile (1575-1632) used the related Neapolitan word *uerco*, or in standard Italian, *orco* in some of his tales. This word is documented in earlier Italian works (Fazio degli Uberti, 14th century; Luigi Pulci, 15th century; Ludovico Ariosto, 15th-16th centuries) and has even older cognates with the Latin Orcus and the Old English *Orcnēas* found in Beowulf. All these words may derive from a shared Indo-European mythological concept. The *Dictionnaire de l'Académie Française* (1932-'35) alternatively states that the name is derived from the word *Hongrois*, which means Hungarian, as of western cultures referred to Hungarians as a kind of monstrosity.

Ogre could possibly also derive from the biblical *Og*, last of the Giants (or from the Greek river god *Oiagros*, father of Orpheus). The word Ogre came into wider usage in the works of Charles Perrault (1628-1703) or Marie-Catherine Jumelle de Berneville, Comtesse d' Aulnoy (1650-1705), both of whom were French authors. The first appearance of the word Ogre in Perrault's work occurred in his *Histoires ou Contes du temps Passé* (1696). It later appeared in several of his other fairy tales, many of which were based on the Neapolitan tales of Basile. The first example of a female Ogre being referred to as an Ogress is found in his version of *Sleeping Beauty*, where it is spelled Ogresse. Madame d'Aulnoy first employed the word Ogre in her story *L'Orangier et l'Abeille* (1698), and was the first to use the word Ogre to refer to the creature's offspring.

Oilar

Oilar or *Ollaar* means "rooster" in Basque. It is not uncommon to meet the rooster in Basque legends. Its crowing announces the retreat before daylight of the nocturnal *Ireluak* like the *Laminak*. Sometimes however, a *Gaiskiñe* (evil spirit) takes on the appearance of this animal. If someone suffers from a mysterious illness, the feathers of his/her pillow or bolster should be examined. If a cluster is found that fits the shape of a whole rooster, the disease is regarded to be incurable. If the head of the rooster is not formed, the feathers must be taken to a crossroads and burned there: then the disease will be cured.

Ojáncanu

In Cantabrian mythology, the *Ojáncanu* (Sorrow of Cantabria) or *Ojáncano* (female: *Ojáncana* or *Ojánca*) is a 10 foot tall *Ogre* or Bigfoot-look alike found in Cantabrian mythology. The Ojancanu has a yellowy color and very long reddish, brown or black hair covering most of his body, except his round face, which like a *Cyclops*, has only one eye. It is an embodiment of cruelty, with a wild and beast-like temperament and the most well-known entity in Cantabrian mythology. It mostly operates nocturnally. The Ojáncanu has superhuman strength, which he measures by fighting bears and bulls. Compared to humans the creature has a double amount of fingers and toes. The strangest thing about these creatures is their reproduction process. Instead of mating, when an Ojancanu gets too old, the other Ojáncanus and Ojáncanas will kill him. Then they distribute certain body parts amongst each other and bury the remains of the corpse under an oak or yew tree. Nine months later, yellow worms grow out of the corpse and the Ojáncana feeds them with blood from her breasts, until they become Ojáncanus or Ojáncanas three years later. Cantabrian mythology holds the Ojáncanus to be the creator of gorges and ravines, as well as the reason for some trees to be found uprooted. It is often depicted with clubs or using small trees as weapons, as well as a sling and a walking stick, which it can turn into a wolf, crow or viper.

Ojáncanus are completely opposite in nature from their opponents: the benevolent *Anjanas*. They are believed to constantly do evil, and are known for stealing sheep, breaking trees, blocking wells, streams and rivers, as well as causing landslides. The Cantabrian farmers fear them the most, for not only their lands suffer but also their families. There are many tales of how an Ojáncanu has come down the valley before dawn, and stolen away young maidens never to be seen again, killing or eating most of the cattle in the process of this kidnapping. However, it is said that all these Ogres have one white hair hidden somewhere in their red beards, and if it was to be pulled out, the creature would die. Yet, the people of Cantabria say that once every 100 years a good Ojáncanu is born, and if taken in by the people of the local communities, this creature would warn the inhabitants against when his kin are near, so the villagers could protect themselves. Beings similar to the Ojáncanu are found in other pantheons such as Extremadurian mythology in which it is the *Jáncanu*, *Pelujáncanu* or *Jáncanas*. It is also found in the Basque mythology as *Tartalo* or *Torto*.

P

Paniskoi

Paniskoi are "little Pans". There appeared not only a great Pan, but also little Pans, Paniskoi, who played the same part as the *Satyrs*. Paniskoi / *Satyrs* are spirits that are totally fused with the vital and sexual forces in nature. They can appear to the clairvoyant eye, during a long-lasting totally absorbing sex-play between lovers. They are half human half animal and do not always have goat horns, but may also have the face of other animals, like lions. As Pan's duplicates they are also linked to the fertility of the plant kingdom.

Papu

The *Papu* or *Papus* is a most famous *Bogey*-figure in Catalan mythology. In Catalan it may also be called *Butoni* or *Marraco*. Related to the Asturian *Papón* and the Portuguese *Papão* and *Bicho-papão*, it shares the concept of swallowing its victims without having to chew on them, indicating that it must be provided with a large mouth and stomach. It may also be related to the French *Babau*, a Bogey present in some Pyrenean valleys in southern France.

Parisette

La Parisette is a very attractive *Forest Nymph*, full of zest for life, who rules over a herb called paris or true lover's knot *(Paris trifolia)*. She used her clean appearance and sensual attractiveness to seduce men. Out of envy, the *Nymph of the Nettle* shrank her height from 166 cm to 126 cm. The goddess *Flora* who rules all plants, took pity on Parisette and made sure her beauty was preserved. This transformation made the Parisette yearn for the days when she effortlessly charmed all men. Since then, her main activity has been to redeem tramps enchanted by the spells of *La Tourmentine*, the evil daughter of the Nettle Nymph.

Paris or true lover's knot, is a species of flowering plant in the family *Melanthiaceae*. It occurs in temperate and cool areas throughout Eurasia, from Spain to Yakutia, and from Iceland to Mongolia. It prefers calcareous soils and lives in damp and shady places, especially old established woods and stream banks. The wearing of the three-leafed Parisette is said to attract "luck in all money matters."

Patuek

Patuek or *Patuak* is a Basque word for familiar *Irelu* – somewhat like the personal *Genius* of the ancient Greeks and Romans, or the *Familiar* of the medieval witch – mysterious beings with whose collaboration extraordinary works are carried out. When someone has little luck in his/her life, the Basques used to say: "*Ez du orrek patu onik*" (This one doesn't have a good patu). Patu means "destiny" in Basque. With the suffix "a", patua is translated as "fate". Considering the nature of the Patuek one would not expect them to be related to the location of Ibarruri (Biscay). It is also believed they are related to the Mamur, small Ireluak who can be captured the night before Saint John's Day.

Pegai

Pegai (Latin: *Pegaeae*) are the *Nymphs* of springs and wells in Greek mythology. Although often described as daughters of one or another river god, they were also considered the great aunts of the *Potamoi* (River gods), thus establishing a mythological relationship between a river itself and its springs. This symbolically depicts the fact that most rivers originate from a spring. Like the *Limnades* and other Nymphs associated with fresh water, they belonged to the *Naiads*. They were closely related to the Crenaeans, Nymphs of springs and fountains, who were counted among the most revered Nymphs. This can be explained by the vital importance of sources of fresh water. According to myths, these Nymphs sometimes possessed the ability to heal people or animals from various illnesses. The *Ionidas,* four Pegai-sisters, could for instance cure various diseases. *Anigridas* – associated with the river of the same name in the Peloponnese (daughters of a river deity) were evoked to cure skin diseases. The river flowed down from Mount Lapita where the medicinal springs of Caiaphas are located. Sometimes they had more unusual abilities. For example, *Castalia* and *Aganyppa* gave literary and poetic inspiration, and are an example of a more common occurring fusion of Nymphs with *Muses*. Nymphs were usually offered milk and honey.

Like other Nymphs, the Pegai were depicted as beautiful girls, with voices as clear as the gurgling of a spring. The Pegai often accompanied Artemis during the hunt. One Nymph, *Salmacida*, who did not like the hunt and continually stayed at her spring, is described rather as an exception to the rule. Pegai and other Nymphs were not immortal and could be killed, but their life span could be thousands of years. In the case of Pegai and other *Water Nymphs*, death was probably something that happened simultaneously with the drying up of their source. A special devotion to springs is characteristic of many cultures. The veneration of the Pegai, Crenaeans and other Naiads was preserved in a certain form under Christianity as many springs now bear the names of Christian saints.

Thriaí

The *Thriaí* (ancient Greek: Θριαί, Romanized: *Thriae*) were three sisters; *Melaina* (The Black), *Kleodora* (Famed for her Gift), and *Corycia* or *Daphnis* (Laurel) were *Pegai* Mountain Nymph cross-overs. They were three virginal sisters, guarding the sacred springs of the Corycian Cave of Mount Parnassus in Phocis, and were the patrons of bees. The Thriaí presided over a special kind of (lower) divination by means of stones (θριαί), under the authority of the messenger-god *Hermes*, that were cast into an urn. The higher form of divination was by Hermes himself, and only reserved for *Zeus*. Melaina was linked to subterranean streams, hence her name "Black". Their appearance was unusual for the average Nymph. These Pegai had women's heads and torsos and lower bodies, but the wings of a bee instead of arms. They were fond of honey, which in one version of the stories was offered to them, before they spoke their prophecies. A passage from Plato connects honey with the fountains that give poetic inspiration *(Ion, 534a-b)*:

> *"For surely the poets who offer us songs tell us that, like bees, they are released into the fountains from which honey flows in some gardens and dens of the muses, and they too flock in the same way."*

Honey, according to a Greek myth, was discovered by a Nymph called *Melissa* (Bee); and honey was offered to the Greek gods from Mycenean times. Bees were also associated with the Delphic oracle and the prophetess was sometimes called a bee. Apart from Hermes, the *Thriaí*, or Bee-Sisters, were associated with the gods Apollo and Poseidon.

Pegasides

Pegasides (Greek: Πηγασίδες, sing.: Pegasis) were the *Nymphs* of Greek mythology connected with wells and springs, specifically those that were believed to have been created by the mythical winged horse *Pegasus* by striking the ground with his hooves. According to Greek mythological tradition the winged horse Pegasus was the son of *Poseidon*. The hero *Bellerophon* needed the untamed Pegasus to help him defeat the monster *Chimera*. Hence, while Pegasus was drinking at the spring Pirene in Corinth, Bellerophon caught him. Pegasus, startled, struck a rock with his hoof, creating the spring *Hippocrene* on Mount Helicon.

The term *pegasides* (plural form of the Greek feminine adjective *pegasis*) literally means "originating from or linked with Pegasus". Therefore, in poetry, the waters and streams of Hippocrene and other springs that arose from the hoofprints of Pegasus are called *Pegasides*. The *Muses* are likewise sometimes called *Pegasides* because the spring Hippocrene was sacred to them. Nymphs in general, if associated with springs and brooks, may be called Pegasides: thus *Pegasis*, the singular form, is applied by the Roman poet Ovid as a by-name or adjective to the Nymph *Oenone*, daughter of the river-god *Cebrenus*. *Pegasis* is used by the Greek author Quintus Smyrnaeus as the name of a Nymph who had sex with the Trojan prince Emathion and gave birth beside the river *Granicus* to a son: *Atymnius*, who was eventually killed by *Odysseus* in the Trojan War.

Peix Nicolau

Peix Nicolau (Fish Nicolau) is a creature that, just like *Mermaids*, is half man half fish, in Mediterranean folklore related to the *Melusine*-stories. The different legends and tales of the Mediterranean contain diverse stories about enchantments and marine mysteries.

Penates

The *Penates* (Latin: *Dii Penates*) were among the *Dii Familiares*, or household deities, invoked most often in domestic rituals in ancient Rome. Together with other gods, they protected the family and its household. The Penates were in charge of the stove and the pantry – they made sure that the precious embers did not cool down, that rats did not get at the food supplies at night, and they had to stimulate the cook to cook something tasty. Their name is derived from the Latin word for "pantry": *penus*. When the family had a meal, they threw a bit into the fire of the hearth for the Penates. They were thus associated with *Vesta*, the *Lares*, and the *Genius* of the *paterfamilias* in the "little universe" of the Domus. Since Penates were the souls of deceased ancestors, they were tied to their family and went with them when the family moved. Indeterminate in gender and nature, they always appeared in twos or threes and divided their jurisdiction between hearth, food and drinks. The hearth was their altar. The Penates were transmitted like an inheritance, from father to son. In each home they were reserved a place, at least a small room, often an altar and sometimes a sanctuary (named *Laraire*).

Public Penates

The Penates of Rome (*Penates Publicis Populi Romani)* had a temple on the Velia near the Palatine. Dionysius of Halicarnassus says it housed statues of two youths in the archaic style. The public cult of the ancestral gods of the Roman people originated in Lavinium, where they were also closely linked with Vesta. One tradition identified the public Penates as the sacred objects rescued by Aeneas from Troy and carried by him to Italy. They, or perhaps rival duplicates, were eventually housed in the Temple of Vesta in the Forum. Thus the Penates, unlike the localized Lares, are portable deities.

Perro del Urko

In (Spanish) Gallician folklore the *Perro del Urko* (Dog of Urko; Gallician: *Can do Urco*) or *Huerco* is an animal that takes the form of a huge black dog, with large ears and horns. It emerges out of the sea dragging heavy chains. Its presence is considered a very bad omen, often announcing a coming death. In Galicia the animal is also called *Urco* and *Can do Mar*, while in Asturias it is called *Güercu*. However the Güercu is not necessarily a dog-shaped entity, but a being that has no place or defined form at all. When someone is going to die, he may appear before a loved one or relative in the shape of that person, or as a bird. There are not many writings in which this being is mentioned, although there are many people who claim to have witnessed a Güercu during their lives, who came to inform them of the death of someone. According to popular belief, the Urcos lived on the banks of the Lérez river, coming from a dark place known as Borrón, a place of the Other World, that was under the

Sea. In Pontevedra, the legend of the Urco was included in the Entroido celebrations. According to Antón Fraguas, from 1876 on, this monster began to be honored, in the form of a huge and ferocious dog capable of swallowing in one bite twenty sacks of small change as easily as a donkey swallows two grains of barley.

Pesadilla

Pesadilla is a local name for a *Nightmare* or *Alp* in the Spanish Pyrenees; a creature that attacks people in their sleep by sitting on their chests and obstructing their breathing, causing panic and sleep paralysis.

Pesanta

In Catalan folklore, the *Pesanta* (heavy one) is an *Alp*-like creature in the shape of a huge dog (rarely a cat), that visits bedrooms at night and places itself on people's chests, making breathing difficult and causing fear and nightmares. The Pesanta has a furry and black appearance, with steel legs, so perforated that it cannot pick up anything from the ground without falling. The creature is difficult to observe, because when someone wakes up, it runs away, and the victims only see a shadow shooting away. Joan Amades (in: *Los ogros infantiles – Revista de Dialectología y Tradiciones Populares*, 1957) gives the following description of a Pesanta, in which instead of having four perforated legs, one of its legs is entirely made of iron:

> *"La Pesanta, a black dog, as thick and heavy as lead, intensely hairy, with a terrible iron paw, with which it spanks all those who pass through the street at night. It goes through keyholes, under doors and, if necessary, seeps through walls. It pleases itself by placing itself on the chest during sleep, and and obstructs breathing, causing nightmares and very agitated and desperate dreams."*

The figure of the Pesanta, like all Alp-type creatures, is related to a parasomnia called sleep paralysis. The victim awakens from sleep but cannot move. In this state, there is hyperacusis (hypersensitivity to outside noise) and hallucinations may be experienced. Different cultures give similar explanations for this phenomenon. Always there is an entity sitting on the chest exerting a heavy pressure; sometimes in the form of a *Hag*.

Pie-pie van-van

In northern France in the Valley of the river Meuse, in the vicinity of Braux and Sécheval, according to local lore, the marshes used to be infested with evil spirits or Goblins. The population called them *Pie-pie van-van*; these spirits watched for travelers at night and tried to lure them into the water to drown them. Afterwards, they would dance over their corpses, shouting *"drowned, drowned"*.

Pilous

Pilous or *Er-pilour-lann* are noisy entities, native to Brittany and Ile-et-Vilaine. They are probably some kind of *Lutins*, but lack any reliable description. They only get noticed because of their *poltergeist*-like behavior. Locals tell of their annoying habit of hammering at the walls of farm houses and barns. Pilous also make a strange noise as they walk. Their footsteps sound like apples being smashed on the floor. They manifest themselves at night, in the attics, in the rafters, in the walls, and begin to march, disturbing the sleep of the farmers and their family.

Prakagorri

Prakagorri is the Basque word for "red pants" and represents a demon of Basque mythology in Guipúzcoa and Vizcaya, just like *Galtzagorri*, which also means the one with "red pants".

Puigmal

In Catalan mythology, a *Puigmal* is considered the protector of trees and animals, who defends them against attacks from humans. He is said to inhabit the mountains overlooking the valley of Ribes (Ripollés).

Q

Quarantamaula

The *Quarantamaula* is a demonic creature and a type of *Bogey* from the folklore of Valencia that preys on children. It is also known as *Cucamaula, Quicamaula* and *Corantameula*. The creature slithered across the rooftops at night, looking for boys and girls, it pounded and made other terrifying noises. Especially at risk were the children who misbehaved and disobeyed. The demon threw stones at the houses where the children lived, so that the adults, hearing the noise, came out to see what was going on. At that moment, the Quarantamaula took the opportunity to come in and abducted the children who had misbehaved. If anyone heard the creature, he or she had to shout, "*La Quarantamaula!*". Then all activity ceased. Stores closed their doors and people stopped their daily work. They closed the doors and windows and hid in their houses, stiffened with fear when they heard the typical noise the Quarantamaula made, which sounded like heavy chains being dragged. Besides the pounding and chain clanking, you knew the Quarantamaula was nearby by the putrid smell of its breath. This was so toxic that the facades of houses rotted, iron objects rusted, and weeds invaded the streets and squares. When not sliding across rooftops in search for naughty children, the Quarantamaula mainly haunted the area around the towns of Tibi and Alicante, hiding among the reeds of the Tibi reservoir.

There are varying descriptions of the appearance of the Quarantamaula. Often the creature is described as a monster, part chicken and part human, with half of its body covered in feathers, long legs and a neck like that of a vulture. In other stories, the Quarantamaula is a witch who turned herself into a demonic black cat, the mere sight of which paralyzed people with terror; yet other sources speak of an innocent-looking but dangerous snail or a hairy, black demon. The creature allegedly keeps a fabulous treasure in its lair, which it has amassed over the years during its nocturnal raids.

Satyrs, unknown artist, dated second half of the 16th century

R

Ramidreju

In Calabrian folklore, the *Ramidreju* is a mythical creature, described as a hybrid of the *monuca galana* (weasel) and the *rámila* (marten), thin and long, with skin striped in black and green, with the face of a wild boar and yellow eyes. It was described by the Cantabrian writer Manuel Llano, according to an account in which he claims to have heard a neighbor from Viaña (Cabuérniga) talk about it. It is said that the Ramidreju is born every hundred years, digs deep tunnels, and that its gall – which is drunk by the *Anjanas* in the valley of Cieza – has the ability to cure all illnesses and reveal hidden treasures.

Rongeur d'Os

On mainland Normandy the *Rongeur d'Os* wanders the streets of Bayeux on winter nights as a phantom dog, gnawing on bones and dragging chains along with it.

S

Sarramauca

In in the folk-beliefs of Occitania and the Pyrenees a *Sarramauca* is a kind of female *Alp* or *Cauchemar*. The creature was a *Hag*-like figure who was dangerous to children. Sarramauca means in Occitan "tighten (the) chest (or the belly)". It is the equivalent of the *Chauchevieille* or *Caucavielha* that can be found as far away as Lyon, the *Pesadilla* of the Spanish Pyrenees, or a host of other Alp-like entities, whose characteristic is to intervene in sleep and provoke sensations of oppression and suffocation, of crushing, which can lead to death. The Sarramauca was often seen as the hidden cause of unexplained deaths of people, especially the deaths of children. The protection against Sarramauca or its equivalents was the same as that was used against witchcraft: prayers and formulas to recite, branches of fennel or hawthorn, etc. A legend says that a woman, tormented by the Sarramauca, imagined to protect herself by placing penches on her chest; carding combs with long sharp teeth. In the night, she heard a frightening voice shouting at her: *"What if I turn them over?"*, and after that she was pierced by her own combs. Several witchcraft trials have involved accusations of night-time suffocation, notably in Seix, in Couserans (Ariège).

Sarvanot

According to the folklore of the Northern Italian part of Occitania, in Piedmont, the *Sarvanot* lives in the woods and appears as a hybrid between a *Kobold* and a *Faun* or *Satyr*. It is a small hairy creature with goat-legs. Pretty harmless, although it likes to play small pranks when it enters houses. Local lore tells of trips to stables and houses, of stolen cream, of walnuts scattered on balconies at night, of salt exchanged for sugar, of braided ponytails and manes, of clothes scattered on the ground. These creatures have a fickle nature, sad with the sun, happy with the rain, sometimes spiteful, but never bad. They live in so called *barme*, natural shelters made up of protruding rocks.

Satyr

A *Satyr* (ancient Greek Σάτυρος *Sátyros*, pl. Σάτυροι *Sátyroi*; Latin *Satur*, *Saturus*) or *Silen* (Σιληνός, Σειληνός *Silēnós*, *Seilēnós*, pl. Σιληνοί, Σειληνοί *Silēnói*, *Seilēnói*, Doric Σιλανός *Silanós*; Latin *Silenus*, *Silanus*) is a playful and usually sexually aroused fertility daemon in the retinue of Dionysus in Greek mythology. Satyrs are among the hybrid beings of Greek mythology. They appear at the end of the 7th century BC as a single figure, and Silenos in particular stands out. A distinction is made between the Silene (*Silenoi*, older Satyrs with fat bellies and bald heads) and *Satyrisci* (Satyriskoi, juvenile and childlike Satyrs), although it is often not possible to make a clear distinction in pictorial representations. Roman poets identified them with the *Fauns*.

Little is known about the origin of the Satyrs; according to Hesiod they are descended from five daughters of Hekateros. They represented the male principle, opposite to the Nymphs. As similar nature-spirits, they bore attributes of the "all-god" Pan as well as some of Priapus. Their name meant "the full ones" in a dialect of ancient Peloponnesus, referring both to their physique and to their erotically aroused state. In most cases they are depicted with erect penises. Skilled occultists who invoke fertility entities, accompanied by an abnormal sexual state, sometimes see Satyr-like figures appear, with both human and animal features.

The Satyrs and Silenes are said to have fought as Dionysus' troops in the *Gigantomachy*, terrifying the giants with the braying of their donkeys. Otherwise, little is found in Greek mythology about the Satyrs as a whole, very little compared to their presence in art, especially vase painting. Some is found in relation to individual Satyrs, for example in the Dionysiaka, the great epic of Nonnos of Panopolis about the myths surrounding Dionysus, especially his campaign to India. Several Satyrs are mentioned by name, but these remain largely without contour and their names are mostly derived from epithets of Dionysus. Satyrs with whom separate myths are associated:

- *Ampelos*, lover of Dionysus, was killed by a bull and transformed into a vine by Dionysus.
- *Krotos*, inventor of the bow and clock generator in the singing of the Muses, was transferred to the sky as the constellation of Sagittarius.
- *Marsyas*, who lost a musical contest with Apollo, was flayed alive by the god for it.
- *Silenos*, leader of the chorus of Satyrs and Silenes in the Satyr play, educator of Dionysus.

Appearance

Usually Satyrs or Silenes are depicted snub-nosed, bald-headed, unclothed and ithyphallic (with erect penis). As hybrid beings, they are usually equipped with ears and tails of horses or donkeys, and often with animal extremities. Their pictorial representation begins in the 6th century BC in the vase painting of Attica, Crete and Thasos. As the retinue of Dionysus, they are often depicted with the Maenads, who also belong to the Dionysian retinue. In representations of the Archaic period they are equipped with horse or donkey features and are depicted only in connection with a few mythological motifs; with the development of the Satyr play they then increasingly appear in other contexts. They are also more humanized as inventors of viticulture and music and thus as bringers of culture, but nevertheless they always remain animalistic. They do not acquire their buck characteristics until Hellenism, probably under the influence of representations of the *Panes* and the *Paniskoi*, who appeared in the same role as the Satyrs. They appear sometimes with the *goblet*, sometimes in a bacchanalian frenzy with the *thyrsus* (a wand or staff, signifying prosperity, fertility and hedonism), sometimes devoted to sleep, sometimes drinking wine, also playing the flute or beating the cymbal, often united with the Nymphs in rapid dances or lustfully pursuing them.

Satyrs of the wilderness in the Book of Isaiah

In the Bible, Satyrs are creatures who express the soul of the wilderness. The word *Satyr* or *Satyrs* occurs twice in the King James version, both times in the *Book of Isaiah*. Isaiah, speaking of the fate of Babylon, says that:

> *"Wild beasts of the desert shall lie there; and their houses shall be full of doleful creatures; and owls shall dwell there, and satyrs shall dance there."*
> (Isa. 13:21; 2 Ne. 23:21)

In another passage about judgment against the wicked, we read:

> *"The wild beasts of the desert shall also meet with the wild beasts of the island, and the satyr shall cry to his fellow; the screech owl also shall rest there, and find for herself a place of rest."*
> (Isa. 34:14)

In his autobiographic story *Deep Water* (chapter: *The Night of Fear*), the Australian metaphysic Robert Bruce reports a solitary stay in the wilderness in order to get rid of an evil entity that tried to overtake him.

> *"And then came the spirits, dozens of them. First it was just ghostly faces and smokey trails, but soon I was able to see everything. These were not strictly human spirits. They were spirits native to this land. They were like big trails of glowing smoke with heads and faces, and sometimes chest and shoulders too. Some had aboriginal faces with beards, some were part human and part animal."*

Saurimonde

The story of the *Fée Saurimonde* is set near the river Arnette, below the village of Hautpoul, near the larger town of Mazamet in the Tarn department. The town is situated on a rocky peak overlooking the vast forests of the Montagne Noire mountain range. There are two versions of the story:

• First version

According to the first legend, on the banks of the Arnette lived an extraordinarily beautiful woman with long blond hair and her three-year-old daughter. Their refuge was a cave, a palace for them, at the foot of a waterfall, where they lived hidden from humans. The woman was in reality a Fée named Saurimonde. She kept away from the people because she did not like the inhabitants of the village, then a prosperous medieval town. The most obnoxious of these citizens was the leader of the archers, named Rivière, greedy, arrogant and insolent, who liked nothing better than to hunt. One day, as he was returning from one of these hunting parties, carrying a deer over his shoulders, he heard laughter coming from the river. As he approached, he saw the woman and her daughter, both naked on the river bank. The mother was trying to comb her daughter's hair with a large golden comb encrusted with precious stones. Rivière recognized the Fée Saurimonde, because the troubadours of Occitania sang of her in their songs. Her beauty did not interest him. He only desired the precious golden comb she possessed, *"a jewel of a queen, the work of the devil"*. He waited quietly, but when the sun set and they emerged from the water, he could not hold out any longer and prepared to seize the object. However, he stepped on a wobbly stone, which fell into the water, alerting the Saurimonde. The Fee then fled, with her child in her arms, into her cave. From that moment on, Rivière got possessed by the comb, and wanted nothing more than to own it. He even lost interest in hunting, and all the villagers saw that he had changed. So one evening, overcome with his desire, he ran to the waterfall, armed with his crossbow. When he got there, he discovered to his delight that the Fée was still there. Hidden away, he placed an arrow in the weapon and took aim at her. But he failed to hit his target, which had never happened to him before. Meanwhile, the naked woman mocked him, and he was forced to return to Hautpoul. He returned every night, but never succeeded in hitting the Fee, who seemed magically protected from all his efforts. Furious, he then decided to visit the priest of the church of Saint-Sauveur and convinced him that Saurimonde was a daughter of the devil. The cleric advised him to place a gold coin from the Count of Toulouse on his arrow before firing it at Saurimonde, for she, *"struck dead, will drop her jewel"*.

The next morning, at the first light of day, Rivière went to the waterfall with a determined step. There the Fee and her daughter, who had seen him, were already laughing at him. Without even taking time to aim, he fired, but did not hit the woman. However, he mortally wounded her little daughter. Saurimonde, mad with grief, took her child into the cave, dropped the golden comb, which disappeared into the waterfall. But before she crossed the threshold, she turned and cursed Rivière: *"Murderer, be cursed! You are a great river, but you will become a small stream!"* Then she disappeared forever. Rivière, the murderer, spent his days in the Arnette, searching for the precious comb, losing sleep, appetite and even his mind. His prosperous family languished and his name disappeared from the streets of Hautpoul. The curse of Saurimonde was a fact.

• Second version

Another version of the legend tells of a woman who could talk to birds and who combed her hair with a golden comb, using the Arnette as a mirror. One day, when she bent down too much, the comb fell from her hand and took some of her long blonde hairs with it. She was distraught by the loss and lay there crying for a long time. When she finally got up, she discovered to her surprise that the banks of the river were covered with houses: the city of Mazamet had appeared, the city that – after the comb slipped into the river – became very rich because of the textile industry that settled there on a large scale in the 19th century.

The historical background

This legend of Saurimonde shares many characteristics with other attractive *water* and *spring spirits* in European folklore. These elements seem to have blended with a story that took place after the Albigensian Crusade. A female Cathar preacher, fleeing persecution, took refuge in a cave near Hautpoul, with her child. She was then betrayed by a resident named Rivière, who wanted to obtain a reward. She was handed over to the Inquisition and died as a result of the torture inflicted on her. The people of Hautpoul, very sympathetic to Catharism, but oppressed by the Catholics in power, could not take revenge on Rivière. This is perhaps why this legend appeared, to keep the memory of the young woman alive and to take revenge on her traitor, who thus saw his name linked to a crime against a Fée. Moreover, the golden comb in the legend recalls the greed he showed in suing the Cathar woman in exchange for money.

Sbilfs

The *Sbilfs* are protagonists of many legends of Carnia, Northwest Italy. They are *Elves* of the woods, living in the undergrowth but in some cases also close to man, in stables and barns. Their favorite refuge remains the forest and in particular a hollow tree. They are said to be small in size, intelligent, elusive and often playful, but at the same time ready to help those in the woods who find themselves in difficulty. Sbilfs are eternally childlike, fond of games, dance and music. Although they have a very changeable character, they are generally not evil inclined. Sbilfs are very fond of the color red, so much so that many of them dress in clothes of this color. They also like *Zûf* (a local preparation of milk and cornmeal that was once used for breakfast). Sbilfs are known by different names, that are related to their pranks. Thus, there is the *Licj*, intent on knotting ropes and threads that it finds in the houses, or the *Brau*, who loves to unravel clothes and curtains. The *Bagan*, the *Elf* of the stable, who if annoyed, will knock over the buckets full of milk and hide the work tools. The *Maçarot*, very skilled at playing tricks. The *Maçarot* anticipates the prank with a hissing sound, then, once the prank is over, he wiggles into a shrill laugh. A particularly weird Sbilf is the *Massaroul*, who, although wearing red tights, cannot stand this color. In Forni di Sopra, the Maçarot is often accompanied by his wife, *Ridùsela*, who is also intent on playing mischievous pranks. In Gemona, on the other hand, there is the *Pamarindo*, always intent on blocking the passage by widening itself out of proportion. Then there is the *Boborosso*, one of the baddest, absorbed in causing nightmares to children. The area of Paularo would be instead inhabited by the *Guriùz*. These ones, particularly pranksters and greedy, are often intent on stealing sweets and delicacies from the kitchens. A legend speaks, however, of their extinction. The Guriùz are said to have built a half-buried castle in which they hid an enormous treasure. Attacked by a foreign army, they were all killed. The hiding place was never detected and the treasure was never found.

Sèrvan

The *Sèrvan* is, in Alpine folklore, a beneficial *Goblin*, protector of livestock and the home. He is known throughout the Alps, including the Pays de Vaud, Dauphiné, Bugey, Savoie, Haute-Savoie, Bauges, and the Chambéry region, where this belief is almost as widespread as that of the *Fées*. Folklorist Pierre Dubois attributes to them a height of 25-35 centimeters, blond curly hair and a swarthy complexion. They would be dressed in a green shirt, an embroidered flowered vest and leather breeches, with a knitted cap. The *Sèrvans* were fond of haylofts, hollowed-out tree stumps and rocks, and would feed on soup, bread, cheese, butter and milk donated by the inhabitants in exchange for his services. In nineteenth century Switzerland, where the Sèrvans were attached to the guarding of the herds, the shepherds still offered them a libation of milk.

Sgranf

A Bergamasque *Folletto* called *Sgranf* has, besides playing all kinds of tricks (such as overturning the milk pan), the strange characteristic of having libertine and a bit frivolous interests. In Bergamo dialect the term *sgranf* means "cramp", but in this case the association with the name of the creature is improbable. More likely his name is derived from the Bergamasque term, *sgrafe* which means "claws"; in fact the verb *sgrafà* means "to scratch", a physical characteristic that would denote its limbs. In Valtellina one of the nicknames given to the Folletto is *Sgriful*, a term that would denote the same characteristic. The Sgranf is a voyeur, who loves to spy on beautiful women while they bathe or undress themselves or have other intimate moments. Very often, taking advantage of its tiny size, it curls up on itself and hides under the skirts to watch the legs of unsuspecting unfortunate girls, and if it is irritated it ruins their stockings by scratching them. In order to spy even better on the girls, he may also turn himself into a little ball of wool to let himself be picked up and carried in the cleavage. Only then does he moan with pleasure. Other times he takes advantage of the darkness and the sleep of attractive girls to get into their beds and grope them. If he falls in love with a girl, he becomes very jealous, and sometimes moves the clothes of the "beloved" from one room to another insinuating suspicion and creating dark situations. In a strange way he can also be a faithful friend of the person he cares the most about, and warns this person in case of imminent danger.

Silvanus

Silvanus or *Sylvanus* (of the forest) was originally a *Genius loci.* The Tyrrhenian Pelasgians are said to have dedicated a forest and a festival to him in ancient times. In Roman folk mythology Silvanus becomes a guardian spirit and fertility god of fields, forests and cattle. On the one hand, like *Faunus*, he was a good god, but sometimes he manifested himself as a haunting demon, who uttered his terrifying screams from the forest and who was especially feared by childbearing women. He is said to have taken most of his characteristics from the Etruscan deity *Selvans*. The Celtic god *Sucellos* was equated with Silvanus, and the Slavic god *Borevit* bore resemblances to him. The Pyrenean apparition *Tantugou* is also regarded as a Silvan and later spin-off of Silvanus. Silvanus was usually depicted as an aged man with a rough and peasant appearance. In his hand he carried as a club a pine tree, which he had pulled out of the ground by its roots, an image that resembles the medieval *Wilder Mann* (Woodwose) of Germany. Sometimes he was also depicted as a gardener or with the same appearance as the god *Pan*, including the goat feet. In Latin poetry, but also in artistic works, he often appears as an old but cheerful man in love with *Pomona*, the goddess of fruit trees, and later more specifically of apples. The offerings brought to Silvanus consisted of grapes, ears of corn, milk, meat, wine and pigs, especially wild boar, which were often responsible for ruining the fields. Silvanus watched over these fields and farmers in general, and was also considered a protector of field borders and gardens. Hyginius Gromasticus relates that *Silvanus* was the first to place stones to mark the boundaries of fields and that he manifested himself in three forms:

- *Silvanus domesticus,* a domestic god, in inscriptions also called *Silvanus Larum* and *Silvanus sanctus sacer Larum*,
- *Silvanus agrestis*, also called *Silvanus salutaris*, who was worshipped by the shepherds, and
- *Silvanus orientalis*, a border god in the narrower sense of the word, to whom one dedicated a private forest at the place which constituted the division between different properties.

Therefore, instead of one Silvanus, there was often talk of several *Silvani*. In connection with the forests (as *Sylvestris deus*) he was especially lord and master of the plantations. In Rome itself, too, he was worshiped as a forest god. There, the parks and gardens of the emperors and wealthy Romans were especially hallowed to him. Silvanus loved the wild trees, hence he is depicted carrying the trunk of a cypress (δενδροφόρος, *Tree bearer*).

The following story is told about the cypress: On the island of Keos lived youth named Kyparissos (Lat. Cyparissus) who was a lover of Silvanus, or according to other sources, of the god *Apollo*. The best known lore of the myth was recorded by P. Ovidius Naso. He describes the special bond of Kyparissos with a mythical deer, living in the forests around Cartheia. The animal is tame and Kyparissos is very fond of him. One afternoon, the boy is hunting and throws his spear at a deer that is resting in the shady foliage. It turns out to be his favorite deer. Kyparissos, despite Apollo's numerous attempts, is inconsolable and begs the god to let him grieve forever. Apollo thereupon painfully transforms him into a cypress tree, the symbol of mourning.

Silvanus is the protector of herds of cattle, which he guards against wolves and whose fertility he promotes. He also loves music: the syringa was dedicated to him and he is mentioned along with the Pans and the Nymphs. Later people therefore identify Silvanus with Pan, Faunus, Inuus and Egipan. Cato the Elder calls him *Mars Silvanus*, so it is clear that he must have been related to the Italian *Mars*. Not in the context of war, but that of manhood, because it was also stated that his relationship to agriculture involved only the labor performed by men, excluding women from his cult. In *De agri cultura* of Cato the Elder, a sacrifice to Mars Silvanus is described, to ensure the health of livestock.

Simeot

A *Simiot* is, in Pyrenean and Catalan mythology, a devilish creature resembling an ape, known mainly around Arles-sur-Tech, in Vallespir, as well as in Haut Ampurdan. Traditionally, the descriptions are not very detailed and leave much to the imagination. Folklorist Joan Amades stated that Simiots are a kind of *Satyrs*, who would have lived in Llivia, in Cerdanya. In any case, the Simiots seem related to the *Wild Men* and the many versions that exist of them in European folklore from forested and mountainous regions – demonized by Christianity and gradually downgraded to a *Bogeyman* to scare children. In the carnival of Arles, the character of the hunted bear is still called Simiot.

Sirens

In Greek mythology, the *Sirens* (Ancient Greek: sing.: Σειρήν, Seirên; pl.: Σειρῆνες, Seirênes) were dangerous creatures, who evolved from winged daemons, thus aerial beings, into the later concept of the Siren or *Mermaid*. These creatures, half woman half fish, lured nearby sailors with their enchanting music and singing voices to shipwreck on the rocky coast of their island. It was also believed that they could even charm the winds. Roman poets placed them on some small islands called *Sirenum scopuli*. Cape Pelorum and the islands known as the Sirenuse, near Paestum, or in Capreae, were believed to be the home of the Sirens. All such locations are surrounded by cliffs and rocks. Etymologically most experts believe the origin of the word *Seirên* comes from a connection of σειρά (*seirá*, rope, cord) and εἴρω (*eírō*, to tie, join, fasten), resulting in the meaning "binder, entangler", interpreting Seirên further as one who binds or entangles through magic song. This could be connected to the famous scene of Odysseus being bound to the mast of his ship, in order to resist their singing. The English word "siren", of course refers to a noise-making device, derived from the same name.

From bird-woman to fish-woman

Sirens were believed to look like a combination of women and birds in various different forms. In early Greek art, they were represented as birds with a large women's head, bird feathers and scaly feet. Later, they were represented as female figures with the legs of birds, with or without wings, playing a variety of musical instruments, especially harps and lyres. Originally, Sirens were depicted as male or female, but the male Siren disappeared from art around the 5th century BC. In the later Middle Ages, the figure of the Siren definitely transformed into the *Mermaid* figures as we still know them today. The 10th century Byzantine encyclopedia *Suda* still says that from their chests up, sirens had the form of sparrows, and below they were women or, alternatively, that they were little birds with women's faces. In the Renaissance Leonardo da Vinci wrote, "*The siren sings so sweetly that she lulls the mariners to sleep; then she climbs upon the ships and kills the sleeping mariners*". The 7th century Anglo-Latin catalogue *Liber Monstrorum* says that Sirens were women from their heads down to their navels, and that instead of legs they had fish tails.

Number and names of Sirens

Sources differ about their number and names. A marginal note in the Odyssey points out that there are four different Sirens whose names he gives:

- *Aglaophemis* (Ἀγλαοφήμη / Aglaophḗmê – she of brilliant reputation),
- *lxiepie* (Θελξιέπεια / Thelxiepeia – she who meditates through epic song),

- *Pisinoé* (Πεισινόη / Peisinóê – she who persuades), and
- *Ligia* (Λιγεία / Ligeía – she of the shrill cry).

For Apollodorus, the Sirens are three and are called *Pisinoé*, *Aglaopé*, *Thelxiépie*. Other names are given in the sources, and they always refer to the feminine power of the Sirens:

- *Aglaophonos* (Ἀγλαοφώνος / Aglaophṓnos – the one with a beautiful voice),
- *Aglaopé* (Αγλαόπη / Aglaópê – the one with a beautiful face),
- *Thelxinoé* (Θελξινόη / Thelxinóê – the one who enchants);
- *Thelxiope* (Θελξιόπη / Thelxiópê – she who meditates by speech),
- *Molpé* (Μόλπη / Mólpê – the musician),
- *Raidné* (the friend of progress),
- *Télès* (the perfect one).

Another tradition followed by Apollonius of Rhodes, Lycophron or Strabo, considers the Sirens to be three and their names are *Leucosia* (Λευκωσία / Leukôsía – the white creature), *Ligia* and *Parthenope* (Παρθενόπη / Parthenópê – the one with a maiden face). Traditionally, there are three of them: one plays the lyre, another the flute, and the third sings.

Sorginak

In Basque folklore there exists an interchangeability between human and demon concerning the Basque witches or *Sorginak* (sing.: Sorgin; *Bruja(s)* in Spanish). The Sorginak were regarded as neither pure human, nor spirit, as is often the case in European folklore, as witches (and sorcerers and shamans) usually practiced astral traveling or the projection of their etheric doubles, the latter being perceived by the more mediumistic and sensitive people as spirits or demons. The term Sorginak was also used for the servants of the goddess Mari and for demons that could turn normal women into witches. To make it even more complex, sometimes Sorginak are confused with the *Nymph*-like *Lamiak* or even the *Jentilak*, who according to tradition built the local megaliths. In time, the usage of the term Sorginak for a human witch prevailed.

Sorsain

Sorsain is a Basque word, meaning “Sorgin who watches” in Basque mythology. It is the Sorgin (witch) who is waiting for a birth, in order to kill the child. In Soule she is called *Belagile*.

Sottai or Sotré

The *Sottai* or *Sotré* is a small legendary creature from Ardennes and Vosges folklore, brother of the Walloon *Nuton* and comparable to the French *Lutin*. This small whirling or swirling creature, which probably appeared somewhere between the 10th and 12th centuries, can help a household with routine work, do ordinary household chores like repairing things that are damaged, and perform an exceptionally good cleaning job in the house or stables. The Sottai can also help with the milking of cows or feeding domestic animals that have been temporarily abandoned. Originally these creatures live in caves, depending on the version, alone or in a group. According to the local population, if you see him, you must not make fun of his physical characteristics or incongruous clothing. He is on the other hand sensitive to compliments, but never in a direct way. His emblem is the wheel or the spinning wheel. The appearance of the Sottai differs according to each county or region.

Etymology and terminology

The Sottai fuses the qualities of a classical *household-spirit*, of which there are many European variations, with the traditional field-spirits that move like small whirlwinds, yet the etymology and terminology is even more interesting. Whether it is called *Sottai*, *Sotê*, *Massotê*, *Sotay* or *Sotré*, *Sotrê*, *Satré*, *Soltrait*, *Sotret*, *Sotreut*, *Sottrait*, *Sottré*, *Soutrait*, *Souttré*, all these names come from the Greek *Satyr*. It is known of the Walloons that they worshipped the god Pan (the chief of all Satyrs). A small Walloon statue of the god was discovered in the Black Forest region. The Walloons are mainly a mixture of Celtic and Italo-Greek/Etruscan ancestry, which probably explains the Sottai as a derivate of the classical Mediterranean Satyr to the regions of the Vosges and Ardennes. The Walloon language of the Liège region most often calls it Sotê, the variant *Massotê* being specific to the Haute-Ardenne region as in La Gleize or Grand-Halleux. This name comes from the Liège pronunciation of the Walloon *Sotea*, which could etymologically mean *little fool* – comparable to the Dutch-Flemisch word *zot*, derived from the French *sot*, also meaning *fool*, *silly*, *stupid* or *weird*. Of the extremely variable spelling, the version Sotré (or Sotrê, Sotret, Souttré, Soltrait) comes from the Vosges region. In Champagne, the name used is Sotrê. It was also called *spin* or *spinule* (small wheel or living wheel), being a creature that moved in a spinning or cyclonic way, as small turbulence, whirlpool or winding current. In the Vosges, the expression *"voilà le sotré"* refers to the little whirlwinds in the field, the

Sylvanus (1565) by Cornelis Cort(1533-1578) after Frans Floris I

swirling currents in the river, or even to little tornadoes. *Saint Spinule* is the patron saint of the funeral church of the counts of Vaudémont in Lorraine.

Squàsc

The *Squasc* (also: *Squass*, *Squàs*, *Quagg*) is a mythological being from the folklore of eastern Lombardy, Italy. It is said to be a small, hairy, tawny being, similar to a squirrel without a tail, but with an anthropomorphic face. Its function lies somewhere between that of an evil spirit (equate to the *Bogeyman*) and an *Elf*. He is called upon to scare children, while lore also has it that he likes to play pranks and all kinds of practical jokes on adults, with a certain predilection for young women and girls.

Strix

The *Strix* (from Greek στρίγξ / *strígx* – night bird; also στριγός; pl.: *Striges* or *Strixes*; Latin: *Striga* with the plural *Strigae*), are winged female demons, half-woman, half-bird, that utter piercing cries. The Strix was a creature of ill omen, the product of metamorphosis, that fed on human flesh and blood. It also referred to witches and other related malevolent folkloric beings. In Ovid's *Fasti* the Strix is described as a large-headed bird with transfixed eyes, rapacious beak, grayish white wings, and hooked claws. This is the only thorough description of the Strix in Classical literature. Elsewhere, it is mostly described as simply being dark-colored. It was a nocturnally crying creature which – while flying – positioned its feet upwards and head below, according to a pre-300 BC Greek origin myth (Antoninus Liberalis, *Μεταμορφώσεων Συναγωγή*). It is probably meant to be (and translated as) an *owl*, but is also highly suggestive of a *bat*, which hangs upside-down. Striges are also associated with cemeteries. Despite this, the most endurable animal association remains the owl. There are even several examples of the Strix's plumage, etc., said to be used as an ingredient in magic. Propertius, and his contemporary Horace, wrote in his *Epodes* that the Strix's feathers are an ingredient in a love potion. Medea's rejuvenating concoction which she boiled in a cauldron, used a long list of ingredients, including the Strix's wings. Striges also came to mean "witches". One paper speculates that this meaning is as old as the 4th century BC, on the basis that in the origin myth of Boios, various names can be connected to the Macedonian/Thracian region, well known for witches. But more concrete examples occur in Ovid's *Fasti* (early 1st century AD) where the Striges as transformations of Hags is offered as one possible explanation, and Sextus Pompeius Festus (late 2nd century) glossed as *maleficis mulieribus* (women who practice witchcraft) or "flying women" (witches by transference).

The Strix in later folklore became a bird which squirted milk upon the lips of (human) infants. Pliny, in his *Naturalis Historia*, dismissed this folk-assumption as nonsense and remarked it was impossible to establish what bird was meant by this. However, the same habit, where the Strix lactates foul-smelling milk onto an infant's lips is mentioned by Titinius, who noted the placement of garlic on the infant was the prescribed amulet to ward against it. In the case of "Ovid's Striges", they were also said to disembowel an infant and feed on its blood. Ovid allows the possibilities of the Striges being birds of nature, or products of magic, or transformations by witches using magical incantations. The goddess *Carna*, who watched over the hinges of the doors of the houses, had the function of removing these monsters through magical incantations. The word "strige" was also used as an insult in the Roman world. Among the pre-Islamic Arabs, the Stryge is called *Goule* or *Ghole* and feeds on the corrupting flesh of corpses.

Writers of Antiquity on the Strix

According to Antoninus Liberalis, the Strīx was a metamorphosis of *Polyphonte*; she and her bear-like sons *Agrios* and *Oreios* were transformed into birds as punishment for their cannibalism. Here the Strix is described as (a bird) *"that cries by night, without food or drink, with head below and tips of feet above, a harbinger of war and civil strife to men"*. This tale only survived in the form as recorded by Antonius who flourished in 100-300 AD, but it preserved an older tale from the lost *Ornithologia* by Boios, dated to before the end of 4th century BC. In this Greek myth, the ill-omened Strix herself did not perpetrate harm on humans. But according to Samuel Grant Oliphant (in *The Story of the Strix*, 1913) one paper suggests guilt by association with her sons, and seeks to reconstruct an ancient Greek belief in the man-eating Strix dating back to this age (4th century BC). In an opposing view, one study failed to find the ancient Greeks subscribing to the Strix as a "terror" to mankind, but noted a widespread belief in Italy that it was a *"bloodthirsty monster in bird form"*. The first Latin allusion is in Plautus' comedy *Pseudolus*, dated to 191 BC, in which an inferior cook's cuisine is metaphorized as the Striges (vampyre owls) devouring the diners' gastrointestinal organs while still alive, and shortening their lifespan. Commentators point to this as attestation that the Striges were regarded as man-eating. Petronius' novel *Satyricon* (late 1st century AD) includes a tale told by the character Trimalchio, describing the Striges that snatched away the body of a boy who had already died, substituting his body for a straw doll. The Striges made their presence known by their scream, and a manservant attending to the intrusion, discovered a woman and ran her through with a sword so that she groaned, but his whole body turned livid and would die a few days later. Seneca the Younger's links the Strix to the Underworld. In his tragedy *Hercules Furens* there are Striges, vultures, and bubo owls which cry in the marshes in Hades, by the edge of Tartarus. Also, according to the legend of Otus and Ephialtes, they were punished in Hades by being tied to a pillar with snakes, with a Strix perched on that column.

Becoming a demon and Vampire

The legend of the Strix survived into the Middle Ages, as recorded in Isidore's *Etymologiae*. In the 7th-8th century John of Damascus equated the *Stiriges* (Greek pl.: Greek: στρίγγαι, Στρῦγγαι) with the *Gelloudes* (plural of *Gelllo*) in his entry *Perī Stryggōn*, Greek: περί Στρυγγῶν). He wrote that they sometimes had corporeal bodies and wore clothing, and sometimes appeared as spirits. In the era after the discovery of the vampire bats of America, the term *Stryge* of Greco-Latin origin tends to be supplanted by the term *Vampire* of Slavic origin. The dictionaries of the time established an equivalence between the terms. *Strygians* were believed to mainly attack newborns, either sucking their blood or grabbing the babies with their sharp claws and kidnapping them, and therefore they are often confused with Vampires. After the publication of Augustin Calmet's *Traité sur les vampires* (1746), which introduced these creatures to the French-speaking world, the third edition of the *Dictionnaire de Trévoux*, published in 1752, referred to the word "stryge" to explain the concept of *Vampire* to the French reader. At that time, in Russia, the term *Stryge* referred to dead people whose soul or astral body remained visible after their death. The Saxons were convinced that Stryges ate or sucked the blood of the living; and that to preserve themselves from them it was necessary to burn those they had caught, and eat their flesh.

Sugaar

Sugaar (also: *Sugar*, *Sugoi*, *Maju* or *Suar*) is a pre-Christian god or nature-daemon in Basque mythology, associated with storms and lightning. He is the husband of goddess Mari and usually represented by a dragon or snake. The essence of his existence is to periodically join Mari in the mountains (on Fridays, at two o'clock in the afternoon, to be precise), in order to generate storms. The name Sugaar or Sugar seems to derive from the combination of the words *suge* (snake) and *ar* (male), therefore meaning "male snake". However, it can also be formed by an agglutination of the words *su* (fire) + *gar* (flame). Sugoi, another name of the deity, has the same dual interpretation: either from *suge* and *oi* (old snake) or *su* and *goi* (high fire). In Ataun, he is described as living in the cellars of Amunda and Atarreta. It is said that he was seen crossing the sky in the form of a fire, which is considered to be a sign of storms. In the same area it is also said that Sugaar punishes children who disobey their parents. In Azkoitia, Sugaar met Mari on Fridays (the day of Akelarre or the Sabbath), designing the storms. In Betelu, he is known as *Suarra* and considered a demon. It is said there that he travels through the sky in the form of a fireball, between the Balerdi and Elortalde mountains.

T

Tantugou

Tantugou is a character from Pyrenean folklore. He is said to live in the valleys of Comminges near Luchon (Haute-Garonne), the valleys of Larboust and Oueil, and in the valleys of Aure and Louron. Tantugou appears as a tall, bearded old man, dressed in a hooded tunic, sometimes in animal skins and armed with a club, much like his counterpart beyond the Spanish border, the Aragonese *Silvan.* His role is to ensure the continuity of pastoral and agricultural life, he watches over the harvests and the flocks. Sometimes he sleeps on a rock not far from a herd, hunting thieves or defending the cattle against predators. He knows all the secrets of nature. He is therefore one of the avatars of the Roman *Silvanus*, but he is also associated with the Gallic god *Sucellos.* Tantugou rarely shows himself to people who respect and fear him, and there is no evidence of any malice on his part. However – most likely due to Christian demonization politics – he evolved into a *Bogeyman* who would threaten children. Since then, Tantugou is said to prowl around the lakes of Nère in the Val d'Aube, grabbing children who come to fish there, taking them to his cave and devouring them. Tantugou is known from the great survey of linguistics and toponymy in the Pyrenees made by the scholar Julien Sacaze (1847-1889) in 1887. Sacaze writes of the wife of one *Sajous de Jurvielle*, whom Tantugou saw for three consecutive days in the woods of Trémesehoues, and that he himself spoke to her. He also mentions a shepherd from Gouaux, who had fallen asleep while herding his sheep. When he awoke, he saw Tantugou fleeing in the direction of the forest.

Tarasque

The *Tarasque*, a strange kind of amphibious dragon with red eyes and rotten breath, is a creature of Provençal folklore. It lived on the rock where the castle of Tarascon was built, and haunted the marshes near Tarascon. The monster lurked on travelers crossing the Rhone, to feed on them and cause terror in Tarascon. It had six short legs like those of a bear, a torso like that of an ox, covered with a tortoise shell and fitted with a scaly tail ending in a scorpion-sting. The head was described as a lion's head with horse ears and the face of an old man. Jacques de Voragine describes the Tarasque in *la Légende Dorée* (the Golden Legend), which he wrote between 1261-1266, as follows:

> *"At that time, on the banks of the Rhone, in a marsh between Arles and Avignon, there was a dragon, half animal, half fish, fatter than an ox, longer than a horse, with teeth equal to swords and as large as horns. It hid in the river from where it took the life of all the passers-by and sank the ships."*

The Tarasque of Tarascon was included in the *Inventaire du patrimoine culturel immatériel en France* (Inventory of Intangible Cultural Heritage in France) in 2019. Since November 25, 2005, the Tarasque festivals in Tarascon had already been declared by UNESCO as part of the oral and intangible heritage of humanity.

Tartaro

Tartaro (in unified Basque, *Tartalo*) is a character from Basque mythology who is a Cyclops. Tartaro is the name that is most known at the moment, but, according to different times and places, he was/is also known as *Torto* or *Tartalo*. Torto, *Anxo* and *Alarabi* were the forms listed in Jose Migel Barandiaran's *Basque Mythology*, with "Tartalo" described as a local variant particular to the Zegama region. Anxo or *Ancho* is by some sources however explained as an alternate name for *Basajaun*. Folklorist Jean-François Cerquand (1816-1888) mentiones the form *Tartare*. According to the legends, Tartaro is an enormously strong one-eyed giant, very similar to the Greek Cyclops that Ulysses faced in Homer's *Odyssey*. He is said to live in caves in the mountains and catches young people in order to eat them; in some accounts he eats sheep also, and in one oral account, Tartaro ate one whole sheep each day. The origin of the name Tartaro and its variants is unknown. While it has remained specific to the Basque tradition, it is not certain that it is of Basque origin, and it has probably exceeded the current geographical limits of this area. A character called *Tartari* was attested beyond Gascony, on the right bank of the Garonne, in the Agenais region. Tartari is always described as an *Ogre* or at least an evil character. There was even a saying that said *"bad as Tartari"*. In some tales, the Ogre's wife is called *Tartarino*. Many places in the Basque mountains attest to Tartaro's habitation, for example *Tartaloetxeta*.

The Polyphemus-theme

The characteristics and adventures attributed to Tartaro correspond quite closely to those of the Cyclops *Polyphemus*. Like him, he lives in a cave, raises sheep, and eats the men he can catch, until the day one of the prisoners escapes by gouging Tartaro's eye and hiding among his sheep. The motif of the hero blinding Tartaro has both a classical and a Celtic (Irish) parallel: Odysseus blinding the Cyclops Polyphemus in Homer's *Odyssey*, and *Lug* hurling a spear into the eye of *Balor*. Basque tradition usually opposes him to a boy called *Mattin Ttipi* (Little Martin), or *Mattin Txirula* (Martin the flute player), often considered a fool, but whose actions contradict this.

Tchén al tchinne

In Wallonia, the southern region of Belgium, folktales mentioned the *Tchén al tchinne* (Chained Hound – in Walloon), a hellish dog, bound with a long chain, that was thought to roam in the fields at night.

Telchines

On Rhodes, *Telchines* or *Rhodian Dactyls* were the names given to chthonic spirit-men, nine in number, remembered by Greeks as dangerous Underworld smiths and magicians, and multiplied into an entire autochthonous race, that had reared Poseidon, but had been supplanted by Apollo in his Helios role. In Greek mythology, the Telchines (Ancient Greek: Τελχῖνες, *Telkhines*) were the original inhabitants of the island of Rhodes and were known in Crete and Cyprus. They were regarded as the cultivators of the soil and ministers of the gods and as such they came from Crete to Cyprus and from thence to Rhodes. By some accounts, their children were highly worshiped as gods in the ancient Rhodian towns of Cameirus, Ialysos, and Lindos.

Demons

The Telchines were also regarded as wizards and envious demons. Their very eyes and aspect were said to have been destructive. They had it in their power to bring on hail, rain, and snow, and to assume any form they pleased; they further produced a substance poisonous to living things. Thus, they were called *Alastores* for supervising the ceaseless wanderings of people, and Palamnaioi for pouring the water of the river Styx with their bare hands in order to make the fields infertile. The Telchines were described to have stings and as being rough as the echinoid (sea urchin), and thus their name *Teliochinous*, meaning: *"having a poisonous telos* (here: sting) *like an echinoid"*.

Tentirujo

In the Spanish folklore of Cantabria, *Tentirujus* (plural) are small malignant *Duendes*, or *Goblins*, with long hands and a brownish skin, pointed ears, dressed in red with a beret on their head. The *Tentirujo* lives in the basins of the rivers Saja and Besaya. His main mission, in a state of invisibility, is to pervert lonely, obedient and good young women by means of caresses that he performs with the help of a human-shaped root of a young mandrake plant, with which he always accompanies himself when he goes out to carry out his misdeeds. The woman who goes through this trance, wakes up very horny and wants to orgasm. He also drastically changes her behavior, as she may go from being solitary, introvert or even depressed to cheerful and passionate. Tentirujo is sometimes seen as a creature related to the Hebrew she-devil of lust *Masabakes* and it is even believed that she is the one who indicates the place where he should act, helping him, even transporting him to that place. Thus, when a young woman becomes shameless overnight, it is said: "*¡Esa ya tropezó con el Tentirujo!*" (That one has already stumbled upon the Tentirujo!).

Tourmentine

La Tourmentine (the Tormentor) is the daughter of the *Nympf of the Nettle* and also known as *The Grass of Distraction* in French folklore. She manifests herself as grass or a herb that causes the bewilderment of anyone who steps on it. The victim could then circle around for hours, unable to find his way back home. Pierre Dubois has described La Tourmentine as a kind of *Pixie*.

Tramontino

The *Tramontino* (pl.: *Tramontini*) is a legendary creature belonging to the popular tradition of the Upper Valdarno, in central-eastern Tuscany, generally described as a tiny being of anthropomorphic appearance, equipped with insect wings and animated by a malevolent intent. However, the sources do not all agree on the appearance of the Tramontini, often described as a tiny hairless humanoid with membranous wings and armed with long sharp knives, while elsewhere – while maintaining the same appearance and size – they are described as equipped with an abdominal protrusion, similar to the belly of an hymenoptera (class of stinging insects, like bees, wasps etc.), from which protrudes a sharp stinger. Unlike the common *Goblins*, believed to be able to sometimes work for the welfare of man, the Tramontini are generally malevolent, openly opposing the people and their activities in rural areas, especially if operated during the hours of sunset, when the Tramontini are said to abandon their homes to devote themselves to their specific favorite pastimes.

Tranganarru

In Basque folklore *Tranganarru* is the *Irelu* of the waterspouts – especially in Busturialdea – which have caused dread in ancient times to the men of the sea.

Trasgo

The *Trasgo*, *Trasno* or *Trasgu* is a *Duende*, typical of the classical mythology of northern Spain. From the Latin *transgredī* (he who transgresses, he who breaks the law) he is called *Trasgo*, *Trasno* or *Tardo* in Galicia; *Trasgu*, *Cornín* or *Xuan dos Caminos*, *Pisadiel el de la Mano Furada*, *Gorretín Coloráu*, *El de la Gorra Encarnada* or *Sumiciu* in Asturias, León, Cantabria and Eastern Galicia; *Trasgo* or *Martinico* in Castile and León; *Strago* or *Demonio da mano furada* in Portugal. In Spain Trasgos are among the most hated *Duendes*. They are mischievous creatures. They love to enter people's homes through chimneys and live within the hidden spaces of a home. They move things around, or right out steal things from the homes they inhabit so they are never to be found again by the humans who owned them. They love to climb up trees and throw pebbles, seeds and branches at people. They may turn good human boys into mischievous ones. Boys who are improperly raised may even become Trasgos themselves. A special feature of the Trasgo is his ability of causing absent-mindedness and is he also associated with the disappearance of indispensable objects. They are mischievous and sometimes malevolent creatures, destroying household goods or deceiving humans. At night they make noises, or do other mischief such as moving objects around. When the Trasgo is in a bad mood, he breaks pots, chases cattle away, scrambles clothes, messes with water, or ruffles the hair of sleeping housemates. Presumably, it momentarily disappears when religious invocations are made, sometimes a: "*¡Jesús!, ¡Virgen Santa!*" or "*¡Dios Mío!*" (Jesus Christ!, Holy Virgin! or My God!) is enough, but it is very difficult to get rid of it definitively, as the Trasgo almost always accompanies the family in the move. They usually announce themselves by saying: "*Yo también ando de casa mudada*" (I'm also moving house).

The Trasgo is usually represented as humanoid; a familiar *Goblin*, small or totally invisible, who lives in the home; generally represented with a dark complexion, wearing a blouse and a red beaked cap. He has a hole in his left hand. He is described at times as having horns, a tail, sheep ears and long legs, and wearing a long black and gray cloak; at other times he is described as small, with long thin legs and wearing a tight dark brown dress. It is a restless, mischievous and playful creature. Sometimes it has a lame right leg. Especially in Asturian mythology the Trasgu is often represented as a tiny man who limps with his right leg. In Cantabria, the Trasgo is a small Goblin with a black face and green eyes that inhabits forests. His main activity is to mock people and carry out pranks, especially against girls who are engaged in a specific activity, like sheepherding. Because he must hide from humans, his clothes are made of tree leaves and moss. In Galicia the *Trasno* (the term is probably derived from the Latin *trans gradi*, meaning "on the other side of the pass", dwells in the home and is dedicated to playing practical jokes. He is said to be a mischievous and bouncy dwarf with brown skin and a beard. He wears red, is lame and has a hole in his left hand. He is active at night inside houses. He throws the dishes around, shuffles the clothes, frightens the cattle in the stable, makes noises in the attic. During the day it disappears. In Galicia it is very typical to call children "Trasnos" when they are very restless or unruly. It is also a term applied to those who walk alone on the roads or in the woods.

In order get rid of a Trasgo it is necessary to request of him an impossible task, like bringing a basket of water from the sea, picking up millet from the floor (it falls through the hole in his hand) and whitening a black sheep. Because he thinks himself capable of doing anything, he accepts the challenge. In his stubbornness, he will try until he becomes exhausted. When he fails to accomplish the tasks, his pride is hurt. He leaves and does not return.

Trastolillos

The Trastolillos are small *Duendes* that live in the dwellings of man. They make wheat flour in troughs bloom back into wheat, forcing farmers to remill them into flour. They love to drink milk and will drink all the stores of milk. They also open windows during windy storms and cause stews to overcook and burn. They will apologize for the damage they have done, but cannot help themselves and will do it again.

Trenti

In Cantabrian folklore the *Trentis* (plural) are small mischievous *Duendes* or *Goblins* of the forests. They either made up of – or clothed in – leaves, moss, roots and twigs. Trentis hide in the bushes or behind trees so they can pull the girls' skirts, pinch their calves and buttocks, and then escape by running back into the bushes. Although they are pranksters, they can also help people without their knowledge and they are especially fond of children. They help the shepherd find his cattle after a storm or when the cattle is chased away by the *Ojáncanu* and assist old women who can no longer fend for themselves. During the winter, the Tendris sleeps in the shelter of the torcas (natural sink holes) and in summer under the coolness of the trees. It feeds on panicles and blackthorn berries (sloes), but it never drinks water, as it is poison for it.

Tronantes

In Spanish folklore the *Tronantes* (Thunderers) are weather-spirits or weather-Duendes. They are related to storm-elementals in the occult tradition and have the ability to create thunder and lightning.

Truffandec

The *Truffandec* (from: *truffar* "joke", "laugh") is a *Lutin* in the folklore of Béarn, one of the traditional provinces of France, located in the mountains of the Pyrenees and in the plain at their feet, in southwestern France. Truffandec has two aspects: on the one hand, he is a benevolent household-spirit like those found throughout Europe and beyond. On the other hand, he is considered a prankster, stealing things from houses, especially kitchen utensils from the hostess. In particular, he is held responsible for bad batches of bread. He imitated the voice of the village baker (nicknamed: *Pan-Coque*) to encourage the inhabitants to put their dough in the village oven that was not hot enough, thus ruining the dough beyond repair. To prevent these unfortunate incidents, the housewives recited an incantation against Truffandec the day before:

"A la boutz soule de Pan-Coque
Moun Diu, hètz-me bous desbelha
Que Trufandèc que-s biengue esbrigalha
Lou nas sus ma porte, si ey toque."

(Only in the voice of Pan-Coque;
My God, wake me up, so that
Truffandec will come and smash his nose
against my door, when he touches it.)

Txaalgorri

Txaalgorri, *Txalgorri* or *Txahalgorri* is a Basque word for a "red calf". The term is used for an *Irelu* living in the caves of the abysses of Askaeta and the Usategi. The Irelu likes its peace and quiet and when it is provoked to come out of its cave, when people throw rocks at it, for instance, the perpetrators will be severely punished. A story from the Murumendi region tells of three young people who violated this rule during festive days in the Agaoz. A Txaalgorri came out of its cave and haunted them to death. One of them died of fatigue in Agaoz, the other in the meadow of Aralegi, the third arrived in Urrestarazu and died there three days later.

U

Urtzi

Urtzi (*Ortz, Ortzi, Ostri, Ostri, Ost*) represents the spirit, or god, of the *thunder sky* in Basque mythology. There are many demonic derivatives that are used to identify all sorts of natural weather-phenomena related to a sky-god. Thus, *thunder* is represented by *Odei, Ortzantz, Ozkarri. Rays of light and lightning* are represented by *Iñizitu, Tximistarri, Oaztagi* or *Ostargi* (ortzi + argi = sky of light). *Rainbows* are represented by *Ostadar, Ortzadar* or *Ortzeder.* Urtzi or Ortzi means *sky, firmament* or *thunder* in Basque. *Orzgorri* means *red sky*: *ortzi* (sky) + *gorri* (red). Ostegun or *Thursday* comes from *ortzi* (thunder) + *egun* (day) = Thunder Day.

Ventolines

Ventolines are creatures found in Cantabrian and Asturian folklore. The Ventolines are benevolent *weather-Duendes*, spirits of the air, that help those who live on the Cantabrian coast. They act as the opposite force of the malevolent *Nuberos*. In Cantabria they are described as having large green wings, and eyes the color of the waves as they unravel, with an angelic face, living above the sea, in the reddish clouds of the west. When an old fisherman got tired of hauling up the nets, the Ventolines would come down from the clouds at sunset and load the fish into the boat and wipe the sweat off the men, or wrap them with the green wings when it was cold. Then they would take the oars and bring the boat close to the docks. At other times they would hoist the sail. If there was no wind, they would blow into the sails, flying behind the boat and creating a breeze that was enough for the boat to sail... a romance was sung that began like this:

> *"Ventolines, Ventoline*
> *Ventolines de la mar,*
> *Este viejo está cansado*
> *Y ya no puede remar."*

Tartaro (2022) by Benjamin Adamah

(Ventolines, Ventoline
Ventolines of the sea,
This old man is tired
And can no longer row.)

Then a swarm of little Ventolines would appear, like tiny angels, with big green wings, who began to blow in the sail of the boat with all their might, thus bringing a fisherman in distress closer to dry land.

Voirloup

The *Voirloup* is an evil, nocturnal creature, mentioned in French folklore. Contrary to a widespread belief, it is not a kind of Werewolf, but rather its "cousin", since it can transform itself into other animals than the wolf. The Voirloup is specific to the Pays d'Othe. This massif extends between Sens, Troyes and Joigny, uniting the departments of Aube and Yonne; it forms a strip of about twenty kilometers wide and fifty kilometers long. The region between Maraye-en-Othe and Bercenay-en-Othe is the most fertile in legends about the creature. Voirloups are originally men or women with black souls, guilty of the seven deadly sins and who let themselves be possessed by Satan or Belial. During their period of transformation, these creatures can take the form of wolves, but also of foxes, boars, goats or cats, in fact, of all the beasts in whose skin it is easy for them to do harm with impunity. The Voirloups metamorphose at midnight, after coating their lower limbs, front and back, with a mixture called amalgam (composed of human semen obtained in the sabbaths, the nuptial blood of a virgin, the fat of a pig killed on Good Friday at three o'clock in the afternoon which has become rancid, and a trickle of the Devil's slime). They address a supplication to Satan and are covered by the coat of the desired animal while keeping the human understanding. They walk through the forest from midnight to dawn without making a sound, slit the throats of dogs and cattle and quench their thirst with the blood of their victims. Voirloups are generally solitary, but they know how to get together to combine their evil powers.

Voirloups are often seen as invulnerable. They are very dangerous opponents for the human beings they attack; however, they do not kill them, but sometimes suck their blood, like Vampires. It is impossible to kill Voirloups; however, when they are wounded, even though they are insensitive to pain and heal very quickly, they always retain scars. The eyes of the Voirloup can light straw or fodder from a distance, on the hillside, in fields or barns. Several testimonies report night fires in the vicinity of Maraye-en-Othe and Bercenay-en-Othe; each time, a furtive and disturbing silhouette, half-beast, half-man, would appear on the ridge. The Voirloups dread the first light of day because when the sun rises and the rooster begins to crow, their animal skin bursts and they take on human form again. They spend their days spying on mortals to make sure that nothing is said or written about them. Those who dare to describe them in their animal form meet them at nightfall. They are difficult to trap; they have no ability to cast spells, but Voirloups are by nature driven to do as much evil as possible in the name of Satan. In their human form, they are easily recognized by the reddish spot on their lower spine or the image of a two-pronged fork on their left shoulder.

Vrykólakas

The term *Vrykólakas* or *Wrykólakas* (Greek βρυκόλακας also *Vorvolakas, Vourdoulakas, Wrukólakas* or *Brukolák*, masculine) denotes a *Vampire*, or livestock attacking *Revenant* in Greek and Salentine folk-belief. Originally of Slavic origin, it denoted a *Werewolf*. According to Greek folklore, a sacrilegious lifestyle, excommunication, apostasy from the Orthodox faith, burial in unconsecrated ground, and especially eating the flesh of a sheep killed by a Werewolf caused a person to become a Vrykólakas after death. According to certain beliefs, a killed Werewolf also transformed into a Vrykólakas, taking on fangs, hairy palms and glowing eyes. The Vrykólakas knocked on the front door at night and called the inhabitants by name. If he did not get an answer the first time, he passed by without causing any harm. Therefore, in certain areas, people answered knocks or calls only the second time. Legends also say that the Vrykólakas crushes or suffocates the sleeping by sitting on them, much like *Alp*-type or *Incubus* (sleep paralysis) – as does a Vampire in Bulgarian folklore. Unlike Vampires, in Greek folklore, the Vrykólakas are described more as cannibals than bloodsuckers, with a taste in particular for human livers. Victims of the Vrykólakas became Vampires themselves. Since the Vrykólakas becomes more and more powerful if left alone, legends state that one should destroy its body as soon as possible. According to some accounts, this can only be done on Saturday, which is the only day when the Vrykólakas rests in its grave (the same as with Bulgarian Vampire legends). This may be done in various ways, the most common being exorcising, impaling, cutting into pieces, decapitation, tearing out the heart with subsequent boiling in vinegar and especially cremating the suspected corpse. In the process, victims afflicted by the Vrykólakas were also freed from the curse of begetting the same fate as their destroyed undead attacker. The bodies of Vrykólakas have the same distinctive characteristics as the bodies of Vampires in Balkan folklore. They do not decay; instead, they swell and may even attain a "drumlike" form, being very large, have a ruddy complexion, and are, according to one account, *"fresh and gorged with new blood"*. People with red hair and gray eyes were thought to be Vampires – according to accounts near the region of modern Serbia. In the Greek Orthodox rites, it was customary to open the grave of a deceased person after 40 days and to check, in the presence of the priest, whether decomposition had progressed so far that the dead person could no longer be expected to return as a Vrykólakas. However, if decomposition did not seem to have set in, the corpse was generally believed to be possessed by the devil and it therefore had to be destroyed. Any dead body that could not be redeemed was considered incorruptible. It is often reported that the Orthodox Church exploited this popular belief to keep believers from converting to Islam. The fear of not being able to be redeemed dominated the people of the Balkans.

Between Vampire and Werewolf

The word vrykólakas is derived from the Slavic word *vărkolak*. The term is attested in other Slavic languages such as Slovak *vlkolak*, Serbian *vukodlak*, ultimately derived from Proto-Slavic vьlkolakъ and cognates can be found in other languages such as Lithuanian: *vilkolakis* and Romanian: *vârcolac*. The term is a compound word derived from the Slovak *vlk*, Bulgarian вълк (*vâlk*) and Serbian вук (*vuk*), meaning "wolf", and *dlaka*, meaning *(strand of) hair* (i.e. having the hair, or fur, of a wolf), and originally meant *Werewolf* (it still has that meaning in the modern Slavic languages, and a similar one in Romanian). However, the same word (in the form *Vukodlak*) has come to be used in the sense of *Vampire* in the folklore of Croatia and Montenegro while the term *Vampir* is more common in Bosnia and Herzegovina, Serbia and Bulgaria. Apparently, the two concepts have become mixed. Even in Bulgaria, original folklore generally describes the *Vârkolak* as a sub-species of the Vampire, without any wolf-like features. One reason for this switching between Werewolf and Vampire could very well be the folk-belief, widespread throughout eastern

Europe, that a person who harmed others in the form of a Werewolf during his or her lifetime, and remained unrecognized and was not punished, would return after his/her death as a Vampire or harm the living as an afterthought from the grave, unless appropriate measures were taken to banish or destroy the fiend. The original Greek word for Werewolf was *Kallikántsaros*, while the term *Lykanthropos* (literally: wolf-man), often found in literature, was found only in scholarly language, such as among physicians. An ancient Greek term for Vampire, dating from before the adoption of the Slavic word, is not known, which has led to the assumption that the Greeks adopted the Vampire belief only through contact with the immigrating Slavs. So far, all attempts to determine the different roots of the Greek belief in Vampires have not brought satisfactory results. In any case, it is not certain that other blood-sucking beings known to us from ancient mythology are to be regarded as precursors of Vampires, for they are demons (*Lamia* or *Empusa*) and not recurring dead, that is, human beings. Therefore, they have a different mythical background, even if some of the characteristics attributed to them are merged with those of Vampires.

Washerwomen

Washerwomen, *Les Lavandières*, or the *Midnight Washerwomen*, are three old laundresses in the folklore of several Celtic areas. They are known as *Kannerezed noz* in Brittany and *Bean nighe* in Scotland. They can also be found in the Celtic folklore of Iberia as *Las Lavanderas* in Cantabria, as *Lavandeiras* in Galicia or *Les Llavanderes* in Asturias. The three old women go to the water's edge at midnight to wash shrouds or the bloodstained clothing of those about to die, according to the folklore of Brittany. The Midnight Washerwomen may be related to the old Celtic tradition of the triple goddess of death and slaughter. The washerwomen are described as small, dressed in green and have webbed feet like the Basque Lamia. Their webbed feet may be the reason they are also sometimes called the *Cannard noz* (night ducks) in Breton folklore. In the nineteenth century, the belief in *Night-Washerwomen* was very present in Brittany and Normandy, but it is also attested in many other regions of France: Berry, Pyrenees, Alps, Alsace, Morvan, Creuse, Burgundy and Ariège.

In Brittany, legends of the *Lavandière de la nuit* were attested by Jacques Cambry as early as the 18th century *(Voyage dans le Finistère, ou État de ce département en 1794 et 1795).* In Breton, the Washerwomen are collectively known as *Ar c'hannerezed-noz, Ar c'houerezed-noz* or *Ar vaouez o welc'hin.* According to the Breton legends, the washerwomen can either be ghosts whose names are known to all, or anonymous supernatural beings appearing in human form. In some versions they can be encountered during the whole year in the evening, or in the middle of the night, in places like a launderette or creek. In other versions they are only seen on full moon nights, or even only on the eve of the *Feast of the Dead* (Halloween/All Saints' Day). They can be an ominous portent, foretelling death, either one's own or a death in the family, although this is rare – just like they are not always represented as old women, although they always have very pale skin, being creatures of the night, and are often dressed in white, or in traditional clothing. They are very agile and physically strong even when they don't seem so. The Breton washerwomen wash grave-clothes, usually at night, under the moonlight, and are notable for their intense dislike of being disturbed, cursing those who dare to do so. They are known to ask passers-by for help in wringing clothes, breaking the arms of those who do so reluctantly and drowning those who refuse. More rarely, they can also be involved in charity.

In Ireland, they are an ominous portent, foretelling death, either one's own or a death in the family. The washerwomen of Ireland wash the bloodied shirts of those about to die. In Wales and Cornwall a passerby must avoid being seen by the Washerwomen. If they do get seen however, they are required to help wring out the sheets. If they twist the sheets in the same direction as the washerwomen, the individual's arms will be wrenched from their sockets and they will get pulled into the wet sheets and killed instantly. If, however, they twist in the opposite direction, the washerwomen are required to grant the person three wishes.

In Scotland, if one can get between the Washerwomen and the water, they are required to grant three wishes in exchange for three questions answered truthfully. There is also a tradition in Scotland of a single *Washer* at the ford, the goddess *Clotha*, who gives the River Clyde its name. The washerwomen rarely appear in England, although lonely pools are often haunted by some supernatural creature, which may have derived from the same original root.

X

Xana

In Asturias (northern Spain), there is a legend about the *Xana*, a sort of *Nymph* who used to live near rivers, fountains and lakes, sometimes helping travelers on their journey. The Xanas may promise treasures and "love-water" to travelers and can be enchanting. Their hypnotic voices can be heard during spring and summer nights. Those who have a pure soul and hear the song will be filled with a sense of peace and love. Those whose souls are not pure will feel they are being suffocated and may be driven insane. As a benevolent creature she is usually described as small or slender, with long blonde or light brown hair (most often curly), which she tends to with gold or silver combs woven from sun or moonbeams. There are also tales in which the Xanas are small, thin and dark and enter homes to bite or kidnap children. Thus, in some stories she is the Spanish variant on the *changeling-Fairy* theme that has representatives throughout Europe (*Wechselbalg*, *Mamuna*, etc.). The Xanas were conceived as little female *Fairies* with a supernatural beauty. They could give birth to babies called X*aninos* (sing.: *Xanín*) which were sometimes swapped with human babies – some legends claim this was in order for them to be baptized, while others claim this is because the Xana cannot produce milk. According to legend, in order to distinguish a Xanino from a human baby, some pots and egg shells should be put close to the fireplace; a Xanino would then say: *"I was born one hundred years ago, and since then I have not seen so many egg shells near the fire!"*. The use of fire and the egg shells is the most common European apotropaic measure for determining whether or not a child is a changeling.

The origin of the Asturian word *xana* is unclear, although some scholars see it as a derivation of the Latin name for the goddess *Diana*. References to the place where the mythological Xanas lived are still common in Asturian toponyms. They also appear in eastern Galician and Cantabrian mythology (*Anjanas*).

Yan-gant-y-tan (1863) illustration for *Dictionnaire Infernal* by Louis Le Breton

Yan-gant-y-tan

Yan-gant-y-tan is the name of a demon from France. The creature bears similarities to the Anglo-Saxon *Will o' the Wisp* and roams in the night through Finistère (Penn-ar-Bed) the department in the far western tip of Brittany that consists of the historic region of Léon and parts of Cornouaille and Trégor. Collin de Plancy, in his *Dictionnaire Infernal* has translated Yan-gant-y-tan as "Wanderer in the Night", but a more acurate translation of his Breton name is "John with the Fire". He is often depicted as a wiry old *Goblin* or hairy savage, but the only way he really stands out as a unique spirit being are the five candles on his hand. He holds these five candles on the five fingers of his right hand (compare *Hand of Glory*) and makes them spin like a flaming wheel, which prevents him from turning around quickly for fear that their light will go out. The Hand of Glory is the dried and pickled hand of a hanged man, often referred to as the "left hand" (Latin: *sinister*), or, if the person was hanged for murder, the hand that "did the deed". Ancient European beliefs attributed great powers to a Hand of Glory when combined with a candle made of fat from the corpse of the same evildoer who died on the gallows. The candle thus made, lit and placed (as in a candlestick) in the Hand of Glory, is said to have rendered motionless all those to whom it was presented.

Unlike the Will o' the Wisp, the German *Irrlicht* or *Sumpflicht* and other European variants, the Yan-gant-y-tan does not necessarily lure people into a dangerous swamp. An encounter with the Yan-gant-y-tan is however said to be a bad omen. One way to ward off the bad omen of Yan-gant-y-tan is to leave a small bag of gold or a gold chain at a traveler's post, which the Yan-gant-y-tan will steal, after which one will not be bothered by him for a while. Despite the fact that his presence is associated with a bad sign, he is also said to sometimes appear, and give five candles, to a nocturnal traveler, so that this person can light the way for the rest of the night.

Youdic

The *Youdic* is not a spirit creature but what was believed to be a terrifying access to hellish regions, a malicious *Genius Loci*, often mentioned in Breton lore. The actual Youdic is a deep pit in the flat, black swamp of Yeun (also Yeun-Elez, Yeunn Ellez) in the Arrée mountains of Finistère, northwestern Brittany. Ignorant people peering into the Youdic, risked being grabbed and dragged down by unseen forces below. Countless stories circulate about this weird haunted maelstrom of mud and bubbling water. It was once the custom to throw animals suspected of being evil spirits into its black depths. Malevolent fiends, it was thought, would materialize in the form of large black dogs and one would hear them barking at night. Another sound one heard floating on the night wind was believed to come from the mad revels of lost souls. In Christian folklore the Youdic was thought to be a place for confining the possessed. It was thought that only St Michael could prevent souls from falling in.

Z

Zakur

Zakur is the Basque word for dog. This animal is hardly mentioned in Basque myths. According to a story from Beizama (Gipuzkoa), in the cave of Olanoi lives an *Irelu* in the shape of a dog, who acts as the guardian of that cave. In a legend from Mutriku, also in Gipuzkoa, there are two dogs or supernatural beings that appear in this guise. They would appear to the locals and frighten them when they returned home at an ungodly hour. In another legend, in Berriz (Biscay), a dog-Irelu appeared one day in the guise of a dead man, participating in a wedding banquet the next day.

Zaldi

Zaldi (horse in Basque) also denotes an *Irelu* in the shape of a horse. In the region of Tardets (Soule), from the cave of Laxarrigibel, located in one of the buttresses of Ahüski, near Alçay-Alçabéhéty-Sunharette a white phantom-horse is sometimes seen. Both a white horse and a headless horse haunt the Basque mountains (Navarre, Bastan Valley, Aldudes,

Luzaide, Esterenguibel ridges). Seeing either one of them is either a death omen or a sign of imminent doom. The evil white phantom-mare is common in Navarre and Souletin legends.

Zamari zuria

In Basque folkore *Zamari zuria* is a *field-spirit*, representing the spirit of corn. Zamari zuria is usually represented by a dancer in the festivals of Soule and Gipuzkoa.

Zezen or Zezengorri

In Basque folklore Zezen or Zezengorri is a nature-spirit or *Irelu* that appears as a terrifying ghostly bull. *Zezen* simply means "bull" in the Basque language; *Zezengorri* means "red bull". It is believed that some caves, but also chasms, are inhabited or guarded by him. These underground geniuses would come to the surface of the earth at night. Belief in the Zezen could go back to the Paleolithic era. The Betizu, a wild breed of cattle in the Basque Country, is said to have had a special relationship with the Zezen phenomena in the past. There are several Zezen guarding different entrances to caves. The bull that lived in the cave Lezia de Sare (Labourd) frightened and chased away those who wanted to enter the cave with its bellows. Sometimes the sound of his clarinet could also be heard in the depths of the tunnels. In Gatika (Vizcaya), one of these bulls chased someone from the village who was returning from Mungia at night. In Pipaon (Alava) one night a mysterious bull appeared to a group of young people, causing them a terrible fright. They blamed its appearance on the fact that they had insulted an elderly person in the village.

Zirri Mirri, Zirpi Zarba and Zirpi Zirbi

Zirri Mirri is the Basque name of a mysterious *Jentil* or *Mairu,* a giant hairy creature of the Oiartzun region (Guipuscoa). Exactly what his nature was remains very vague, and what is left over of a legend of Oiartzun seems to have intermingled in folklore with what remained from a legend about the *Jentilak* Zirpi Zarba and Zirpi Zirbi. The only remaining interesting thing about two tiny incomplete fragments of a Basque legend is that humans and *Jentilak* are described, working together in the household and on the fields, as if this is the most normal thing in the world, and the dead *Jentil* Zirpi Zarba acting in a way which suggest that being dead as *Jentil* is not such a very big deal. *Jentilak* remain mysterious creatures. Some theories state that they were an unusual strong, big and hairy humanoid race, a bit like the Sasquatch or Yeti, that lived in peace alongside the Basque people. Other legends identify them with the *Lamia*-related *Mairuak* of which it is unclear whether they were of the same race as the *Jentilak* or nature-spirits. The Oiartzun-story is about a female *Jentil*-servant, who worked in the house of Aramburu. One night a scream was heard at the door. The *Jentil* asked what was going on. A voice answered: *"Zirri mirri ill dun!"* (Zirri mirri is dead). The *Jentil*-maid went out, and she never came back.

Zirpi Zarba is the name of a male Jentil from Ataun (Guipuscoa). It is said that a family from Ayarre (probably Aiarre) was weeding corn on their land in Kiskarre. A *Jentil*-woman called Zirpi Zirbi was assisting them in their work. Several Jentilak had their home in the nearby Ai-Iturrieta, and they suddenly warned the farmers of Kiskarre by shouting: *"Zirpi Zarba is dead, tell Zirpi Zirbi that she should come right away"*. The *Jentil*-woman Zirpi-Zirbi left at night. When she returned to Ayarre, she announced that the dead man was her companion. Zirpi Zirbi continued to frequent Ayarre, especially in winter. She spent her nights spinning with the women of the neighborhood.

LITERATURE AND DIGITAL SOURCES

- Abercromby, John – *The Pre- and Proto-historic Finns, both Eastern and Western with the Magic Songs of the West Finns – in two volumes*, published by David Nutt in the Strand, London, 1898
- Árnason, J.; Powell, G. E. J. and Magnússon, E. trans. – *Icelandic Legends* – Richard Bentley, London, 1864
- Arrowsmith, N. – *Field Guide to the Little People: A Curious Journey Into the Hidden Realm of Elves, Faeries, Hobgoblins & Other Not-so-mythical Creatures* – Llewellyn Worldwide., 1970/2009
- Barb, A.A. – *Antaura. The Mermaid and the Devil's Grandmother: A Lecture* – Journal of the Warburg and Courtauld Institutes, 1966

- Bardon, Franz – *Die Praxis der Magische Evokation* – Rüggeberg Verlag Wuppertal, 2003
- Bartsch, Karl – *Sagen, Märchen und Gebräuche aus Meklenburg*, vol. 1 – Vienna, Wilhelm Braumüller, 1879
- Beaumont, William Comyns – *Britain The Key To World History* – London, 1948
- Benwell, G. and Waugh, A. – *Sea Enchantress: The Tale of the Mermaid and her Kin* – Hutchinson, London, 1961
- Blau, Lajos (Ludwich) – *Das Altjüdische Zauberwesen* – 1897-98 Budapest / Graz, 1974
- Blécourt, W. de, – *"I Would Have Eaten You Too": Werewolf Legends in the Flemish, Dutch, and German Area* – 2007
- Bonnefoy, Yves, – *Asian Mythologies* – University of Chicago Press, 1993
- Bottiglioni, Gino – *Leggende e tradizioni di Sardegna (testi dialettali in grafia fonetica)* – 1922
- Briggs, Katharine – *An Encyclopedia of Fairies – Hobgoblins, Brownies, Bogies and Other Supernatural Creatures* – Pantheon Books, USA, 1976
- Calmet, Dom Augustine – *The Phantom World: The History and Philosophy of Spirits, Apparitions &c. Two Volumes in One* – Philadelphia: A Hart, Late Carey & Hart, 1850
- Campbell, J.G. – *Superstitions of the Highlands and Islands of Scotland* – James MacLehose and Sons, Glascow, 1900
- Conway, Moncure Daniel -*Demonology and Devil-Lore 1 & 2* – revised publication of the 1897 editions by VAMzzz Publishing, Amsterdam, 2015
- Conybeare, Frederick Cornwallis – *Testament of Solomon – Jewish Quaterly Review of October 1889* – revised edition VAMzzz Publishing, Amsterdam, 2015
- Corstorphine, Kevin & Kremmel, Laura R – *Horror in the Medieval North: The*

Troll, The Palgrave Handbook to Horror Literature - ed., 2018
- Courtney, M.A. - *Cornish Feasts and Folklore* - Beare and Son, Penzance, 1890
- Craigie, W.A. - *The Oldest Icelandic Folklore,* 1893
- Davidsson, O. *The Folk-lore of Icelandic Fishes,* 1900
- Dennison, W. Traill - *Orkney Folklore, Sea Myths* - Edinburgh University Press, 1891
- Dörler, Adolf Ferdinand (collected and edited by) - *Sagen aus Innsbruck's Umgebung, mit besonderer Berücksichtigung des Zillerthales* - Innsbruck, 1895
- Edmondston, Thomas - *An Etymological Glossary of the Shetland & Orkney Dialect* - Adam and Charles Black, 1866
- *Encyclopedia Brittanica online*
- Folkard, Richard - *Plant Lore Legends & Lyrics* - 1884, revised edition by VAMzzz Publishing, Amsterdam, 2021
- Frazer, Sir James George - *The Golden Bough: A Study in Magic and Religion* - edition 1906-15
- Genesin, Monica & Rizzo, Luana (Hrsg.) - *Magie, Tarantismus und Vampirismus; Eine interdisciplinäre Annäherung* - Verlag Dr. Kovač, Hamburg, 2013
- Gibbings W. W. - *Folk-lore and Legends - Germany,* London, 1892
- Gieysztor, Aleksander - *Mitologia Słowian* - Warszawa: Wydawnictwo Uniwersytetu Warszawskiego, 2006
- Gill, W. Walter - *A Second Manx Scrapbook* - Arrowsmith, London Bristol, 1932
- Grimm, Jacob - *Deutsche Mythologie* - Göttingen: Dieterich, 1835
- Hageland, A. van - *La Mer Magique* - Marabout, Paris, 1973
- Hall, Manly Palmer - *The Secret Teachings of All Ages: An Encyclopedic Outline of Masonic, Hermetic, Qabbalistic and Rosicrucian Symbolical Philosophy* - 1928
- Hanaur, J.E. - *Folk-Lore of the Holy Land - Moslim, Christian and Jewish* - Edited by Marmaduke Pickthall, London Duckworth & Co, 1907
- Henderson, William - *Notes on the folk-lore of the northern counties of England and the borders* - Longmans, Green, 1866
- Hlidberg, J. B. and Aegisson, S.; McQueen, F. J. M. and Kjartansson, R., trans. - *Meeting with Monsters* - JPV utgafa, Reykjavik, 2011 .
- Huizinga-Onnekes, E.J. - *Groninger Volksverhalen* - bewerkt door K. ter Laan, J.B.Wolters' Uitgevers Maatschappij N.V. Groningen - Den Haag, 1930
- *Jewish Encyclopedia online*
- Johnston, Sarah Iles - *Restless Dead: Encounters Between the Living and the Dead in Ancient Greece* - University of California Press, Berkeley-Los Angeles-London, 2013

- Karakurt, Deniz – *Türk Söylence Sözlüğü* (*Turkish Mythological Dictionary*) (OTRS: CC BY-SA 3.0), 2011
- Kivilson, Valerie A. & Worobec, Christine D. – *Witchcraft in Russia and Ukraine, 1000–1900: A Sourcebook* – Cornell University Press, Northern Illinois University Press, 2020
- Kreuter, Peter Mario – *Der Vampirglaube in Südosteuropa. Studien zur Genese, Bedeutung und Funktion. Rumänien und der Balkanraum* – Weidler, Berlin, 2001, (Dissertation Universität Bonn, 2001)
- Lachower, Fischel & Tishby, Isaiah; translations by David Goldstein – *Wisdom of the Zohar – An Anthology of Texts* – London, 1994
- Landt, George – *A description of the Faroe Islands, containing an account of their situation, climate, and productions, together with the manners and customs of the inhabitants, their trade etc.* – 1810

- Lawson, John Cuthbert, M.A. – *Modern Greek Folklore and Ancient Greek Religion – A Study in Survivals* – Cambridge: at the University Press, London: Fetter Lane, E.C., 1910
- Lecouteux, Claude:
  - *Witches, Werewolves and Fairies: Shapeshifters and Astral Doubles in the Middle Ages*, Inner Traditions (Rochester, Vermont) transl. Clare Frock, 2003
  -*The Return of the Dead: Ghosts, Ancestors and the Transparent Veil of the Pagan Mind*, Inner Traditions (Rochester, Vermont) transl. Jon E. Graham, 2009
  - *The Secret History of Vampires: Their Multiple Forms and Hidden Purposes*, Inner Traditions (Rochester, Vermont) transl. Jon E. Graham, 2010
  - *Phantom Armies of the Night: The Wild Hunt and Ghostly Processions of the Undead*, Inner Traditions (Rochester, Vermont) transl., Jon E. Graham, 2011
  - *The Tradition of Household Spirits. Ancestral Lore and Practice*, Inner Traditions (Rochester, Vermont) transl. Jon E. Graham, 2013
  - *Demons and Spirits of the Land: Ancestral Lore and Practices*, Inner Traditions (Rochester, Vermont) transl. Jon E. Graham, 2015
  - *The Hidden Historie of Elves and Dwarfs – Avatars of Invisible Realms*, Inner Traditions (Rochester, Vermont) transl. Jon E. Graham, 2018
- Libera, Roberto – *Storie di streghe, fantasmi e lupi mannari nei Castelli Romani, Genzano di Roma* – Consorzio SBCR editore, 2010
- Lindley, Charles, Viscount Halifax – *Lord Halifax Ghost Book* – first edition Glasgow, 1936
- Lomas, Adriano Garcia – *Mitología y supersticiones de Cantabria* – 1964
- Luzel, François-Marie – *Contes populaires de Basse-Bretagne* – 1881
- Mackenzie, Donald Alexander
  - *Wonder Tales from Scottish Myth and Legend* – Blackie and Son Limited,

London, Glasgow, Bombay, 1917
- *Scottish Folk-Lore and Folk Life. Studies in Race, Culture and Tradition* – 1935
- *Elves and Heroes* – 1909
- *Teutonic Myth and Legend* – 2nd Ed. 1934
- Mannhardt, Wilhelm:
- *Roggenwolf und Roggenhund – Beitrag zur Germanischen Sittenkunde* – Verlag von Constantin Ziemssen, Danzig, 1865
- *Die Korndämonen, – Beitrag zur Germanischen Sittenkunde* – Harrwitz und Gossmann, Berlin 1868
- *Wald- und Feldkulte. Band 1: Der Baumkultus der Germanen und ihrer Nachbarstämme: mythologische Untersuchungen* – Gebrüder Borntraeger, Berlin, 1875
- *Wald- und Feldkulte. Band 2: Antike Wald- und Feldkulte aus nordeuropäischer Überlieferung erläutert* – Gebrüder Borntraeger, Berlin, 1877
- *Mythologische Forschungen* – Karl J. Trüber, Strassburg – London 1884
- Marliave, Olivier de – *Trésor de la mythologie pyrénéenne* – Toulouse, Esper, 1987
- Marliave, Olivier de et Pertuzé, Jean-Claude – *Panthéon Pyrénéen* – Toulouse, Loubatières, 1990.
- Masani, R.P., M.A – *Folklore of Wells, being a study of Water Worship in East and West* – Bombay, D.B. Takapokevale Sons & Co, 1918
- Mathers, S.L. MacGregor / Knor von Rosenroth – *Kabbala Denudata / The Kabbalah Unveiled* – Samuel Weiser Inc. York Beach, Maine, 1989
- McAnally, David Russell – *Irish Wonders: The Ghosts, Giants, Pookas, Demons, Leprechawns, Banshees, Fairies, Witches, Widows, Old Maids, and other marvels of the Emerald Isle* – The Riverside Press Cambridge, 1888
- McIntosh, A – *Faerie Faith in Scotland* (2005) in *The Encyclopaedia of Religion and Nature* – edited by Bron Taylor, 2006
- McPherson, Rev. J. M. – *Primitive Beliefs in the North-East of Scotland – London, New York and Toronto* – Longmans, Green and Co., Ltd., 1929
- Meyer, Elard Hugo – *Mythologie der Germanen,* Straszburg, Verlag von Karl J. Trübner, 1930
- Nadmorski, Dr – *Kaszuby i Kociewie. Język, zwyczaje, przesądy, podania, zagadki i pieśni ludowe w północnej części Prus Zachodnich* – Poznań, 1892
- Paracelsus – *Four treatises of Theophrastus von Hohenheim, called Paracelsus* (1493-1541) – English translation of the German, Baltimore: Johns Hopkins Press, 1941
- Petiteau, Frantz-E. – *Contes, légendes et récits de la vallée d'Aure* – éditions Alan Sutton, 2007

- Plancy, Collin de, – *Dictionnaire Infernal* – 1818
- Podgórscy Barbara and Adam – *Wielka Księga Demonów Polskich. Leksykon i antologia demonologii ludowej* – Katowice: KOS, 2005
- Rajki, Andras – *Mongolian Ethymological Dictionary* 2006-2009 – via *academia.edu*
- Ralston, W. R. S., M.A.
  - *Russian Fairy Tales – A choice collection of Muscovite folk-lore* – New York: Hurst & Co., 1872
  - *The songs of the Russian people, as illustrative of Slavonic mythology and Russian social life* – London, Ellis, 1872
- Ritter, Johann Nepomuk von Alpenburg – *Deutsche Alpensagen* – Vienna, 1861

- Rose, C. – *Giants, Monsters, and Dragons* – W. W. Norton and Co., New York, 2000
- Rosenthal, Bernice Glatzer (editor) – *The Occult in Russian and Soviet Culture* – Cornell University, 1997
- Rhys, John – *Celtic Folklore Welsh and Manx* – Library of Alexandria, 2020
- Ryan, W.F. – *The Bathhouse at Midnight – An Historical Survey of Magic and Divination in Russia*, Pennsylvania State University Press, 1999
- Sacaze, Julien – *Le dieu Tantugou, légende du pays de Luchon* – (in Revue de Comminges, Tome III, 1887, p. 116-118), texte « patois » et traduction littérale
- Saxby, Jessie Margaret Edmondston – *Shetland Traditional Lore* – Edinburgh, Grant and Murray, 1932
- Sébillot, Paul – *Le Folk-Lore de France, Tome Premier: Le Ciel et la Terre* – 1904
- Sikes, Wirt – *British Goblins: Welsh Folk-Lore, Fairy Mythology, Legends and Traditions* – London, 1880
- Simpson, J. – *Icelandic Folktales and Legends* – University of California Press, Berkeley and Los Angeles, 1972
- Sinastrari of Ameno – transl. Liseux, Isidore 1876 – *Incubi and Succubi or Demoniality – A Historical Study of Sexual contacts with Demons* – Revised edition by VAMzzz Publishing, Amsterdam, 2017
- Sluijter, P.C.M. – *IJslands Volksgeloof* – H. D. Tjeenk Willink & Zoon N.V., Haarlem, 1936
- Spada, Dario – *Gnomi, Fate e Folletti e altri esseri fatati in Italia* – SugarCo, Milano, 2007
- Spiesberger, Karl – *Naturgeister wie Seher sie schauwen – wie Magier sie rufen* – Richard Schikowski Verlag, Berlin 1978
- Stefánsson, V. – *Icelandic Beast and Bird Lore* -1906
- Summers, Montague – *The Vampire in Lore and Legend* – Toronto 2001 (previously published as: *The Vampire in Europe*, London, 1929)

- Ter Laan, K. – *Groninger Overleveringen* – Erven B. van der Kamp, Groningen, 1930
- Thompson, Francis – *The Supernatural Highland* – Robert Hale, London, 1976
- Thorpe, Benjamin – *Northern mythology : comprising the principal popular traditions and superstitions of Scandinavia, North Germany, and the Netherlands* – 1852
- Veen, Abe J. van der – *Witte wieven, weerwolven en waternekkers - Een beschrijving van alle geesten, elfen en andere wondere wezens uit Nederland* – 2017
- Vries, A. de, – *Flanders: a cultural history* – Oxford University Press, Oxford, 2007
- Wippel I. – *Schabbock, Trud und Wilde Jagd* – Verlag für Sammler, Graz 1986
- Wikimedia Commons Licence folklore data via *Armenian, Austrian, Basque, Belarusian, Catalan, Dutch, Estonian, Danish, German, Finnish, Icelandic, Italian, French, Latvian, Lithuanian, Norwegian, Polish, Portuguese, Russian, Spanish, Swedish, Swiss, Turkish, and Ukrainian* Wikipedia-files
- Wlislocki, Dr Heinrich von – *Volksglaube und religiöser Brauch der Zigeuner* – Aschendorffsche Buchhandlung, Münster, 1891

FROM THE SAME SERIES

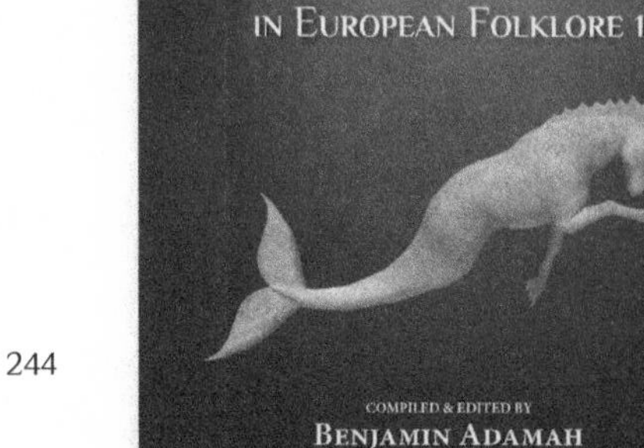

Spirit Beings in European Folklore 1
Ireland, England, Wales, Cornwall, Scotland, Isle of Man, Orkney's, Hebrides, Faeroe, Iceland, Norway, Sweden and Denmark
by Benjamin Adamah, 250 pages,
Paperback, ISBN 9789492355553
www.vamzzz.com

Compendium 1 of the *Spirit Beings in European Folklore*-series covers the northwestern part of the continent where Celtic and Anglo-Saxon cultures meet the Nordic. This book catalogs the mysterious creatures of Ireland, the Isle of Man, England, Wales, Cornwall, Scotland, Hebrides, Orkneys, Faroe Islands, Iceland, Norway, Sweden and Denmark. For centuries, the peoples of these regions have influenced each other in many ways, including their mythologies and folklore. The latter is perhaps most evident in the various species of *Brook-horses* or *Water-horses.* These semi-aquatic ghostly creatures come in all kinds of varieties and are typical of the English or Gaelic speaking parts of Europe and Scandinavia. Many other ghostly entities occur only in specific areas or countries. Some even became cultural icons, such as the Irish *Leprechaun*, the *Knockers* from Wales, the Scandinavian *Trolls* and *Huldras* or the Icelandic *Huldufólk*. England has its *Brownies*, several kinds of *Fairies* and locally famous *ghost dogs*. Iceland and Scandinavia seem to "specialize" in spirit beings who appear fully materialized, such as the different species of *Illveli* (Evil Whales) and *Draugr*, the returning dead.

Compendium 1 discusses 292 spirit beings in detail, including their alternative names, with additional references to related or subordinate beings and a unique selection of illustrations.

CONTENTS:

FROM THE SAME SERIES

Spirit Beings in European Folklore 2
Germany, Austria, Alpine regions, Switzerland, Netherlands, Flanders, Luxembourg, Lithuania, Latvia, Estonia, Finland, Jewish influences
by Benjamin Adamah, 256 pages,
Paperback, ISBN 9789492355560
www.vamzzz.com

Compendium 2 of the *Spirit Beings in European Folklore*-series covers the German-speaking parts of Central Europe, the Low Countries, the Baltic region and Finland. Via the Ashkenazi Jews, spirit beings from the Middle East entered Central European culture, which are also included. This originally densely forested part of the continent is particularly rich in nature-spirits and has a wide variety of beings that dwell in forests and mountainous areas (*Berggeister*) or act as atmospheric forces. Also dominant are the many field-spirits and variations of *Alp*-like creatures (*Mare, Nightmare*). There is an overlap with the Nordic and Eastern European *Revenant* and *Vampire*-types, and we find several water- and sea-spirits. Among the German-speaking and Baltic peoples, invoking field-spirits was an integrated part of agriculture, with rites continuing into the early 20th century. The Alpine regions have spirits who watch over cattle. In general, forest-spirits are prominent. Germany has its *Moosweiblein* and *Wilder Mann* (*Woodwose*), the Baltic region has its *Mātes*, and Finland its *Metsän Väki*. Then there are ghostly animals, and earth- and house-spirits such as the many kinds of *Kobolds*, the Dutch *Kabouter*, and the *Kaukas* of Prussia and Latvia.

Compendium 2 discusses 228 spirit beings in detail, including their alternative names, with additional references to related or subordinate beings and a unique selection of illustrations.

CONTENTS:

FROM THE SAME SERIES

Spirit Beings in European Folklore 3
Russia, Belarus, Ukraine, Poland, Romania, Hungary, Bulgaria, Czechia, Slovenia, Serbia, Croatia, Albania, Georgia, Turkish regions, Roma-culture
by Benjamin Adamah, 246 pages,
Paperback, ISBN 9789492355577
www.vamzzz.com

Compendium 3 of the *Spirit Beings in European Folklore*-series offers an overview of the mysterious, sometimes beautiful and often shadowy entities of the Slavic countries, the Balkans, the Carpathians, Albania, Georgia, and the Turkish and Romani peoples. Many types of *Vampires* and vampiric *Revenants* are included – in their original state and purged of later applied disinformation. The undead are prominent in the folklore of Eastern Europe and Albania. Also typical are farm- and household-spirits such as the *Domovoy*, water-spirits and forest demons like the Russian *Leshy*, the *Chuhaister*, or the evil Polish *Bełt*, who like the Ukrainian *Blud*, leads travelers off their path until they are lost in the deepest part of the forest. Unique is the Russian *Bannik* or spirit of the bathhouse. Amongst the Slavs, some 'demons', like the *Boginka* for example, originally belonged to the pre-Christian pantheon. Eastern Europe, in contrast to its returning dead, is rich in seductive female spirits such as the Romanian *Iele*, the Russian *Russalka*, the *Vila* of the Eastern and Southern Slavs and the Bulgarian *Samodiva*. Via the Balkans, Greek influences entered Slavic culture, while there are also spirits that intersect Germanic and Nordic folklore.

Compendium 3 discusses 255 spirit beings in detail, including their alternative names, with additional references to related or subordinate beings and a unique selection of illustrations.

CONTENTS:

CPSIA information can be obtained
at www.ICGtesting.com
Printed in the USA
BVHW041648301122
653125BV00021B/308